★★★★★★★★★★★★★ ★★★★★★★★★★★★★

Recipe Hall of Fame
One-Dish
Wonders

———————— ★ ————————

*Winning Recipes
from Hometown America*

The Grand Canyon. Arizona.
One of the Natural Wonders of the World.

Best of the Best

★★★★★★★★★★★★ ★★★★★★★★★★★★

Recipe Hall of Fame
One-Dish
Wonders

★

*Winning Recipes
from Hometown America*

EDITED BY
Gwen McKee
AND
Barbara Moseley

QUAIL RIDGE PRESS
Preserving America's Food Heritage

Recipe Collection ©2011 Quail Ridge Press, Inc.

ALL RIGHTS RESERVED
Recipes reprinted with permission from the publishers,
organizations, or individuals listed on pages 247 to 256.

Library of Congress Cataloging-in-Publication Data

Recipe hall of fame one-dish wonders : winning recipes from hometown America
   / edited by Gwen McKee and Barbara Moseley.
   p. cm. — (Recipe hall of fame cookbook collection).
   Includes index.
   ISBN-13: 978-1-934193-68-6
   ISBN-10: 1-934193-68-2
1. One-dish meals--United States. 2. Casserole cooking--United States. 3. Cooking,
   American. 4. Cooking--Competitions--United States. 5. Cookbooks.
I. McKee, Gwen. II. Moseley, Barbara. III. Title: One-dish wonders.
   TX840.O53R43 2011
   641.82—dc23   2011028358

ISBN-10: 1-934193-68-2 • ISBN-13: 978-1-934193-68-6

Cover photo by Greg Campbell • Back cover photo by Emily Burkett
Printed in Canada

On the front cover: Truck Stop Potatoes, page 76
On the back cover: Fellowship Hot Dish, page 129

QUAIL RIDGE PRESS
P. O. Box 123 • Brandon, MS 39043 • info@quailridge.com
www.recipehalloffame.com • www.quailridge.com
www.facebook.com/cookbookladies

Contents

★★

Mount Everest. Nepal.
One of the Natural Wonders of the World.

WIKIMEDIACOMMONS.ORG

Don't you just love to cook things that all blend together into one dish? Wonderful tasting foods that you can make ahead? That you can take along to a bring-a-dish occasion? That you can pop in the frig or freezer till you need it? Who doesn't?

I think a combination of ingredients cooked together and served in one dish is so interesting to prepare. It's almost like having a blank canvas in front of you, and you get to create your own masterpiece. And once it's prepared, your creation is ready for the oven, and only a scoop away from your plate. When you hear "What's for dinner?" you don't have to press the panic button . . . because your one-dish wonder has already been prepared!

Barbara Moseley, my co-editor, and I have chosen our favorites from our entire database of BEST OF THE BEST recipes, so that when this kind of all-in-one dish is called for, you will have them all in one book. Whether it's cooked quickly in a microwave, or in a slow pot on the stove all day, or baked in the oven, the convenience and tastiness of these all-in-one dishes is worthy of having a collection of its own. (Please note that the title of each contributing cookbook is listed below the recipe along with the state name in parentheses, indicating the BEST OF THE BEST STATE COOKBOOK where the recipe appears.)

This cookbook started out to be a casserole cookbook including only recipes that fit the definition: A casserole is a large dish used both in the oven and as a serving vessel, and the word itself describes both the food and the cookware. It's about anything that combines different ingredients that are cooked and served in one dish. Casseroles are usually cooked slowly in the oven, often uncovered. They may be served as a main course or a side dish, and may be served in the vessel in which they were cooked.

★★

But as usual with Barbara and me, we wanted to expand the pallet to include soups and desserts and favorite dishes that one might have a hard time calling a casserole! So we present here an expanded version that we call *One-Dish Wonders*. And you will discover that each one truly is! In addition to "What's for dinner?" you'll probably be hearing, "What smells so good?" Just wait'll they taste it!

We have many people to thank for helping us put this cookbook together, including our longtime assistant Terresa Ray, whose energy and enthusiasm inspires us. In addition, Holly Hardy, Melinda Burnham, Chris Brown, Lacy Ward, Cyndi Clark, and Emily Burkett pick up the pieces to make the whole project come together. Thank you all for all you do.

And thanks especially to all the people all over America who have "painted their masterpieces" and shared these masterful recipes with you. Feast your eyes and your taste buds in this gallery of *One-Dish Wonders*. Create, admire . . . and enjoy!

Gwen McKee

P. S. In keeping with the cookbook's title, we have added photographs and facts that highlight some of the natural and man-made "wonders" of our beautiful, *wonder*ful world. (See page 245–246 for lists of "Wonders.") In addition, we are sharing some trivia about the number "one" (also part of the title) that we hope you will enjoy.

Appetizers

The Northern Lights. Arctic Region.
One of the Natural Wonders of the World.

Baked Reuben Dip

1 cup grated Swiss cheese
1 cup drained sauerkraut
½ cup sour cream
2 teaspoons spicy brown
  mustard
1 tablespoon ketchup

2 teaspoons minced onion
1 (8-ounce) package cream
  cheese, cubed
8 ounces corned beef, cut into
  small pieces

Combine all ingredients. Place in greased glass baking dish. Cover and bake 30 minutes at 350°. Uncover and bake for an additional 5–10 minutes until golden. Serve with crackers.

Sharing Traditions from People You Know (Iowa)

Editor's Extra: When a casserole recipe calls for a greased baking dish, it is generally okay to use cooking spray. And some of the newer bakeware doesn't even need greasing!

Hot Chicken Dip

2 (10¾-ounce) cans chunk
  chicken breast packed in
  water, well drained
2 (8-ounce) packages cream
  cheese (light is okay),
  softened
1 egg, beaten

1 (4-ounce) can diced green
  chiles, including liquid
1 (16-ounce) bottle salsa
1–2 cups shredded Cheddar
  cheese (adjust amount to
  your taste)

Combine chicken, cream cheese, beaten egg, and green chiles. Spread in a greased 9x13-inch baking dish, and bake at 325° for 25 minutes. Remove from oven and spread salsa and cheese over top. Return dish to oven and bake until cheese melts. Serve with your favorite dipper. Tortilla chips are a good choice.

Our Sisters' Recipes (Kentucky)

Tarantula Dip

2 pounds hamburger meat
2 packages taco seasoning
1 red onion, diced
1 (16-ounce) can refried beans
1 (16-ounce) jar taco sauce
1 (8-ounce) package grated
   Colby cheese
2–3 jalapeño peppers, diced
24 ounces sour cream
1 (4-ounce) can sliced black
   olives
Tostitos corn chips

Cook hamburger; drain; add taco seasoning and onion. Spread refried beans in a greased 9x13-inch pan. Put hamburger mixture on top of beans. Spread taco sauce on hamburger. Sprinkle cheese over this. Then layer jalapeño peppers on top. Cook in 325° oven for 30 minutes. Take out of oven. Cool 5 minutes. Spread sour cream on top. Sprinkle black olives on top. Serve with Tostitos corn chips.

What's Cooking at St. Stephens? (Michigan)

Editor's Extra: This is hot! And it makes a lot! Great for couple's parties.

Paula's Pizza Dip

1 (8-ounce) package cream
   cheese, softened
1 (14-ounce) jar pizza sauce
1 very small onion, grated
1½ cups shredded mozzarella
   cheese
1 (4-ounce) can chopped black
   olives
1 (3½-ounce) package
   pepperoni, chopped

Spread cream cheese in ungreased 9x13-inch dish. Pour pizza sauce over cream cheese, then layer onion, cheese, black olives, and pepperoni. Bake at 350° for 20–25 minutes. Serve with Frito Scoops.

Munchin' with the Methodists (Mississippi)

Editor's Extra: Whether this classic recipe is baked in a fancy casserole dish or a tin pie plate, it will always come back empty!

Hot Chile-Spinach Dip
in a Bread Round

1 large round loaf unsliced
   Shepherd's bread or French
   bread
2–3 jalapeño chiles, minced
1 (7-ounce) can diced green chiles
1 small onion, chopped
2 tablespoons vegetable oil
2 tomatoes, chopped
1 (10-ounce) package frozen
   chopped spinach, thawed,
   drained and squeezed dry

1 tablespoon red wine vinegar
1 (8-ounce) package cream
   cheese, softened
2 cups grated Monterey Jack
   cheese
1 cup half-and-half
1 teaspoon cumin
Salt and pepper to taste
Tortilla chips

Preheat oven to 325°. Cut top off bread ¼ of the way down. Carefully scoop out inside, leaving a 1-inch shell. Reserve top.

In a medium skillet over medium heat, cook chiles and onion in oil, stirring, for 4 minutes, or until onions are softened. Add tomatoes and cook mixture, stirring, for 2 more minutes. Stir in spinach, vinegar, cream cheese, Monterey Jack cheese, half-and-half, cumin, salt and pepper, and heat gently.

Pour sauce into bread round, replace top and wrap in heavy foil. Place in a baking pan and bake for 1½ hours.

To serve, place the bread round on a platter and surround with tortilla chips for dipping. The dip may also be served in a chafing dish. Serves 8–10.

California Sizzles (California)

A basic definition of aurora borealis is luminous arches or streams of light that appear in the Northern regions of the earth. The Latin words "aurora borealis" are roughly translated as "northern lights"—hence the alternative name. Aurora pertains to the lights (the red dawn) and borealis pertains to the North. It is interesting to note that "Aurora" was the name given to the Roman goddess of dawn.

★ ★ ★ ★ ★ ★ ★ ★ ★ ★ ★   ★ ★ ★ ★ ★ ★ ★ ★ ★ ★ ★

Artichoke Dill Dip

2 (14-ounce) cans artichoke
   hearts, drained and chopped
1 cup grated Parmesan cheese
1 cup mayonnaise

2 teaspoons garlic powder
¼ teaspoon Worcestershire
1 teaspoon dill weed

Combine all ingredients in a 1-quart casserole dish sprayed with cooking spray. Bake at 350° for 20–25 minutes or until heated through. Serve with toast rounds and/or vegetables.

Elko Ariñak Dancers Cookbook (Nevada)

Cheezy Crab Hors D'Oeuvres

1 (8-ounce) package cream
   cheese, softened
1 teaspoon milk
1 tablespoon instant minced
   onion
¼ cup grated Parmesan cheese

½ teaspoon horseradish
1 cup (8 ounces) crabmeat
Salt and pepper to taste
1 (2-ounce) package slivered
   almonds (optional)

Blend together cream cheese, milk, onion, Parmesan cheese, and horseradish. Gently mix in crabmeat. Add salt and pepper. Put in greased shallow 1-quart baking dish; sprinkle almonds over top. Bake at 350° until lightly browned on top, about 20 minutes. Serve hot on crackers or as a dip.

Note: Can be served without cooking. Simply add milk to proper consistency for use as a spread or dip. Keep refrigerated until served.

The Rappahannock Seafood Cookbook (Virginia)

Zucchini Squares

4 eggs, slightly beaten
½ teaspoon seasoned salt
½ teaspoon dried oregano
  (rubbed between palms of
  your hands)
½ cup vegetable oil

½ cup chopped onion
½ cup grated Parmesan cheese
2 tablespoons snipped parsley
1 cup Bisquick Baking Mix
4 cups thinly sliced, unpared
  zucchini

Beat eggs with seasonings; stir in oil. Mix with all remaining ingredients, adding zucchini last. Bake in greased 9x13-inch dish, 350° for 35 minutes, or until a cake tester or toothpick comes out clean. It should be golden brown. Slice in small squares to serve. This will keep several days, refrigerated, and can be reheated in the microwave.

Conducting in the Kitchen (Mid-Atlantic)

Artichoke Nibbles

These are amazingly easy to make, so of course I serve them at practically every party I have. The nibbles taste better when they're hot.

1 (12-ounce) can marinated
  artichoke hearts
1 small onion, finely chopped
1 garlic clove, minced
4 eggs
¼ cup dry bread crumbs
Salt (optional)

Pepper to taste
Oregano to taste
2 dashes Tabasco (or to taste)
2 cups shredded Cheddar
  cheese
2 tablespoons minced parsley

Drain the marinade from the artichoke hearts, and chop them well. Add onion and garlic. Sauté until onion is limp, but not browned. Beat eggs well. Add bread crumbs, salt, pepper, oregano, and a couple of drops of Tabasco—or more if you're brave. Stir in the Cheddar, parsley, and artichoke and onion mixture.

  Bake in a lightly greased 7x11-inch or 8x8-inch pan at 350° for 30 minutes. Serve with any kind of cracker or pita. Serves 6–8.

Hoboken Cooks (Mid-Atlantic)

Artichoke-Tomato Tart

1 refrigerated unbaked pie
  crust
1 (8-ounce) package shredded
  mozzarella cheese, divided
8 Roma tomatoes
1 (14-ounce) can artichoke
  hearts, drained and chopped

1 cup loosely packed fresh
  basil leaves
4 garlic cloves
½ cup Hellmann's
  mayonnaise
¼ cup grated Parmesan
  cheese

Bake pie crust according to package directions in a 9-inch quiche dish. Remove from oven. Sprinkle ¾ cup of the mozzarella cheese over the baked pie shell. Cut Roma tomatoes into wedges; drain on paper towels. Arrange tomato wedges atop the cheese in the baked pie shell. Sprinkle artichoke hearts over the tomato wedges.

In a blender, combine basil leaves and garlic; process till coarsely chopped and sprinkle over the tomatoes. Combine remaining mozzarella cheese, mayonnaise, and Parmesan cheese and spoon over basil mixture, spreading evenly to cover the top. Bake in a 375° oven for 35 minutes or till top is golden and bubbly. Serves 8.

Recipes & Remembrances / Buffalo Lake (Great Plains)

The aurora borealis, or northern lights, is caused when material thrown off the surface of the sun collides with the atmosphere of the Earth. The emission of light from atoms is excited by electrons accelerated along the planet's magnetic field lines.

The appearance of the aurora borealis can be forecast by following events on the sun in relation to the speed of the gaseous matter being thrown off its surface. Various types of forecasts and predictions regarding the appearance of the northern lights are published on several websites on the Internet. The best months to view the phenomena are between October and March.

Sango Sin

2 loaves French bread
1 (8-ounce) package cream
  cheese, softened
1 (8-ounce) container sour
  cream
2 cups shredded Cheddar
  cheese

¾ cup chopped cooked ham
¼ cup chopped green onions
⅓ cup chopped green bell
  pepper
1 tablespoon Worcestershire
1 dash hot sauce

Slice off top of one bread loaf. Hollow out bottom section, leaving a shell. Cut bread top and the other loaf of bread into 1-inch cubes; place onto baking sheet. Bake at 350° for 11 minutes or until lightly browned.

Beat cream cheese until smooth; add sour cream. Stir in Cheddar cheese and remaining ingredients. Spoon into bread shell, wrap with aluminum foil, and place on baking sheet. Bake at 350° for 30 minutes, or until thoroughly heated. Unwrap, place on serving platter, and surround with toasted bread cubes. Serves 16.

Linen Napkins to Paper Plates (Tennessee)

Sausage-Onion Snacks

As quick as can be.

1 pound bulk pork sausage
1 large onion, chopped
2 cups biscuit baking mix
¾ cup milk
2 eggs, divided use

1 tablespoon caraway or
  poppy seed
1½ cups dairy sour cream
¼ teaspoon salt
Paprika

Grease a 9x13x2-inch baking pan. Cook sausage and onion over medium heat until browned. Drain. Mix biscuit mix, milk, and 1 egg together. Spread in baking pan. Sprinkle with caraway seeds. Top with sausage mixture. Mix sour cream, salt, and remaining egg. Pour evenly over sausage. Sprinkle with paprika. Bake uncovered at 350° until set, 25–30 minutes. Cut into rectangles. Serve warm. Makes 32 rectangles.

Finely Tuned Foods (Missouri)

Bacon Onion Cheesecake

⅔ cup stone-ground wheat
  cracker crumbs
⅓ cup finely chopped walnuts
2 tablespoons butter, softened
8 slices bacon
½ cup chopped onion

1 tablespoon bacon drippings
3 (8-ounce) packages cream
  cheese, softened
3 eggs, beaten
¼ teaspoon garlic powder
½ teaspoon cayenne pepper

Combine cracker crumbs, walnuts, and butter until well blended. Press crumbs evenly in bottom of springform pan. Bake in preheated 350° oven for 10 minutes. Cool on rack.

Fry bacon until crisp, reserving drippings, then crumble. Sauté onion in drippings until tender and set aside. Beat cream cheese. Gradually add eggs, garlic powder, and cayenne. Beat until smooth. Stir in bacon and onion. Spoon mixture into pan. Spread level. Bake 45–60 minutes or until cheesecake is almost set and cracks on top. Cool completely. Store in refrigerator covered with plastic wrap. Just before serving at room temperature, remove sides of pan. Serve with crackers or carrot slices. Serves 10–12.

Best Taste of Fairmont (West Virginia)

The Seven Wonders of the Ancient World

The historian Herodotus (ca.484–425 BCE), and the scholar Callimachus of Cyrene at the Museum of Alexandria (ca. 305–240 BCE) made early lists of seven wonders but their writings have not survived, except as references. The seven wonders included:

1. Great Pyramid of Giza – Egypt
2. Hanging Gardens of Babylon – Babylon, Present Day Iraq
3. Statue of Zeus at Olympia – Greece
4. Temple of Artemis at Ephesus – Turkey
5. Mausoleum of Maussollos at Halicarnassus – Turkey
6. Colossus of Rhodes – Greece
7. Lighthouse of Alexandria – Egypt

The earliest lists had the Ishtar Gate as the seventh wonder of the world instead of the Lighthouse (sometimes called Pharos) of Alexandria.

The list known today was compiled in the Middle Ages, by which time many of the sites were no longer in existence. Today, the only ancient world wonder that still exists is the Great Pyramid of Giza.

Firecracker Chile Cheese Pie

Light up your taste buds with this festive appetizer.

1 cup crushed tortilla chips
3 tablespoons melted butter
16 ounces cream cheese,
  softened
2 eggs
1 (4-ounce) can chopped green
  chiles
2 fresh jalapeños, minced

4 ounces shredded Colby cheese
4 ounces shredded Monterey
  Jack cheese
¼ cup sour cream
Chopped green onions, chopped
  tomatoes, and sliced black
  olives for garnish

Mix crushed tortilla chips and melted butter in a bowl. Press over bottom of a 9-inch springform pan. Bake at 325° for 15 minutes.

Beat cream cheese and eggs in a mixing bowl. Mix in green chiles, jalapeños, Colby cheese, and Monterey Jack cheese. Pour over baked layer. Bake at 325° for exactly 30 minutes. Cool for 5 minutes.

Place on a serving plate. Loosen side of pan with a knife and remove. Spread sour cream over pie. Garnish with green onions, tomatoes, and olives. Serve with additional chips. Serves 8–10.

Savor the Moment (Florida)

Chili Cheese Shrimp

16 ounces cream cheese, softened
2 tablespoons Worcestershire
¼ teaspoon grated lemon peel
1 tablespoon lemon juice
½ cup sliced green onions

⅛ teaspoon Tabasco
12 ounces bottled chili sauce
1 tablespoon horseradish
12 ounces small cooked shrimp

In a bowl, beat the first 6 ingredients together until smooth. Spread into the bottom of a shallow one-quart dish. Mix the chili sauce and horseradish. Spread this over the cream cheese mixture. Top with shrimp. Serve cold with crackers.

The Lafayette Collection (California)

Shrimp Mold

Big hit on a cocktail table!

1 package unflavored gelatin
¼ cup water
1 cup mayonnaise
1 (8-ounce) package cream
   cheese, softened
Juice of ½ lemon
Dash of Worcestershire
1 pound cooked shrimp, cut
   in small pieces

1 cup finely chopped celery
1 small onion, minced
1 very small bottle of olives,
   sliced or chopped
½ cup chopped green bell
   pepper

Dissolve gelatin in water. Whip mayonnaise, cream cheese, lemon juice, and Worcestershire until creamy. Add dissolved gelatin and rest of the ingredients, mixing well. Pour into lightly greased mold.

Note: If using a fish-shaped mold, save 1 olive slice to make an eye.

The Smithfield Cookbook (Virginia)

Spinach Bars

½ stick butter
3 large eggs
1 cup all-purpose flour
1 cup milk
1 teaspoon baking powder
6 medium mushrooms, chopped
1 small onion

2 packages frozen, chopped
   spinach, thawed
   and squeezed till dry
1 teaspoon salt
1 pound Cheddar cheese, finely
   grated

Melt butter in a 9x13-inch glass baking dish. Combine remaining ingredients and pour over butter in pan. Bake at 350° for 35 minutes. Cool a bit before cutting into 1-inch cubes. Can be frozen and reheated.

Holy Chow (Kentucky)

Vegetable Pizza

2 (8-count) cans crescent rolls
2 (8-ounce) packages cream
  cheese, softened
1 cup mayonnaise
1 envelope ranch salad
  dressing mix
¾ cup chopped green bell
  pepper

¾ cup chopped onion
¾ cup chopped broccoli
¾ cup chopped cauliflower
½ cup chopped tomato
1 (2-ounce) can sliced black
  olives, drained
1 carrot, shredded
1 cup shredded Cheddar cheese

Spread crescent roll dough over ungreased 7x11-inch baking sheet. Bake at 375° for 10–12 minutes or until golden brown. Beat cream cheese, mayonnaise, and salad dressing mix in mixer bowl until light and fluffy. Spread over cooled crust. Top with green pepper, onion, broccoli, cauliflower, tomato, olives, carrot, and cheese. Cover with wax paper, pressing down slightly. Chill; cut into squares to serve. Serves 20.

The Pennsylvania State Grange Cookbook (1992 Green Edition)
(Pennsylvania)

Victoria Falls, located in southern Africa on the Zambezi River, is said to be the largest falls in the world. The large sheet of water measures 5,604 feet wide with a height of 354 feet. Victoria Falls is nearly twice the width and height of Niagara Falls.

★★★★★★★ ★★★★★★★

Victoria Falls. Africa.
One of the Natural Wonders of the World.

Sausage Coffee Cake

1 pound bulk sausage
½ cup chopped onion
¼ cup grated Parmesan cheese
½ cup grated Swiss cheese
1 egg, beaten
¼ teaspoon Tabasco
1½ teaspoons salt

2 tablespoons chopped parsley
2 cups Bisquick
¾ cup milk
¼ cup mayonnaise
1 egg yolk
1 tablespoon water

Brown sausage and onion; drain. Add next 6 ingredients. Make batter of Bisquick, milk, and mayonnaise. Spread half of batter in greased 9x9x2-inch pan. Pour in sausage mixture, then spread remaining batter on top. Mix egg yolk and water and brush top. Bake at 400° for 25–30 minutes or until cake leaves edges of pan. Cool 5 minutes before cutting into 3-inch squares. This recipe doubles easily in a 9x13-inch pan. Freezes well. Makes 9 squares.

Louisiana Entertains (Louisiana)

Versatile, Variable, Dependable, Commendable Coffee Cake

1 cup sugar
4 eggs
1 cup oil
2 cups all-purpose flour
¼ teaspoon salt
1 teaspoon baking powder

1 teaspoon vanilla
1 can apricot (or other) pie
   filling
Sugar and cinnamon
Powdered sugar frosting

Mix sugar, eggs, oil, flour, salt, baking powder, and vanilla. Spread half of mixture in greased 9x13-inch pan. Spread can of pie filling over this evenly. Spread remaining batter over pie filling. Sprinkle with sugar and cinnamon. Bake 30–40 minutes at 350°. Drizzle powdered sugar frosting (powdered sugar and water) over top. Serves 8 or more.

Dorthy Rickers Cookbook: Mixing & Musing (Minnesota)

Coffee Cake with Cinnamon Walnut Topping

CINNAMON WALNUT TOPPING:

1¼ cups brown sugar 1¼ cups chopped walnuts
1 tablespoon cinnamon

Combine Topping ingredients. Set aside.

COFFEE CAKE:

1 (18¼-ounce) box yellow cake 4 whole eggs
  mix, with pudding in the mix ¼ cup oil
1 stick butter, melted 1½ cups sour cream

Mix cake mix, butter (or margarine), eggs, oil, and sour cream together. Batter will be thick; don't overmix. Grease 9x13-inch pan or 2 square glass pans. Pour in batter, then top with Cinnamon Walnut Topping. Swirl topping into batter with tip of knife. Bake at 350° for 40–45 minutes. This freezes well and is good served warm or cold. Serves 8–12.

Recipe by Otters Pond Bed & Breakfast of Orcas Island
Another Taste of Washington State (Washington)

The Victoria Falls are just over a mile wide and are made up of five different "falls." Four of these are in Zimbabwe and one is in Zambia. They are known as The Devil's Cataract, Main Falls, Rainbow Falls, and Horseshoe Falls in Zimbabwe, and the Eastern Cataract in Zambia.

The Devil's Cataract name comes from the adjacent island in the river where the local tribes used to perform sacrificial ceremonies. When the missionaries arrived in the area, they referred to these ceremonies as "devilish" and hence the name was given to this cataract.

Main Falls is the largest waterfall and certainly the most majestic view of the falls. A wide curtain of water, it has a peak flow rate of 700,000 cubic meters per minute. The sheer volume over the height of the falls is so great that before getting anywhere near the ground, the water is buffeted by the strong rising winds and turned into mist.

Rainbow Falls is the highest point of all the falls. On a clear day a beautiful rainbow can normally be viewed at this point. A lunar rainbow may also be seen on a full moonlit night.

Horseshoe Falls, as the name suggests, is shaped like a horseshoe. This is the section with the least volume of water and will be the first to dry up, usually between October and November.

The Eastern Cataract is the second highest falls and is situated completely on the Zambian side of Victoria Falls, but you can have a stunning view of the falls from the Zimbabwean side at Danger Point.

Streusel Coffee Cake

Everyone always wants this recipe—easy, delicious, and freezes well!

**2 cups graham cracker crumbs
  (approximately 15 graham
  crackers)
¾ cup chopped nuts
¾ cup firmly packed brown
  sugar
1¼ teaspoons cinnamon**

**¾ cup butter, softened
1 (18-ounce) package yellow
  cake mix
1 cup water
¼ cup vegetable oil
3 eggs**

Preheat oven to 350°. Grease and flour a 9x13x2-inch pan. Combine crumbs, nuts, brown sugar, cinnamon, and butter. Mix and set aside. Mix the cake mix, water, oil, and eggs in a large mixer bowl on low speed until moistened. Beat 3 minutes on medium speed, scraping sides occasionally.

Put ½ batter into pan; sprinkle with ½ crumbs. Top with remaining batter in an even layer. Top with remaining crumbs. Bake 38–45 minutes in a 350° oven or until toothpick inserted in center comes out clean. Cool. Serves 24–30.

GLAZE:
1 cup powdered sugar   **1½ tablespoons water**

Combine ingredients, adding more water to reach consistency for drizzling over cake.

Treat Yourself to the Best Cookbook (West Virginia)

Blueberry French Toast

2 cups fresh or frozen
  blueberries
2 tablespoons cornstarch
½ cup orange juice
¼ cup sugar
½ cup plus 3 tablespoons
  water, divided

3 eggs, beaten
6 slices bread
2 tablespoons butter, melted
Cinnamon sugar

Place blueberries in a 9x13-inch pan. Blend cornstarch, orange juice, sugar, and ½ cup water together and place over blueberries. In shallow dish or pie pan, beat eggs and 3 remaining tablespoons water together. Dip slices of bread in egg mixture, allowing time for bread to absorb eggs, then place on top of blueberries. Brush bread with butter. Sprinkle with cinnamon sugar. Bake at 350° for 15–20 minutes until bread is lightly toasted and blueberries are bubbly and thickened. Serve with syrup. Serves 6.

Taste of Clarkston: Tried & True Recipes (Michigan)

Pineapple Cream French Toast

3 eggs
¾ cup half-and-half
¼ teaspoon ground nutmeg
1 (8-ounce) can crushed
  pineapple, with juice

½ cup brown sugar
⅔ loaf French bread, cut into
  ¾-inch slices
¼ cup butter, for frying
Powdered sugar

In small bowl beat eggs, half-and-half, nutmeg, pineapple, and brown sugar. Place bread in single layer in 9x11-inch glass baking dish (may need an extra dish). Pour egg mixture over bread, lifting to let liquid run under bread. Refrigerate overnight.

In the morning melt 2 tablespoons butter in frying pan. Add 3 or 4 slices bread and cook over moderate heat until golden brown on each side. Melt 2 more tablespoons butter and cook remaining slices. Dust with powdered sugar; serve with syrup. Serves 3–4.

Recipe from Creekside Cottage Bed & Breakfast, Hill City, South Dakota.
South Dakota Sunrise (Great Plains)

Overnight Apple-French Toast

1 cup brown sugar
1 stick butter
2 tablespoons light corn syrup
3–4 large tart apples such as
  Granny Smith, peeled and sliced

1 loaf French bread
3 eggs
1½ cups milk
1 teaspoon vanilla

Cook sugar, butter, and corn syrup at low temperature until thick. Pour into a 9x13x2-inch baking dish sprayed with nonstick cooking spray, or buttered well. Place apple slices on top. Cut bread in ¼-inch slices and place on top of apples, pressing bread together tightly. Whisk together remaining ingredients and pour over bread; cover and refrigerate overnight. Bake uncovered 40 minutes in 350° oven. Serve hot with Apple Syrup.

APPLE SYRUP:
1 cup applesauce
1 (10-ounce) jar apple jelly
½ teaspoon cinnamon

⅛ teaspoon ground cloves
Dash of salt

Cook over medium heat, stirring constantly, until apple jelly melts and is consistency of syrup. Serves 8–10.

Note: The French toast can be prepared ahead, and freezes well.

Encore! Encore! (Mississippi)

On May 21, 1921, Taggart Baking Company of Indianapolis, Indiana, debuted its Wonder Bread. This bread was named by the vice president, Elmer Cline, who was filled with "wonder" by the scene of hundreds of balloons at the International Balloon Race.

French Toast Casserole

1 loaf day-old French or
  Italian bread, sliced
1 cup sweet cream
1 cup milk
8 eggs
1 tablespoon sugar
1 teaspoon vanilla
½ teaspoon nutmeg
1 cup butter, softened
1 cup brown sugar
1 cup finely chopped pecans

Layer bread in a buttered 9x12-inch pan. Mix the cream, milk, eggs, sugar, vanilla, and nutmeg and pour over the bread. Mix the butter, brown sugar, and pecans. Dot this mixture over the egg/bread. Cover with foil. Refrigerate overnight. Bake at 350° for 45 minutes, covered.

Sharing Our Best Volume II (Michigan)

Cheese Danish

2 packages refrigerated crescent
  rolls
2 (8-ounce) packages cream
  cheese, room temperature
1 egg, separated
1 teaspoon vanilla
¾ cup sugar

Grease 9x13-inch pan. Spread 1 package rolls on bottom, stretching to cover. Mix cream cheese, egg yolk, vanilla, and ¾ cup sugar. Spread on top of rolls. Spread out other package of rolls on top of cream cheese; brush with egg white and sprinkle with additional sugar. Bake at 350° for 25 minutes or until golden brown. Cool before cutting.

Our Daily Bread (West Virginia)

Easy Caramel Rolls

2 loaves frozen bread
Pecans (1 cup or more)
Cinnamon
½ cup butter

1 (3-ounce) box vanilla
  pudding, not instant
1 cup brown sugar
2 tablespoons milk

Butter a 9x13-inch pan. Cut bread into 6 slices each. Put pecans in pan and place slices of bread on top. Sprinkle cinnamon on top of bread. Heat butter, pudding, brown sugar, and milk until butter is melted. Pour sauce over bread. Let rise until double. Bake at 350° for 30 minutes. Serves 8–12.

St. Charles Parish Cookbook (Wisconsin)

French Bread with Cheese

1 long loaf French bread
1 (8-ounce) package sliced Swiss
  cheese, cut into thirds
½ cup margarine, softened
1 tablespoon prepared mustard

¼ cup minced onion
2 tablespoons poppy seeds
2 slices bacon, cooked and
  crumbled

Preheat oven to 375°. Cut bread into individual servings by slicing almost all the way through the loaf vertically. Place cheese between bread slices. Combine margarine, mustard, onion, and poppy seeds. Spread top and sides of bread with mixture. Place loaf in a foil "boat" and top with bacon. Bake 15 minutes. Serves 8–12.

Stir Crazy! (South Carolina)

Scrambled Egg Casserole

Relax and enjoy this one.

CHEESE SAUCE:

2 tablespoons butter
2 tablespoons all-purpose flour
½ teaspoon salt
⅛ teaspoon pepper

2 cups milk
1 cup shredded American
   cheese

Melt butter; blend in flour, salt, and pepper. Add milk; cook and stir till bubbly. Add cheese and cook till cheese melts and sauce is smooth.

1 cup diced Canadian bacon
¼ cup chopped green onions
4⅓ tablespoons butter, melted,
   divided
12 eggs, beaten

1 (4-ounce) can mushroom
   stems and pieces, drained
2¼ cups soft bread crumbs
⅛ teaspoon paprika

In large skillet, cook Canadian bacon and onions in 3 tablespoons butter till onion is tender but not brown. Add eggs and scramble just till set. Fold mushrooms and cooked eggs into Cheese Sauce. Turn into a 7x12-inch baking dish. Combine remaining 1⅓ tablespoons melted butter, crumbs, and paprika; sprinkle atop eggs. Cover; chill till 30 minutes before serving. Bake, uncovered, in 350° oven for 30 minutes.

Easy. Do ahead. Serves 8–10.

Culinary Classics (Georgia)

Bayfield Eggs

1½ pounds sausage
12 eggs
¾ pound shredded Cheddar
  cheese, divided
½–1 cup chopped green onions
½ green bell pepper, chopped
1 (4-ounce) can sliced
  mushrooms, drained
½ teaspoon salt
½ teaspoon pepper
½ pint whole cream

Fry sausage and drain well. Grease 9x13-inch pan. Break eggs into pan. Poke the yolks. Top with all the sausage, ½ the cheese, and all the onions, green pepper, and mushrooms. Sprinkle with salt and pepper. Cover all with cream and remaining cheese. Refrigerate overnight. Bake at 350° for 1 hour. Serves 8.

Sharing Our Best (Alaska)

Sunshine Casserole

1 (20-ounce) package frozen
  hash brown potatoes
½ pound sausage links, cooked
  and cut into ½-inch
  slices
1½ cups shredded Monterey
  Jack or Cheddar cheese
6 eggs
4 cups milk
4 tablespoons finely chopped
  onion
2 teaspoons Dijon-style mustard
Paprika
2 medium tomatoes, sliced
  (for garnish)

Grease a 9x13-inch baking pan. Cook hash browns according to package directions. Spread them in a single layer in the prepared pan. Spread sausage and cheese evenly over the potatoes.

Combine the eggs, milk, onion, and mustard in a large bowl; pour the mixture over the top. Sprinkle with paprika. Cover and refrigerate for at least one hour or overnight.

When ready to cook, heat oven to 325°. Bake the casserole, uncovered, for about one hour or until a knife inserted in the center comes out clean. Let stand for 10–15 minutes before serving. Garnish with tomato slices and serve. Serves 8.

What's Cookin' (Michigan)

Elegant Brunch Eggs

2 (3-ounce) packages dried
  beef, torn into pieces
1 cup all-purpose flour
½ cup butter
1 pound bacon, cooked,
  drained, and crumbled
1 quart milk
16 eggs, beaten
Salt and pepper to taste
1 (12-ounce) can evaporated
  milk

Place dried beef, flour, butter, bacon, and milk in large skillet. Cook and stir over low heat until thickened. Place eggs in another skillet that has been oiled and heated. Add salt, pepper, and evaporated milk. Cook and scramble gently. In an ungreased 11x14-inch deep casserole, layer half the sauce, then all of the eggs, then remaining sauce. Refrigerate overnight. Bake in a 325° oven for one hour. Serves 16–20.

Special Fare by Sisters II (Iowa)

Baked Eggs with Three Cheeses

7 eggs, beaten
1 cup milk
2 teaspoons sugar
1 pound small curd cottage
  cheese
4 ounces cream cheese, cubed
1 pound shredded Monterey
  Jack or muenster cheese
⅔ cup butter or margarine,
  melted
½ cup all-purpose flour
1 teaspoon baking powder

Beat together eggs, milk, and sugar. Add cheeses and melted butter and mix well. Mix in flour and baking powder, then pour into a 3-quart baking dish sprayed with non-stick pan coating. Bake 45–50 minutes at 350°, or until knife inserted in center comes out clean.

  May be prepared in advance and refrigerated, covered. If put in oven directly from refrigerator, uncover, and bake up to 60 minutes. Cut into rectangles to serve. Serves 12.

The Queen Victoria® Cookbook (Mid-Atlantic)

Eggs Kennett Square

1½ cups hash brown potatoes,
   frozen
½ cup diced onion
½ pound fresh mushrooms
½ cup shredded Cheddar cheese

4 eggs, beaten
½ cup half-and-half
Salsa for garnish

In a skillet, brown hash brown potatoes and onion in hot oil. Slice and sauté mushrooms. Grease 2 (8-ounce) casserole dishes. Arrange potatoes and onion evenly in dishes. Top with mushrooms. Sprinkle with cheese.

In a small mixing bowl, beat eggs and half-and-half. Pour egg mixture over potato/mushroom/cheese mixture. Bake, uncovered, at 350° for about 25 minutes or until centers appear set. Let stand 5 minutes. Garnish with salsa. Serves 2–4.

Note: This recipe is very flexible—can be made with bacon, sausage, peppers, artichoke hearts, or tomatoes.

Submitted by Kennett House Bed & Breakfast, Kennett Square
Inncredible Edibles (Pennsylvania)

Eggs Gifford

10 eggs
½ cup all-purpose flour
½ teaspoon salt
1 tablespoon baking powder
½ cup butter, melted
1 (16-ounce) carton small curd
   cottage cheese

½ pound Monterey Jack
   cheese, shredded
½ pound Cheddar cheese,
   shredded
8 ounces diced green peppers
   (or jalapeños)

Beat eggs. Mix in remaining ingredients. Pour into greased 9x13-inch baking dish. Bake at 350° for 35 minutes. Let rest 5–10 minutes before cutting. Serve with a dollop of salsa, if desired.

Aliant Cooks for Education (Alabama)

Eggsistentialist Stuffed Eggs
with Hollandaise

6 hard-boiled eggs, halved
3 green onions, diced
½ stick butter
¼ pound mushrooms, minced
½ cup light cream

¼ cup white wine
¼ cup chopped parsley
1 cup prepared Hollandaise
Salt and pepper to taste
½ cup shredded Swiss cheese

Remove yolks from eggs; chop fine.

In a saucepan, cook green onions in ½ stick butter over medium heat. Add mushrooms, light cream, and white wine. Cook mixture for 15 minutes until liquid is reduced. Remove from heat and let cool. Stir in egg yolks and parsley and blend until smooth. Season to taste.

Pour enough Hollandaise sauce in the bottom of a greased flat casserole to keep eggs from sticking to pan. Fill egg whites with mushroom-yolk mixture and place in casserole dish. Pour remaining Hollandaise over eggs to cover. Sprinkle top with grated cheese. Place casserole on the bottom rack of the oven and broil eggs 15 minutes or until golden brown. Serves 4–6.

Preparation: 20 minutes. Cooking: 15 minutes. Difficulty: Average.

Juicy Miss Lucy Cookbook (Florida)

The unique geography of Victoria Falls means you can watch them face-on and get to enjoy the full force of the spray, noise, and spectacular rainbows that are always present. The best time to view Victoria Falls is during the rainy season from March to May, when they are at their most impressive.

Eggs Benedict Casserole

2½ cups cut-up cooked ham

10 eggs, poached

¼ teaspoon black pepper

¼ cup butter, melted

1 cup crushed cornflakes or

    fine bread crumbs

Put ham in a 9x13-inch baking pan; place poached eggs on ham. Sprinkle with pepper. Prepare Mornay Sauce and pour over eggs. Toss butter and cornflakes; sprinkle over sauce in rectangle around each egg. Refrigerate no longer than 24 hours. Heat in 350° oven until sauce is bubbly. Serves 8–12.

MORNAY SAUCE:

¼ cup butter

¼ cup all-purpose flour

½ teaspoon salt

⅛ teaspoon nutmeg

2½ cups milk

1½ cups shredded Gruyère

    or Swiss cheese

½ cup grated Parmesan

Heat butter over low heat till melted. Stir in flour, salt, and nutmeg. Cook, stirring constantly, till bubbly. Remove from heat, then stir in milk. Heat to boiling, stirring constantly. Boil 1 minute. Add cheese, and stir till smooth.

Dawn to Dusk (Ohio)

Lewis Carroll's famous story *Alice's Adventures in Wonderland* was published in 1865 and is still in print today. There have now been over a hundred editions of the book, as well as countless adaptations in theatre and film. It is commonly referred to by its abbreviated name, *Alice in Wonderland,* and is beloved by adults and children alike.

Enchiladas de Huevos

This wonderful luncheon or brunch dish can be prepared the night before.

8 hard-cooked eggs, chopped
1½ cups shredded Cheddar or
   Monterey Jack cheese, divided
1 cup picante sauce, divided
¼ cup sour cream
⅓ cup chopped bell pepper
⅓ cup sliced green onions
   and tops
¾ teaspoon cumin
½ teaspoon salt
8 (6- to 8-inch) flour tortillas
Avocado slices and sour cream

Combine eggs, ½ cup cheese, ¼ cup picante sauce, sour cream, bell pepper, green onion, cumin and salt; mix well. Spoon about ⅓ cup of mixture in center of tortillas. Place seam side down in 11x7-inch dish. Spoon remaining picante sauce evenly over casserole. Cover dish tightly with aluminum foil. Bake in a preheated 350° oven for 15 minutes. Uncover. Sprinkle with remaining cheese. Continue baking uncovered about 10 minutes until hot, and cheese is melted. Garnish with avocado and sour cream. Serve with additional picante sauce. Serves 4.

Holy Chow (Kentucky)

Spinach Strata

Wonderful for brunch or Sunday supper served with spiced peaches.

1 package (4 cups) seasoned
   croutons, crushed
½ cup margarine, melted
½ cup grated Parmesan cheese
2 (10-ounce) packages
   spinach, chopped, thawed,
   and drained
2 cups cottage cheese
8 ounces Monterey Jack
   cheese, cubed
6 eggs, beaten
½ cup chopped onion
2 garlic cloves
4 tablespoons sour cream

Put crouton crumbs in 9x13-inch pan; pour melted margarine over croutons. Mix remaining ingredients together and pour over croutons. Bake 35 minutes at 350°. Let stand 5 minutes before serving. Serves 6–8.

Cooks Extraordinaires (Wisconsin)

Carolina Gentleman's Breakfast Casserole

Good hearty casserole—men love it! Use mild pork sausage for a tamer-flavored casserole; try hot pork sausage to pump up the flavor.

4 English muffins, halved
1 pound sausage, cooked,
  drained
1 (10¾-ounce) can cream of
  mushroom soup

3 eggs
1½ cups milk
1¼ cups shredded Swiss
  cheese, divided

Line a 9x13-inch baking dish with halved English muffins. Add sausage. Mix soup, eggs, and milk together with 1 cup cheese, and pour over sausage. Sprinkle with remaining ¼ cup cheese. Cover and bake in a preheated 350° oven 20 minutes or until warmed through. Serves 8.

Dining Under the Carolina Moon (South Carolina)

Brunch Casserole

This is wonderful to serve to guests for a mid-morning brunch.

6 slices white bread
2 cups shredded Jack cheese
2 cups shredded Cheddar
  cheese
1 pound link sausage, cooked
1 (4-ounce) can mild diced
  chiles
6 eggs

2 cups milk
1 teaspoon salt
½ teaspoon pepper
1 tablespoon oregano
¼ teaspoon dried mustard
¼ teaspoon garlic powder
½ teaspoon paprika

Cut crust from bread. Butter one side and place buttered-side-down in 9x13-inch pan. Layer ½ cheeses, chopped sausage, remaining ½ cheeses, then chiles. Beat together eggs, milk, and spices. Pour over ingredients in pan. Cover and chill overnight.

Bake uncovered at 325° for 50 minutes. Serves 6–8. Serve with fresh fruit.

Home Cooking (Nevada)

★★★★★★★★★★★ ★★★★★★★★★★★

Bacon-Cheese Brunch

1 pound bacon
1 (20-ounce) can apple slices,
  drained
2 tablespoons sugar
2 cups shredded Cheddar
  cheese

1½ cups Original Bisquick mix
1½ cups milk
4 eggs

Heat oven to 375°. Grease a 9x13-inch baking dish. Cut each bacon slice into fourths. Cook and stir over medium heat until crisp, then drain. Set bacon aside.

Mix apples and sugar; spread in dish. Sprinkle with cheese and bacon. Beat remaining ingredients with hand beater until smooth. Pour over top. Bake, uncovered, until knife inserted in center comes out clean, 30–35 minutes. Cut in squares to serve. Serves 8–10.

Trinity Treats (Florida)

Christmas Morning Casserole

1–2 (8-ounce) packages
  crescent rolls
1 pound sausage
6 eggs
2 cups milk

Salt and pepper to taste
1 (24-ounce) package frozen
  hash brown potatoes
1 cup grated cheese

Spray a 9x13-inch baking pan, and place crescent rolls along the bottom. Brown and drain sausage. Beat eggs, milk, salt and pepper together. Layer sausage, egg mixture, potatoes, and top with cheese. Refrigerate overnight.

Bake at 350° for 45 minutes. Serves 6.

Centennial Cookbook (Florida)

Hilltop Manor House Specialty

6 slices bread
Butter or margarine
1 pound pork sausage
1 onion, chopped
1½ cups shredded low-fat
  cheese

2 cups half-and-half (or
  fat-free cream substitute)
6 eggs
Pinch of salt or salt substitute

Remove crust from bread; butter bread, and place buttered-side-up into greased 9x13-inch casserole. Cook sausage and onion together until browned, drain well, and break up. Spoon sausage over top of bread. Sprinkle with cheese. Combine half-and-half with eggs; add a pinch of salt. Pour over bread. Cover and refrigerate overnight. Remove from refrigerator 15 minutes before baking. Bake uncovered at 350° for 45 minutes. Let stand 5 minutes.

Recipe from Hilltop Manor Bed & Breakfast, Cairo
Good Morning West Virginia! (West Virginia)

Baked Cheesy Grits

3 cups water
1 cup grits
½ stick butter
2 eggs, separated
¼ cup milk
½ teaspoon seasoned salt

⅛ teaspoon white pepper
⅛ teaspoon red pepper
¼ teaspoon minced garlic
1 cup shredded cheese
  (Cheddar or mixture of
  Cheddar and Monterey Jack)

Heat water to boiling. Add grits; reduce heat; cook 5 minutes or until thick, stirring often. Remove from heat. Add butter. Beat egg whites and set aside. Add milk to egg yolks and beat; add salt and peppers. Stir garlic and cheese into grits. Add egg mixture to grits. Fold in egg whites.

Bake in greased casserole at 325° for 45 minutes or longer, till firm on top and almost set in middle. Will firm up and settle as it sits. Garnish with sprinkle of cheese or paprika on top. Serves 6–8.

Long Hill Bed & Breakfast (Virginia II)

Tex-Mex Brunch or Supper

12 eggs, beaten
4 cups (1 pound) shredded
  sharp Cheddar cheese
2 (4-ounce) cans green
  chiles, drained and chopped

2 cups cream-style corn
1 tablespoon Worcestershire
1 tablespoon salt
½ teaspoon red pepper

Preheat oven to 325°. In large bowl, combine all ingredients; beat until well mixed. Pour into greased or Pam-sprayed 9x13-inch baking dish. May prepare ahead of use up to this point; cover and can refrigerate up to 24 hours in advance. Bake 1 hour 15 minutes, or until firm to touch, at 325°. Serves 10–12.

Note: Good served with fresh fruit and buttered bread sticks.

Collectibles III (Texas II)

World's Best Baked Oatmeal

¼ cup oil
¼ cup packed brown sugar
2 eggs
3 cups old-fashioned oats
2 teaspoons baking powder
½ teaspoon salt
1¼ cups milk

1 teaspoon cinnamon
Liquid French vanilla coffee
  creamer
Chopped fresh fruit
Chopped pecans
Honey

In a bowl, cream oil, brown sugar, and eggs together. Stir in oats, baking powder, salt, milk, and cinnamon. Pour into a greased 8x11-inch casserole dish. Bake at 350° for 30 minutes.

Place oatmeal in 4 serving bowls and sprinkle with additional brown sugar. Add just enough vanilla creamer to cover and pile on fruit. Top with pecans and drizzle with honey. Serves 4–6.

Tennessee Cook Book (Tennessee)

Chiles Rellenos

1½ teaspoons butter
1 (4-ounce) can whole green
  chiles, drained, split, and
  seeded

½ pound Tillamook or
  Monterey Jack cheese, sliced
5 eggs
¼ teaspoon salt

Melt butter in a 9x9-inch baking pan. Place chiles in pan and cover with cheese slices, leaving about ½ inch between slices. Beat eggs with salt and pour over cheese. Bake in preheated 325° oven until cheese is melted and eggs have set, about 25 minutes. Remove from oven. Let sit for 20 minutes, then cut into squares. Serves 2–4.

The Fruit of the Spirit (Nevada)

The awesome Christ the Redeemer statue, constructed between 1922 and 1931, has become an icon of Rio de Janeiro and Brazil. Weighing 700 tons, it sits atop the 2,300-foot peak of Corcovado mountain. It is visible night and day from most of the city's neighborhoods. In 2007, Christ the Redeemer was named one of the New Seven Wonders of the World.

Soups, Stews & Chilies

★★★★★★ ★★★★★★

WIKIMEDIACOMMONS.ORG

Christ the Redeemer statue. Brazil.
One of the New Wonders of the World.
The Harbor of Rio de Janeiro above which it stands is listed as one of
the Natural Wonders of the World.

★★★★★★★★★★★★ ★★★★★★★★★★★★

Strawberry Soup

First-prize winner—Watsonville Strawberry Festival 1999.

4 cups strawberries	1 cup Rosé wine
1 cup sugar	Oyster crackers
1 cup sour cream	Whole strawberries for garnish
4 cups cold water	

Put ¼ of each ingredient (except crackers) in blender. Blend. Repeat 3 times. Serve in soup bowl; garnish with whole strawberries. Serve with oyster crackers. May be served in glasses for appetizer or dessert. Serves 8.

Apples Etc. Cookbook (California)

Cucumber Soup

1½ pounds cucumbers	¾ teaspoon dill or tarragon
½ cup minced shallots (or combination of shallots, scallions, and/or onions)	4 tablespoons cream of wheat or farina
	Salt and pepper to taste
3 tablespoons butter	1 cup sour cream, divided
6 cups chicken stock (or more)	Fresh dill, tarragon, or parsley
1½ teaspoons wine vinegar	

Peel cucumbers. Cut 18–24 slices paper-thin to serve later. Cut rest in ½-inch chunks; should have about 4½ cups. Cook shallots, scallions, or onions in butter until tender but not brown. Add cucumbers, chicken broth, vinegar, and herbs. Bring to a boil, then stir in Cream of Wheat or farina. Simmer, partially covered, for 20–25 minutes. Purée and return the soup to pan. Thin with more liquid, if necessary; season. Bring to a simmer before serving; beat in ½ cup sour cream.

Ladle soup into bowls; place a dollop of sour cream in each bowl. Float cucumbers and sprinkle with herbs. Serves 4–6.

Three Rivers Cookbook I (Pennsylvania)

Butternut Squash Soup

1 tablespoon butter
1 medium onion, finely chopped
1 small garlic clove, minced
½ teaspoon curry powder
⅙–⅛ teaspoon dried red pepper
  or seeds (crushed)
2½ pounds butternut squash

3¾ cups chicken broth
1 cup water
¼ teaspoon nutmeg
1 tablespoon creamy peanut
  butter
1 teaspoon Worcestershire
½ cup heavy cream

In a small skillet, melt butter and gently cook onion, garlic, curry powder, and red pepper until wilted (not brown). Peel and seed squash and cut into 1-inch cubes (for even cooking).

In a large pot, mix squash, broth, water, and nutmeg. Bring to a boil. Add onion mixture and boil gently, covered, until squash is very tender. Remove from heat and stir in peanut butter and Worcestershire.

Purée mixture in a blender, then add cream. Stir thoroughly. Reheat on low, if necessary. Serves 6–8.

Dining Door to Door in Naglee Park (California)

The awesome Christ the Redeemer statue in the harbor in Rio de Janeiro, Brazil, is 130 feet tall and 98 feet wide and is considered the second largest art deco statue in the world. It is made of reinforced concrete and soapstone, and was constructed between 1922 and 1931.

The left arm of the statue points to Rio de Janeiro's north zone, the right to the south zone. This saintly perch offers spectacular views of Ipanema, the Maracana soccer stadium, and the Serra do Órgãos mountain range. It takes about 220 steps to see the statue up close.

Christ with his arms open is symbolic of the love Christ had for one and all. From the statue, one derives the meaning that He seems to embrace everyone who comes to Him.

Jack-O-Lantern Soup

2 cups unseasoned pumpkin	⅛ teaspoon pepper
3 cups chicken broth	½ teaspoon grated nutmeg
½ cup chopped onion	⅛ teaspoon ground ginger
½ cup chopped celery	⅛ teaspoon cinnamon
1 apple, peeled, chopped	3 tablespoons honey
2 tablespoons butter	1 cup heavy cream
½ cup light rum	2–3 cups milk
1 teaspoon salt	Salt and pepper to taste

In a large saucepan over medium heat, bring pumpkin, broth, onion, celery, and apple to a boil. Cover, reduce heat, and simmer 20 minutes. Purée in a blender or a food processor, 2 cups at a time, or press through a sieve.

Return to saucepan and stir in butter and rum. Simmer, uncovered, 1–2 minutes, stirring constantly. Stir in seasonings and honey. Add cream and enough milk to make 8 cups of soup. Add salt and pepper to taste. Heat, but do not let boil.

To serve, ladle into soup bowls. To make ahead, complete through addition of seasonings. Add cream and milk just before serving. Serves 6–8.

Family Celebrations Cookbook (Illinois)

Editor's Extra: Purée means to grind, press, blend, and/or sieve cooked foods to a soft creamy consistency. This can be done in a blender or food processor, with a potato masher, forced through a strainer, or the food merely crushed in a pot.

Roasted Red Pepper Soup

5 large red peppers
3 tablespoons olive oil,
  divided
2 cups chopped onions
2 garlic cloves, crushed
½ teaspoon cumin (optional)
½ teaspoon salt

5 whole peppercorns
1 (10-ounce) can chicken broth
1 can water
Garnish: sour cream,
  chopped parsley, green
  onions or chives

Preheat oven to broil. Prepare peppers: cut in half, remove seeds, and place cut-side-down on large ungreased cookie sheet. Brush lightly with 1 tablespoon olive oil. Broil 10 minutes (skins should be charred and blistered). Place peppers in paper bag immediately; fold and crease bag to secure. Let stand 10 minutes. Scrape away the blackened skins and rinse well. Slice peppers into strips.

Heat remaining 2 tablespoons olive oil in stockpot; add onions and garlic. Cook over medium to high heat for 5 minutes. Add roasted peppers, cumin, salt, peppercorns, broth, and water. Simmer for 20 minutes. Remove from heat; purée soup with hand blender. Top bowls of soup with sour cream, chopped parsley, green onions or chives. Serves 4–6.

Texas Sampler (Texas II)

Portuguese explorers named the Harbour of Rio de Janeiro "The River of the First of January," because they were convinced they had reached the mouth of a great river when they were gliding toward a narrow opening in the coastline on New Year's Day 1502.

The geology of this amazing place is admired by people who said, "God made the world in six days and on the seventh, he concentrated on Rio." Its climate is wonderful and the beaches are free to everyone.

Meatless Split Pea Soup

1 (l-pound) package green
   split peas
2 quarts chicken broth
2 cups diced onions
2 tablespoons crushed garlic
½ teaspoon oregano

¼ teaspoon thyme
½ teaspoon pepper
1 bay leaf
2 cups diced carrots
1½ cups chopped celery
Mrs. Dash to taste

Wash and sort peas. In a 5-quart Dutch oven combine peas, chicken broth (fat skimmed off), onions, garlic, oregano, thyme, pepper, and bay leaf. Bring to a boil. Reduce heat; simmer 1½ hours.

Stir in carrots and celery. Simmer another 1½ hours or until soup reaches desired thickness. Pick out bay leaf. Put all ingredients through a blender to cream. Serves 6.

Note: To thicken soup, stir in instant mashed potato flakes.

Amount per serving: Calories 165; Grams of fat 4.6; Cholesterol 0mg; Sodium l04mg; % of Fat 25%.

Eat To Your Heart's Content, Too! (Arkansas)

Broccoli Soup III

3 pounds broccoli (about
   3 bunches)
3 (14½-ounce) cans regular-
   strength (not condensed)
   chicken broth
1 medium-size onion, chopped
4 tablespoons butter
½ teaspoon salt
1 cup peeled, chopped potatoes

¼ teaspoon marjoram
¼ teaspoon thyme
1 pint half-and-half (or
   whipping cream)
1 (15-ounce) can evaporated
   milk
Cooked, crumbled bacon for
   garnish

Cut broccoli head from stems, then peel and slice stalks. Simmer broccoli, broth, onion, butter, salt, potatoes, and herbs, covered, until vegetables are tender. Pureé mixture in food processor or blender until smooth. Stir in milk products. Serve hot or cold. Serves 12.

Note: Liquids (broth and milk) can be adjusted to desired consistency without changing basic ingredients.

Gardeners' Gourmet II (Mississippi)

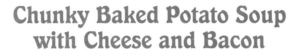

Chunky Baked Potato Soup
with Cheese and Bacon

½ cup butter
½ cup chopped onion
½ cup chopped celery
¾ cup all-purpose flour
5 cups milk
1¼ cups chicken broth
¾ teaspoon salt
½ teaspoon pepper
1½ cups (6 ounces) shredded
  Cheddar cheese

4 large baking potatoes, baked,
  peeled, and cut into large
  chunks
12 bacon slices, cooked and
  crumbled
1 cup sour cream
Toppings: chopped green
  onions, shredded Cheddar
  cheese, crumbled cooked
  bacon

Melt butter in a large Dutch oven over medium heat; add onion and celery, and sauté until tender. Add flour to mixture and cook, whisking constantly, for 3 minutes. Gradually add milk and broth, stirring until thickened. Stir in salt and pepper.

Add cheese to mixture and cook, stirring constantly, until melted. Stir in potatoes and bacon. Add sour cream and cook until thoroughly heated. Add desired toppings to each serving. Serves 10–12.

Absolutely à la Carte (Mississippi)

The Seven Wonders of the Modern World
Complied by the American Society of Civil Engineers

1. Channel Tunnel – Strait of Dover, between the United Kingdom and France
2. CN Tower – Toronto, Ontario, Canada
3. Empire State Building – New York, New York
4. Golden Gate Bridge – Golden Gate Strait, San Francisco, California
5. Itaipu Dam – Parana River, between Brazil and Paraguay
6. Delta Works/Zuiderzee Works – Netherlands
7. Panama Canal – Isthmus of Panama

Creamy Potato Soup

6 medium potatoes, cubed
1 large onion, chopped
2 carrots, diced small
2 ribs celery, chopped
6 cups water or 3 cups water
  and 3 cups chicken broth

1 tablespoon salt
1 teaspoon pepper or to taste
1 (12-ounce) can evaporated
  milk
2 cups cubed Velveeta cheese

In large pot, boil first 7 ingredients until vegetables are tender, about 30 minutes. Add milk and cheese. Lower heat, and cook, stirring, until cheese melts. If you prefer this soup thick, mix 4 tablespoons flour in 1/3 cup cold water. Add 1/2 cup hot soup gradually; return to pot and heat through, stirring gently. Serves 8.

Country Cooking (Oklahoma)

White Bean with Roasted Garlic Soup

2 cups navy or white beans
  (cleaned well)
4–5 cups water or stock
1 bulb fresh garlic
2 tablespoons oil

2 carrots, peeled and diced
1 large onion (diced)
1 bay leaf
1 tablespoon dried thyme
Salt and pepper to taste

Soak beans overnight in water. Drain and rinse well in colander. Place in a soup pot with water or stock. Bring to a boil, then simmer for 1–1 1/2 hours, skimming the surface from time to time.

Separate the bulb of garlic into individual cloves, keeping skin on. Toss garlic in oil and wrap loosely in aluminum foil. Roast in a 450° oven for 10–15 minutes or until cloves become soft. Cool.

Add prepared vegetables, bay leaf, thyme, and salt and pepper, to the beans. Squeeze the cloves out of their skins and mash with a fork. Stir into the soup. Simmer until vegetables are tender. Add more liquid, if too thick. Serve with unseasoned croutons. Serves 6–8.

Washington Street Eatery Cook Book (New England)

★★★★★★★★★★★★ ★★★★★★★★★★★★

Make-A-Meal Soup

1 onion, chopped
1 tablespoon pure vegetable oil
1 pound smoked sausage,
  thinly sliced
3 cups water
2 chicken bouillon cubes
1 teaspoon salt
¼ teaspoon pepper
1 bay leaf
½ teaspoon thyme
3 carrots, chopped
3 celery stalks, chopped
¼ head cabbage, cut in 1-inch
  chunks
2 tablespoons uncooked rice
1 (8-ounce) can tomato sauce
1 (15-ounce) can kidney beans,
  drained
1 (28-ounce) can whole
  tomatoes

In a large saucepan, brown onion in oil until tender. Add remaining ingredients. Cover and simmer for 30 minutes. Serves 8.

Our Best Home Cooking (New Mexico)

Cabbage Patch Soup

1½ pounds hamburger
3 medium onions, sliced
  thin
2 medium stalks celery,
  chopped
1 (16-ounce) can tomatoes
1 (15-ounce) can tomato sauce
2 (15-ounce) cans pinto
  beans, drained, rinsed
½–1 cup chopped bell
  pepper
1½ quarts water
3 teaspoons chili powder
2 teaspoons salt
½ teaspoon pepper
2 cups coarsely chopped
  cabbage

Brown hamburger. Pour off fat. Rinse to remove fat. Add onions, celery, tomatoes, tomato sauce, beans, bell pepper, and water. Add seasonings. Cook 15 minutes. Add cabbage last, and cook until cabbage is tender, 10–15 minutes. More water may be added to make soup the desired thickness. Add more or less seasoning to suit your taste. Serves 8–12.

Jim Graham's Farm Family Cookbook for City Folks
(North Carolina)

Extra Good Vegetable Soup

3 medium onions, chopped
1 pound ground lean beef
1 cup diced potatoes
1 cup diced celery
1 cup diced green beans
1 cup diced carrots
3 cans beef consommé soup

2 large cans tomatoes, chopped
1 cup dry red burgundy wine
2 tablespoons parsley
½ teaspoon basil
¼ teaspoon thyme
1 cup water

Sauté onions. Cook ground meat until done and drain. Simmer onions, ground meat, and all remaining ingredients for 1½ hours. Makes 3 quarts.

Note: A crockpot or slow cooker works well for this soup.

Carolina Cuisine Encore! (South Carolina)

Dorothy's Taco Soup

If you're a taco lover, you'll love this soup!

2 pounds ground beef
1 onion, chopped
2 (15-ounce) cans kidney beans
   with liquid
2 (15-ounce) cans white kernel
   corn with liquid

2 (10½-ounce) cans tomatoes
   with green peppers and
   onions
2 (15-ounce) cans tomato sauce
1 package taco seasoning

Brown ground beef and onion. Add remaining ingredients; cook for 1 hour or so. Serve with corn chips, olives, sour cream, and grated cheese. If too thick, add canned beef broth. Serves 6–12.

Soup's On at Quilting in the Country (Big Sky)

Autumn Soup

1½ pounds ground beef
1 cup chopped onion
4 cups water
1 cup cut-up carrots
1 cup diced celery
1 cup cubed potatoes

1 teaspoon seasoning salt
½ teaspoon Beau Monde
  seasoning
¼ teaspoon lemon pepper
½ teaspoon salt
6 fresh tomatoes, chopped

Cook and stir meat until brown. Cook and stir onion with meat until tender. Stir in remaining ingredients except fresh tomatoes. Heat to boiling, then reduce heat, cover, and simmer for 20 minutes. Add tomatoes. Cover and simmer for 10 minutes more, or until vegetables are tender. Serves 6–8. Soup can be frozen nicely.

Note: A 28-ounce can of tomatoes can be substituted for the 6 fresh tomatoes; use liquid and cut water to 3 cups.

The Crooked Lake Volunteer Fire Department Cookbook (Wisconsin)

Chicken Almond Soup

1¼ sticks butter
1 cup chopped yellow onion
½ cup plus 3½ tablespoons
  all-purpose flour
7½ cups hot chicken stock
2 tablespoons chicken base
  granules
½ cup sliced fresh mushrooms

1 cup diced poached chicken
  breast (¼-inch dice)
1 tablespoon fresh lemon juice
2 teaspoons tarragon
¼ teaspoon thyme
2 cups half-and-half
¼ cup toasted sliced almonds
  for garnish

Melt butter in 5-quart saucepan. Add onion and sauté until translucent. Sift flour into butter and onions and simmer for 5 minutes. Do not let brown!

Mix hot chicken stock with chicken base granules and slowly add to flour mixture, stirring well as you go. Bring soup to a boil; then reduce heat; add mushrooms and chicken, and simmer 10 minutes, stirring occasionally. Turn off heat and stir in lemon juice, tarragon, and thyme. Add half-and-half to soup. Garnish with almonds. Serves 6 or more.

A Cookbook for My Southern Daughter (Alabama)

Williamsburg Turkey Soup

1 turkey carcass or whole
  chicken
4 quarts water
1 cup butter or margarine
1 cup all-purpose flour
3 onions, chopped
2 carrots, diced

2 stalks celery, diced
1 cup long-grain rice
  (uncooked)
2 teaspoons salt
¾ teaspoon pepper
2 cups half-and-half

Place turkey carcass or chicken in water in large Dutch oven; bring to a boil. Cover, reduce heat, and simmer one hour. Remove from broth and pick meat from bones. Set broth and meat aside. Measure broth; add water, if necessary, to measure 3 quarts.

Heat butter in Dutch oven; add flour and cook over medium heat, stirring constantly for 5 minutes. (Roux will be a very light color.) Stir onions, carrots, and celery into roux; cook over medium heat for 10 minutes, stirring often. Add broth, turkey or chicken, rice, salt, and pepper; bring to a boil. Cover, reduce heat, and simmer for 20 minutes or until rice is tender. Add half-and-half, and cook until thoroughly heated. Serves 8–12.

Capitol Cooking (Alabama)

Crab Island Bisque

1 pound Florida blue crabmeat
2 tablespoons finely chopped
  onion
2 tablespoons finely chopped
  celery
¼ cup margarine or butter,
  melted

3 tablespoons all-purpose flour
1 teaspoon salt
¼ teaspoon paprika
⅛ teaspoon white pepper
1 quart milk
¼ cup chopped parsley

Remove any remaining shell or cartilage from crabmeat. Cook onion and celery in margarine until tender, but not brown. Blend in flour and seasonings. Add milk gradually, stirring constantly; cook until thickened. Add crabmeat and heat. Just before serving, sprinkle with parsley. Serves 6.

Crab Island Cookbook (Florida)

Shrimp Gazpacho Soup

This is a cold soup, but is also delicious served hot with melted Cheddar cheese on top.

½ cucumber, diced	2 tablespoons chives
1 stalk celery, diced	2 tablespoons parsley
1 carrot, diced	1 tablespoon basil
1 medium onion, diced	1 tablespoon tarragon
1 green bell pepper, diced	1 tablespoon chervil
1 (46-ounce) can V8 juice	1 tablespoon paprika
1 teaspoon salt	1 tablespoon sugar
1 teaspoon pepper	⅛ cup lemon juice
Tabasco to taste	1 pound boiled shrimp,
Worcestershire to taste	shelled

Combine all vegetables with V8 juice. Add spices and shrimp. Chill for 3–4 hours. Serves 6.

Gourmet by the Bay (Virginia)

Crab Gumbo Point Clear Style

4 tablespoons bacon fat	2 (6-ounce) cans tomato paste
6 tablespoons all-purpose flour	2 quarts chicken stock or stock
1 green bell pepper	made with bouillon cubes
1 stalk celery	2 bay leaves
2 large onions, chopped	2 pounds crabmeat*
2 pounds okra	6 cups boiled rice
2 cups canned tomatoes	Salt and pepper to taste

Brown flour in bacon fat. Add pepper, celery, onions, and okra, all cut into small pieces. Cook about 20 minutes, stirring constantly. Add tomatoes and tomato paste. Mix well.

In a large container, add mixture to stock; simmer gently one hour. Add crabmeat with bay leaves and simmer half and hour more. Season to taste. Serve with rice. This quantity makes 12–15 generous servings.

*More crabmeat may be added if gumbo is to be the main course.

Treasured Alabama (Alabama)

★★★★★★★★★★★★ ★★★★★★★★★★★★

Corn Chowder

4 tablespoons butter
1½ cups finely chopped onions
4 cups peeled and diced
  potatoes
3 cups water (or just enough
  to cover potatoes)
2 (15-ounce) cans cream-style
  corn
2 (10-ounce) packages frozen
  corn kernels

1 (13-ounce) can evaporated
  milk
1 (13-ounce) can water
1 (13-ounce) can fresh milk
Salt and freshly ground
  pepper to taste
3 tablespoons chopped fresh
  parsley leaves

Melt the butter in a 7-quart pot. Cook the onion for 5 minutes over medium heat, stirring often. Add potatoes and 3 cups water and bring to a boil. Cook over medium to high heat for about 15 minutes, or until potatoes are tender. Add remaining ingredients, except the parsley, and bring to a boil. Lower heat and simmer for 5 minutes. Purée ½ the soup, a few cups at a time, in a blender and return to pot. Stir well. Garnish each bowl with a little parsley. Serves 16.

From the High Country of Wyoming (Big Sky)

All American Clam Chowder

3 slices bacon
½ cup minced onion
1 (7½-ounce) can minced clams
  (save clam liquor)
1 cup cubed potatoes

1 (10¾-ounce) can cream of
  celery soup
1½ cups milk
Dash of pepper

Cook bacon in frying pan until crisp. Remove and break into 1-inch pieces. Brown onion in bacon fat. Add clam liquor and potatoes. Cover and cook over low heat until potatoes are done, about 15 minutes. Blend in bacon pieces, minced clams, and other ingredients. Heat, but do not boil. Bacon may be used for garnish. Serves 4.

Recipe by Former First Lady Barbara Bush
First Ladies' Cookbook (Big Sky)

Wood Stove Stew

Put all the ingredients in a Dutch oven in the order given; put the lid on, put it on your wood stove and go chop wood or work in your garden— that's more fun!

1 (10-ounce) can beef broth
1 (28-ounce) can whole or
  stewed tomatoes
1½ pounds trimmed moose
  roast, cut in 1-inch chunks
  (well, beef will do!)
1 onion, chopped
4 carrots, peeled and cut in
  large chunks
1 medium potato, cut in
  bite-size pieces

2 ribs celery, cut in bite-size
  pieces
1 tablespoon Worcestershire
2 tablespoons parsley
1 bay leaf
1 teaspoon garlic salt
¼ teaspoon pepper
2 tablespoons quick-cooking
  tapioca to thicken (or you can
  stir 2 tablespoons flour into
  the beef broth)

Put lid on and set on hottest part of stove and let simmer for 6 hours or until you get the wood chopped or the garden weeded. Serve with homemade bread, real butter, and dill pickles. Serves a bunch.

Note: If you don't have beef broth, you can use water or even, in a pinch, steal a can of your husband's beer.

Grannie Annie's Cookin' on the Wood Stove (Alaska)

Editor's Extra: You can put this in a covered casserole in a 325° oven for 3½ hours. Delicious!

5-Hour Stew

2 pounds stew meat
Flour
1 cup chopped celery
1 pinch salt
Pepper to taste
Basil to taste
Parsley to taste

1 tablespoon sugar
4 or 5 carrots, sliced
3 or 4 potatoes, cubed
1 quart stewed tomatoes
1 medium onion, chopped
¼ cup minute tapioca

Dredge meat in flour. Mix all together in a large casserole. Cover and bake 5 hours at 250°. (I have baked 6–8 hours at 200°, and it was great.) Serves 8.

A Taste of Kennedy Cook Book (Minnesota)

Catfish Stew, Southern Style

2 slices bacon
1 large onion, chopped
1 cup boiling water
1 (14.5-ounce) can tomatoes
2 large potatoes, diced
1 teaspoon salt

2 tablespoons Worcestershire
¼ cup ketchup
¼ teaspoon thyme
1¼ pounds skinned catfish
   fillets, cut into bite-size pieces

In Dutch oven or heavy saucepan, fry bacon; remove, then drain on paper towels, and crumble back into pan with chopped onion. Brown onion lightly, then add water, tomatoes, and other ingredients except fish. Simmer for 30 minutes, covered. Add fish and simmer, uncovered, 15 more minutes. Serves 4.

From Hook to Table (Florida)

Lobster Stew

The lobster feed is enjoyed by inlanders as well as those on the coast. One of the delicious aftermaths of a lobster feed is a lobster stew. The coral (eggs in some lobsters) and tomalley (lobster liver) add good flavor to the meat from claws and body of the crustacean, picked by patient lobster "pickers." We find that it takes about 5 (¼-pound) lobsters to make 1 pound (or 3 cups) of clear meat.

¼–½ cup butter or margarine   **Coral and tomalley**
2–3 cups lobster meat   **Salt and pepper to season**
2 quarts milk

In a kettle, melt butter over low heat and sauté the lobster meat, stirring until meat is pink in color. Add milk and continue cooking, stirring frequently. Reduce heat; do not boil. A double boiler at this stage is recommended. The stew will have blossomed to a rosy color. Add tomalley and coral. Season to taste. Heat to serve hot. Serves 6–8.

Many cooks prepare the stew early in the day; refrigerate and reheat when needed.

Memories from Brownie's Kitchen (New England)

World War I, also called the First World War or Great War, was a major war centered in Europe that began in the summer of 1914 and lasted until November 1918. It involved all of the world's great powers.

More than 70 million military personnel, including 60 million Europeans, were mobilized in one of the largest wars in history. More than nine million combatants were killed, largely because of great technological advances in firepower without corresponding advances in mobility. It was the sixth deadliest conflict in Western history. Germany agreed to a cease-fire on November 11, 1918, later known as Armistice Day. By the war's end, four major imperial powers—the German, Russian, Austro-Hungarian, and Ottoman Empires—had been militarily and politically defeated and had ceased to exist. The former two states lost a great amount of territory, while the latter two were dismantled entirely. The map of central Europe was redrawn into several smaller states.

Spicy Lentil Stew

1½ cups uncooked lentils, rinsed
4 cups chicken broth (homemade, canned, or bouillon-based)
2 garlic cloves, finely chopped
1 cup chopped onion
1 cup chopped green bell pepper (optional)

1 cup large carrot pieces
1 (15-ounce) can diced tomatoes, with juice
1 medium sweet potato, peeled and cut into chunks
¼–½ teaspoon cayenne pepper
½ teaspoon ground cumin

Using a large pot with lid, combine lentils, chicken broth, and garlic. Bring to a boil; lower heat, cover, and simmer for 20 minutes. Turn off heat and let lentils sit for 1 hour.

In the meantime, prepare remaining ingredients. After 1 hour, reduce heat to medium. Add remaining ingredients. Cook, uncovered, until carrots and sweet potato are tender, about 30 minutes. Serves 6.

Variation: Serve over rice or other grain.

Nutrition Facts: Per 1½-cup serving: Cal 270; Cal from Fat 15; Total Fat 1.5g; Sat Fat 0g; Chol 0mg; Sod 660mg; Carb 44g; Dietary Fiber 18g; Sugars 11g; Prot 19g; Vit A 150%; Vit C 80%; Cal 8%; Iron 30%.

Cent$ible Nutrition Cookbook (Big Sky)

Mount Everest in Nepal, also called Mount Chomolungma in Tibet, is the world's highest mountain. To say that it is 29,029 feet high doesn't give you a visual of just how high it is. But try to picture it being higher than 21 Empire State Buildings stacked on top of one another. Now that's high!

The elevation is based on a GPS device implanted on the highest rock point under ice and snow in 1999 by an American expedition. Mount Everest is rising about one-third of an inch a year. Everest is also moving northeastward about three inches a year.

Edmund Hillary from New Zealand and Tenzing Norgay from Nepal became the first climbers to reach the summit on May 29, 1953. Stacey Allison from Portland, Oregon, made the first ascent by an American woman on September 29, 1988. The conditions on the mountain are extremely difficult. By the end of the 2008 climbing season, there had been 4,102 ascents to the summit by about 2,700 individuals.

White Chili

1 pound Great Northern beans, rinsed, picked over	1½ teaspoons crumbled dried oregano
2 pounds boneless, skinless chicken breasts	¼ teaspoon ground cloves
1 tablespoon oil	¼ teaspoon cayenne pepper
2 medium onions, chopped	6 cups reserved chicken broth
4 garlic cloves, minced	3 cups shredded Monterey Jack cheese, divided
2 (4-ounce) cans chopped green chiles	Salt and pepper to taste
2 teaspoons ground cumin	Sour cream
	Salsa

Place beans in large heavy pot. Add enough cold water to cover; soak overnight.

Place chicken in large heavy saucepan. Add cold water to cover, and bring to a simmer. Cook until tender. Drain and reserve broth; cool. Cut chicken into cubes, and set aside. Drain beans.

Heat oil in same pot over medium-high heat. Add onions and sauté until translucent, about 10 minutes. Stir in garlic, chiles, cumin, oregano, cloves, and cayenne; sauté 2 minutes.

Add beans and reserved broth; bring to a boil. Reduce heat and simmer until beans are very tender, about 2 hours, stirring occasionally. Add chicken and 1 cup cheese to chili and stir until cheese melts. Season to taste with salt and pepper. Ladle chili into bowls. Serve with remaining cheese, sour cream, and salsa. Serves 8–10.

Food for Thought (Ohio)

Mount Everest

Picante Chili

1 large onion, chopped
2 tablespoons oil or butter
1 pound steak, cut into cubes
1 pound ground beef
1 (8-ounce) can tomato sauce
1 (28-ounce) can tomatoes
1 tablespoon chili powder
2 tablespoons chopped cilantro
  or parsley
1 cup hot picante sauce
  (or to taste)

1 garlic clove, minced
½ teaspoon salt
½ teaspoon oregano
1 ounce Mexican chocolate,
  grated (or baking chocolate
  with 1 teaspoon sugar and
  ½ teaspoon cinnamon)
1–1½ cups grated Cheddar or
  Monterey Jack cheese
  (optional)

Brown onion in oil or butter in large skillet until soft. Transfer to crockpot. Brown cubed steak and ground beef, a little at a time, in same skillet. Transfer to crockpot.

Combine remaining ingredients and simmer until chocolate melts. Add to crockpot and mix well. Cook for 7–10 hours on LOW setting. Serves 6–8. Serve with cornbread and a green or fruit salad.

Note: Transports well in the crockpot and will stay hot for several hours.

Only in California (California)

The Brave One is a 2007 crime-drama/psychological thriller film directed by Neil Jordan, produced by Joel Silver, and starring Jodie Foster. It was released in the United States on September 14, 2007. The film earned Foster a Golden Globe nomination for leading actress in a drama.

Lori's Firecracker Chili

Cornbread is a great complement!

1 pound cubed round steak	2 (16-ounce) cans tomatoes,
Oil	cut up
2 medium onions, chopped,	1 (15-ounce) can tomato sauce
divided	2–3 jalapeño peppers (¼ cup
2 garlic cloves, minced, divided	chopped)
1½ teaspoons cumin, divided	1½ teaspoons ground red
¼ cup chili powder, divided	pepper
2 cups water, or as needed	1 bay leaf
1 pound lean ground beef	Salt and pepper to taste
1 medium green pepper, seeded	1 (15½-ounce) can red kidney
and chopped	beans (optional)
1 stalk celery, chopped	Grated cheese, chopped onions,
½ teaspoon oregano	and peppers for garnish

In large kettle, brown cubed round steak in oil with ½ the onions, 1 clove minced garlic, ½ teaspoon cumin, and 1 teaspoon chili powder. Add 2 cups water. Bring to boil, reduce heat, and cook down until liquid is almost gone. Set aside.

In saucepan, brown ground beef with remaining onion and garlic, plus green pepper and celery. Combine both meat mixtures in kettle. Add oregano, canned tomatoes, tomato sauce, jalapeño peppers, red pepper, bay leaf, and remaining cumin and chili powder. Bring to a boil and reduce heat. Add salt and pepper and simmer at least 1½ hours. Stir occasionally and add water, as needed. If beans are to be used, add them during the last 20 minutes or so. Remove bay leaf before serving. Serve with grated cheese, onions, and peppers. Serves 8–12.

Our Cherished Recipes Volume II (Alaska)

Texas Chili

The smell of this chili cooking brought my family running.

3 pounds lean beef
¼ cup vegetable oil
6 cups water
2 bay leaves
6 tablespoons chili powder
1 tablespoon salt
10 garlic cloves, minced
1 teaspoon comino seeds
1 teaspoon crushed oregano
  leaves

½ teaspoon red pepper
¼ teaspoon pepper
1 tablespoon sugar
3 tablespoons sweet Hungarian
  paprika
1 tablespoon dried onion flakes
3 tablespoons flour
6 tablespoons cornmeal

In a 6-quart saucepan, sear beef (cubed or coarsely ground) in oil until beef color is gray, not brown. Add water, bay leaves, chili powder, salt, garlic, comino seeds, oregano, red pepper, pepper, sugar, paprika, and onion flakes. Simmer, covered, 2 hours. Cool. Refrigerate overnight so flavors will mellow.

Remove top layer of solidified fat. Reheat. With a little cold water, make a paste of flour and cornmeal. Add paste to chili. To obtain a smooth texture, cook and stir 5–7 minutes after thickening has been added. Remove bay leaves before serving. Serves 6 or more.

Cook 'Em Horns (Texas)

Parícutin is a cinder cone volcano in the Mexican state of Michoacán, close to a lava-covered village of the same name. The volcano began as a fissure in a corn-field owned by a P'urhépecha farmer, Dionisio Pulido, on February 20, 1943. Pulido, his wife, and their son all witnessed the initial eruption of ash and stones first-hand as they ploughed the field. The volcano grew quickly, reaching five stories tall in just a week, and it could be seen from afar in a month.

Salads

WIKIPEDIA.ORG

Parícutin Volcano. Mexico.
One of the Natural Wonders of the World.

"Let Us Entertain You" Salad

Such a versatile salad! The Relish may be used over greens for smaller salads. Ham and/or chicken and cheeses cut into julienne strips may be added to make this a unique chef's salad. Looks great layered in a straight-sided glass bowl.

RELISH:

1 (6-ounce) can pitted ripe olives, drained and sliced
1 (16-ounce) can French-style green beans, drained
1 (17-ounce) can LeSueur peas, drained
1 (12-ounce) can shoepeg corn (or tender young corn), drained
1 medium-size Bermuda onion, sliced into thin rings
1 medium-size red or golden pepper, sliced into thin rings
1 cup thinly sliced celery
½ cup vegetable oil
¼ cup tarragon vinegar
½ cup sugar
2 teaspoons water
½ teaspoon coarsely ground pepper

Toss the first 7 ingredients in a large mixing bowl suitable for marinating. Combine the next 5 ingredients in a jar and shake well. Pour over vegetables, and allow to marinate, refrigerated, for 24 hours.

FETA DRESSING:

1 cup mayonnaise
1 (1.4-ounce) package Good Seasons Buttermilk Farm-Style Dressing
¼ cup sour cream
2 cups buttermilk
4 ounces crumbled feta cheese

Whisk mayonnaise, dressing mix, sour cream, and buttermilk together in a wide-mouth quart jar. Add the feta cheese and refrigerate for 24 hours.

SALAD:

2 large heads iceberg lettuce, washed, drained, and torn into bite-size pieces
1 Relish recipe
3 large fresh tomatoes, peeled and cut into wedges (optional)
1 Feta Dressing recipe

Assemble the Salad in layers, beginning with a layer of iceberg lettuce, then drained Relish, tomatoes if desired, and dollops of Feta Dressing. Serves 12–16.

A Pinch of Salt Lake Cookbook (Utah)

Layered Green Salad

1 medium head lettuce (bite-size
  pieces)
½ cup thinly sliced green onions
½ cup thinly sliced celery
1 (8-ounce) can sliced water
  chestnuts
1 (10-ounce) package frozen
  green peas, uncooked
2 cups mayonnaise or Miracle
  Whip (or combination)

2 teaspoons sugar
1 teaspoon seasoned salt
¼ teaspoon garlic powder
½ cup grated Parmesan cheese,
  or 1 cup shredded Cheddar
  cheese
Tomatoes
3 hard-boiled eggs
⅓ pound bacon, cooked crisp,
  crumbled

In large bowl, preferably glass, layer first 5 ingredients, beginning with lettuce and ending with peas. Mix together well, the mayonnaise, sugar, seasoned salt, and garlic powder. Spread over top of salad. Cover bowl with plastic wrap and refrigerate overnight.

Before serving, layer cheese on top of the dressing. Thinly slice wedges of tomatoes and ring the outside; next add a ring of sliced hard-boiled eggs; fill the center with crumbled bacon.

Variation: Tomatoes and eggs can be chopped. Put a layer of tomatoes, a layer of eggs, then bacon, and cover with cheese. The first one is colorful, but in the variation, the ingredients mix better when dishing it up.

Recipes from the Kitchens of Family & Friends (Oregon)

One Life to Live is an American soap opera that debuted on July 15, 1968, and was broadcast on the ABC television network. On April 14, 2011, ABC announced that it canceled *One Life to Live* after almost 43 years because of low ratings. The final episode aired January 20, 2012.

★★★★★★★★★★★★   ★★★★★★★★★★★★

Swiss Layered Salad

1 package fresh spinach,
  chopped
Salt and pepper to taste
2 teaspoons sugar, divided
1 pound bacon, fried crisp,
  drained, crumbled
6 hard-cooked eggs, sliced,
  divided

½ head lettuce, chopped
1 (10-ounce) package
  uncooked frozen peas
1 large sweet onion, sliced
1 cup mayonnaise
1 cup Miracle Whip
1 cup grated Swiss cheese

In a long, flat 2-quart casserole, place a layer of spinach; over this sprinkle salt, pepper, and 1 teaspoon sugar. Sprinkle bacon on top, then top with half the egg slices, reserving some for top. Over this, put a layer of lettuce; sprinkle again with salt, pepper, and remaining sugar. Spread with frozen peas and onion slices. Mix mayonnaise and Miracle Whip together. Spread over top of salad; sprinkle with cheese and top with remaining egg slices. Refrigerate 12 hours. Serves 12.

Great Lakes Cookery (Michigan)

There are actually several hundred cones of volcanoes in the Mexico area, but Parícutin is the only one known to have erupted. The worst of Parícutin's volcanic activity took place in 1943, with its lava rising to about fifty feet below the crater's rim.

The volcano derives its famous name from the village of Parícutin, which now lies buried under its lava. The entire village was relocated to an uninhabited area nearby. Surprisingly, only three deaths have been registered in the entire history of volcanic eruptions of the Parícutin. Major volcanic activity of the Parícutin was witnessed until 1952. Today, the volcanic mountain stands at a height of 424 meters (1,391.08 ft).

The hardened lava from Parícutin covers an area of ten square miles, and the volcano sand (fragments of volcano material) covers an area of twenty square miles.

The city of Parícutin is located two hundred miles West of Mexico City. Ashes from Parícutin reached distances as far away as Mexico City.

Strawberry Spinach Salad with Poppy Seed Dressing

DRESSING:

½ cup mayonnaise
½ cup sour cream
1 tablespoon poppy seeds
1 tablespoon honey

1 tablespoon orange juice
1 teaspoon grated orange rind
¼ teaspoon ground ginger

Thoroughly mix all Dressing ingredients. Chill several hours to blend flavors.

SALAD:

10–12 ounces fresh spinach
2 small oranges, peeled, sliced

2 cups halved strawberries
⅓ cup sliced, toasted almonds

Wash and drain spinach and tear it into bite-sized pieces. Arrange in large bowl. Top with orange slices, strawberries, and almonds. Drizzle Dressing over Salad. Serves 6–8.

VARIATION FOR POPPY SEED DRESSING:

½ cup sugar
2 tablespoons sesame seeds
1 tablespoon poppy seeds
1½ teaspoons minced
    green onion

¼ teaspoon Worcestershire
¼ teaspoon paprika
½ cup vegetable oil
¼ cup cider vinegar

Thoroughly mix all ingredients. Chill and drizzle over Salad.

The Best of Mennonite Fellowship Meals (Pennsylvania)

★★★★★★★★★★★★   ★★★★★★★★★★★★

Ninth Street House Congealed Spinach Salad with Crabmeat Dressing

9 ounces lime gelatin
6 tablespoons vinegar
1½ cups mayonnaise
3 cups cottage cheese
4 tablespoons minced onion

1 cup diced celery
3 (10-ounce) packages frozen
  chopped spinach, thawed,
  drained, and squeezed dry
Tomato wedges for garnish

Dissolve gelatin in 3 cups boiling water; add ½ cup cold water and vinegar, then all other ingredients, and pour into 9x13-inch pan that has been coated with mayonnaise. Refrigerate until congealed. Cut into squares, garnish with tomato wedges, and serve with Crabmeat Dressing. Serves 12–15.

CRABMEAT DRESSING:
3 cups mayonnaise
¾ cup chili sauce
6 tablespoons horseradish

½ large onion, chopped
Tabasco (optional)
2 cups flaked crabmeat

Mix all ingredients except crabmeat. Fold in crabmeat, and spoon over squares of Congealed Spinach Salad.

Dining in Historic Kentucky (Kentucky)

Pink Champagne Salad

¾ cup sugar
1 (8-ounce) package cream
  cheese, softened
2 or 3 bananas, mashed
1 (14-ounce) can crushed
  pineapple with juice

1 (10-ounce) package frozen
  strawberries
1 (8-ounce) carton whipped
  topping
1 cup nuts (optional)

Cream sugar and cream cheese; add bananas, pineapple, and strawberries. Beat well. Fold in whipped topping and nuts. Freeze in a 9x13-inch pan.

Woodbine Public Library (Iowa)

Pink Arctic Freeze Cranberry Salad

2 (3-ounce) packages cream
  cheese, softened
2 tablespoons mayonnaise or
  salad dressing
2 tablespoons sugar
1 (8-ounce) can (1 cup) crushed
  pineapple, drained

1 (1-pound) can (2 cups) whole
  cranberry sauce
½ cup chopped black walnuts
1 cup whipping cream

Blend together cream cheese, mayonnaise, and sugar. Add pineapple, cranberry sauce, and walnuts. Whip whipping cream until stiff. Fold into cranberry mixture. Pour into 8½x4½x2½-inch pan. Freeze 6 hours, then unmold and serve.

What's Cooking in Kentucky (Kentucky)

Twenty-Four Hour Fruit Salad

4 tablespoons flour
2 tablespoons sugar
4 eggs, beaten
3 cups milk, divided
6 tablespoons vinegar, divided
2 tablespoons margarine
1 teaspoon vanilla
1 large package marshmallows

1 (4-ounce) can almonds
1 (15-ounce) can fruit cocktail,
  drained
1 (20-ounce) can pineapple
  tidbits, drained
2 (15-ounce) cans cherries,
  drained
½ pint whipping cream

Mix dry ingredients in saucepan; add eggs, ⅓ of milk, and ⅓ of vinegar. Cook until thick. Add remaining milk and vinegar; continue cooking until thick. Add margarine and vanilla. Pour over marshmallows, nuts, and fruit in large bowl. Let stand for 24 hours. Before serving, whip cream and toss with salad.

Calhoun County Cooks (Alabama)

Easy Ambrosia Salad

1 (20-ounce) can crushed
   pineapple with juice
1 (6-ounce) box orange Jell-O
2 cups buttermilk

1 cup flaked coconut
½ cup chopped pecans
1 (8-ounce) carton Cool Whip,
   thawed

Combine pineapple and Jell-O in saucepan. Heat just until Jell-O is dissolved. Remove from heat; stir in buttermilk, coconut, and pecans. Fold in Cool Whip. Pour into 9x13-inch pan. Chill until firm. Serves 12–15.

Bell's Best III: Savory Classics (Mississippi)

Apricot Pineapple Salad

1 (20-ounce) can apricots,
   drained and chopped,
   reserve juice
1 (20-ounce) can crushed
   pineapple, drained, reserve
   juice

2 small packages orange Jell-O
2 cups boiling water
2 cups reserved apricot and
   pineapple juice, mixed,
   divided
¾ cup miniature marshmallows

Drain and chill fruit, reserving all juice. Dissolve Jell-O in boiling water. Add 1 cup reserved juice, reserving rest for Topping. Chill until mixture has congealed slightly. Fold in fruit and marshmallows. Pour into 9x13-inch shallow dish. Chill until firm, and spread with Topping.

TOPPING:
½ cup sugar
3 tablespoons flour
1 egg, slightly beaten
1 cup reserved pineapple and
   apricot juice, mixed

2 tablespoons butter
1 cup whipped cream or Cool
   Whip
¾ cup grated Cheddar cheese

Combine sugar and flour; blend in egg, then gradually stir in juice. Cook over low heat until thickened, stirring constantly. Remove from heat; stir in butter. Cool. Fold in whipped cream, and spread over gelatin mixture. Sprinkle with grated cheese. Cut into squares, and serve on lettuce.

A Bouquet of Recipes (Louisiana II)

Apricot Cream Cheese Salad

1 (6-ounce) package apricot
  Jell-O
1 (20-ounce) can undrained
  crushed pineapple
2 small jars strained apricot
  baby food

¾ cup sugar
1 (8-ounce) package cream
  cheese, softened
1 (13-ounce) can evaporated
  milk, chilled
⅔ cup finely chopped nuts

Combine Jell-O and pineapple. Heat until mixture simmers. Add apricots, sugar, and cream cheese. Continue heating, stirring occasionally, until cheese melts. Remove from heat; chill until mixture mounds when dropped from spoon. Whip chilled evaporated milk until stiff peaks form; fold into apricot mixture. Pour into a 9x13-inch pan. Chill until firm. Top with chopped nuts. Serves 15.

Centennial Cookbook (Michigan)

Frosted Cranberry Salad

1 (8½-ounce) can crushed
  pineapple
1 (1-pound) can whole cranberry
  sauce
2 (3-ounce) packages raspberry
  gelatin

1 (8-ounce) package cream
  cheese, softened
2 tablespoons salad dressing
  (Miracle Whip or Ranch)
1 cup heavy cream, whipped
1 tart apple, peeled, chopped

Drain pineapple and cranberry sauce, reserving liquid. Add enough water to make 2 cups liquid. Bring to a boil. Dissolve gelatin in hot liquid. Chill until partially set.

Beat softened cream cheese and salad dressing together until fluffy. Gradually beat in gelatin. Fold this mixture into whipped cream. Set aside 1½ cups of this mixture for topping. Add drained fruit and apple to cheese mixture. Pour into 12x17½x2-inch glass dish. Refrigerate until surface sets, about 20 minutes. Frost with reserved topping. Refrigerate several hours. May freeze for a few days; remove to refrigerator 1 hour before serving. Serves 12.

Our Cherished Recipes (Alaska)

Chicken Mousse

2 (2½-pound) chickens
1 teaspoon salt
1 rib celery, quartered
¼ teaspoon pepper
1 onion, quartered
1 bay leaf
1 carrot, sliced
2 envelopes unflavored gelatin

1 (8-ounce) package cream
  cheese, softened
1 (10½-ounce) can cream of
  chicken soup
1 cup mayonnaise
2 cups chopped celery
2 tablespoons lemon juice
4 tablespoons chopped olives

In a large pot, cover chicken with cold water and add next 6 ingredients. Bring water to a rolling boil, reduce heat, and simmer for 1½ hours, or until chicken is tender. Reserve and strain 1 cup of broth. When chicken is cool, skin, bone, and cut it into small pieces. In a large bowl, soften gelatin in reserved chicken broth. In a saucepan, blend cream cheese with the chicken soup over low heat; add it to gelatin mixture. To this mixture, add chicken and remaining ingredients, and mix well. Pour mixture into a 9x13-inch pan. Refrigerate at least 24 hours.

Cut mousse into squares and serve it on lettuce leaves. The mousse may be topped with homemade mayonnaise. Serves 12–16.

La Bonne Cuisine (Louisiana)

Chicken Pasta Salad

1 (8- to 10-ounce) package
  rotini, cooked, hot
3 cups chopped cooked
  chicken
½ cup Italian salad dressing
½ cup mayonnaise
3 tablespoons lemon juice
1 tablespoon mustard

1 onion, chopped
¾ cup sliced black olives
1 cup chopped cucumber
1 cup chopped celery
1 teaspoon pepper
1 cup quartered artichoke
  hearts
Salt to taste

Combine rotini, chicken, and dressing in a bowl, and mix well. Combine mayonnaise, lemon juice, mustard, onion, olives, cucumber, celery, pepper, and artichoke hearts, and mix well. Add to pasta mixture, and mix well. Season with salt. Chill, covered, 1–2 hours.

Meet Me at the Garden Gate (South Carolina)

Vegetables

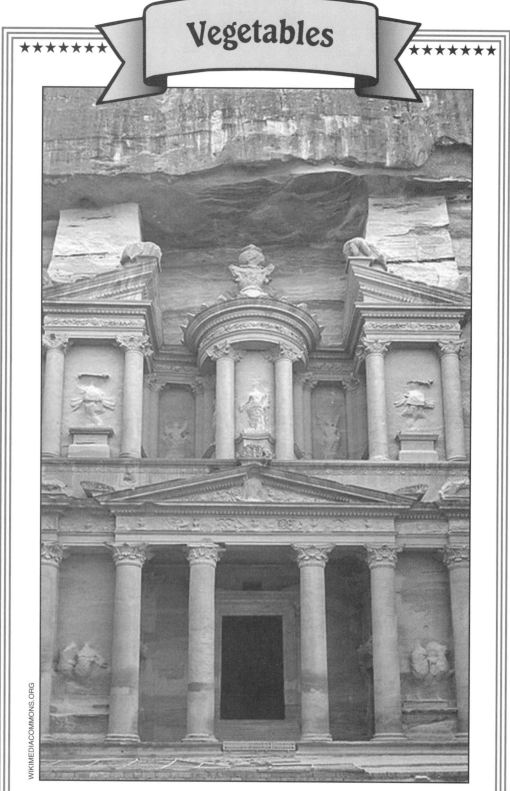

Petra. Jordan.
One of the New Wonders of the World.

Creamy Oven Potatoes

4 potatoes
½ teaspoon salt
1 onion
2 tablespoons butter
2 tablespoons flour

1 cup milk
2 tablespoons chopped fresh
  parsley
¾ cup bread crumbs

Pare and dice potatoes into ½-inch cubes. Gently boil potatoes 10 minutes in 1 cup boiling water; drain. Add salt. Chop onion. Make white sauce by melting butter in saucepan over low heat. Add flour and milk, stirring constantly, until sauce thickens and begins to boil. Place potatoes, parsley, and onion in greased casserole. Pour sauce over all. Sprinkle bread crumbs on top. Bake 35–40 minutes in 350° oven.

Neffsville Mennonite Cookbook (Pennsylvania)

Mashed Potato Casserole

A very tasty dish that you can do ahead of time and pop into the oven at the last minute. Good for a buffet.

10 medium-size potatoes,
  peeled
1 cup sour cream
1 cup cottage cheese
1 tablespoon grated onion

½ cup butter or margarine
¼ teaspoon pepper
1 teaspoon salt
¼ cup grated Parmesan
  cheese

Boil the potatoes in salted water to cover until tender. Mash potatoes or use a potato ricer. While still hot, add the sour cream, cottage cheese, onion, butter or margarine, pepper, and salt. Mix well.

Place in a casserole. Sprinkle Parmesan on top. Bake in a 325° oven for 30 minutes. Serves 8–10.

The Country Innkeepers' Cookbook (New England)

Farmhouse Potatoes 'n' Ham

5–6 large russet potatoes
  (about 2½ pounds),
  peeled and thinly sliced
¼ cup butter or margarine
3 tablespoons flour
1⅓ cups milk
2 teaspoons mustard
⅓ cup minced sweet red onion

1⅓ cups shredded Cheddar
  cheese, divided
1½ cups diced cooked ham
¼ teaspoon salt
⅛ teaspoon pepper
⅓ cup seasoned dry bread
  crumbs

Preheat oven to 350°. Arrange sliced potatoes in 2- to 2½-quart oblong oven-safe casserole and set aside. Put butter in 4-cup glass measure or microwave-safe bowl. Microwave on HIGH about 45 seconds to melt. Blend in flour, milk, and mustard. Microwave on HIGH 3 minutes. Stir and add onion. Microwave on HIGH until sauce thickens. Add one cup cheese and stir until melted. Fold in ham, salt, and pepper. Pour sauce over potatoes. Sprinkle with remaining ⅓ cup cheese and top with bread crumbs. Bake 50–60 minutes, until potatoes are tender. Serves 6–8.

The Des Moines Register Cookbook (Iowa)

The city of Petra, Jorda, takes its name, which is the Greek word for "rock," from the fact that it is most notable for its buildings and tombs that are carved directly into the red sandstone that serves as the city's natural protection from invaders. At its peak, the city of Petra was home to some 20,000 Nabataeans who, in the midst of the desert, built an ingenious system of waterways. Established sometime around the 6th century BC, the site remained unknown to the Western world until 1812, when it was introduced by Swiss explorer Johann Ludwig Burckhardt.

Its popularity with tourists may also have a connection to the city's Biblical significance. It is here where King Aretas called for the arrest of the Apostle Paul at the time of his conversion, which led him to stop persecuting early Christians and become a follower of Jesus Christ himself.

Truck Stop Potatoes

A marvelous addition to brunch or barbecue or just by itself, but not for those counting fat grams.

5 pounds small red potatoes
2 large onions, chopped
¾ cup butter, melted
3 cups sour cream, divided
3 (15-ounce) cans tomato bits, drained
1 (8-ounce) package shredded Monterey Jack cheese
1 (8-ounce) package shredded sharp Cheddar cheese
Salt and cayenne to taste
2 fresh tomatoes, chopped
1 avocado, sliced
1 bunch green onions, cut into small circles

Boil potatoes in water to cover in a saucepan just until tender; drain well. Dice unpeeled potatoes. Combine potatoes, onions, and butter in a baking pan and mix well. Bake at 350° or just until top begins to brown, stirring occasionally. Remove from oven and cool slightly. Combine potato mixture, 2 cups sour cream, tomato bits, and cheeses in a bowl and mix well. Season with salt and cayenne. Spoon into a 3-quart glass casserole. Bake at 350° until heated through. Surround with fresh tomatoes, avocado, and green onions. Spread remaining sour cream down the center of the dish, if desired. Serve immediately. Serves 12–15.

Note: Potatoes will bake in a hurry if boiled in salted water for 10 minutes before popping them into a very hot oven.

Southern Settings (Alabama)

*The Hadrien Gate and the Cardo Maximum
in Petra.*

★★★★★★★★★★★   ★★★★★★★★★★★

Southwest Scalloped Potatoes

8 medium potatoes, peeled
  and thinly sliced
1/3 cup butter
1/2 cup flour
3/4 teaspoon garlic salt
3 cups milk
2 (10¾-ounce) cans condensed
  Cheddar cheese soup

1 (4-ounce) can green chiles
1 small onion, finely chopped
Buttered bread crumbs
1 cup grated Monterey Jack
  cheese
Dash of paprika

Cook potatoes until tender. Melt butter in a saucepan and stir in flour and garlic salt. Cook until bubbly. Stir in milk and cook until it thickens and bubbles, about 3 minutes. Stir soup in with a whisk. Add chiles and onion. Drain potatoes and layer with sauce in a greased 9x13x2-inch pan. Top with bread crumbs, cheese, reserved chiles, and paprika. Cover with foil and bake at 350° for 1 hour; uncover and bake 30 minutes longer. Serves 12.

Per serving: Cal 372; Fat 8g; Carb 47g; Prot 9g.

Diamonds in the Desert (Texas II)

Scalloped Potatoes

4 pounds potatoes, sliced
2 tablespoons minced onion
1 green bell pepper, chopped
2 (10¾-ounce) cans cream of
  celery soup
1½ cups half-and-half

1 (8-ounce) package cream
  cheese, softened
1 teaspoon salt
½ teaspoon pepper
½ pound bacon, cooked crisp,
  crumbled

Stir together potatoes, onion, and green pepper. Heat soup, half-and-half, cream cheese, salt, and pepper. Mix with potato mixture and place all in a greased casserole. Bake at 350° for 1½ hours. About 15 minutes before removing from oven, sprinkle bacon bits over top and return to oven. Serves 6–8.

Our Favorite Recipes (Oregon)

★★★★★★★★★★★★ ★★★★★★★★★★★★

Linda's Baked Potato Casserole

6 large potatoes, peeled
1 pint sour cream
1 cup grated sharp Cheddar
  cheese
½ stick margarine
1 small onion, grated

¼ cup parsley flakes
1 teaspoon garlic powder
Paprika
Salt and pepper to taste
Cheddar cheese

Boil potatoes in saucepan in water to cover until tender. Drain water; add all ingredients. Mix together with mixer. Pour into greased casserole. Sprinkle grated Cheddar cheese on top and cover. Bake 350° for 30 minutes, covered. Serves 4–6.

Entertaining the Louisville Way, Volume II (Kentucky)

Greek Oven Potatoes with Lemon Juice

1 cup chicken or beef broth
½ cup olive oil (or vegetable
  oil)
½ cup freshly squeezed lemon
  juice
1 teaspoon salt
½ teaspoon pepper

2 tablespoons dried oregano
1 tablespoon garlic powder
  (optional)
1 teaspoon dried dill (optional)
6 or 7 white baking potatoes,
  peeled, cut into quarters,
  lengthwise

Combine all ingredients except potatoes in a large bowl, until well blended. Add potatoes and coat thoroughly in mixture. Arrange potatoes in a greased 9x13-inch pan and pour juice remaining in the bowl over top. Cover with aluminum foil. Bake in preheated 375° oven for 1 hour. Uncover and continue baking another 30 minutes, or until potatoes are cooked through. Serves 6–8.

A Festival of Recipes (Ohio)

★★★★★★★★★★★★ ★★★★★★★★★★★★

Hash Brown Potato Casserole

1 (2-pound) package frozen
  hash brown potatoes
1 stick butter or margarine
½ cup finely chopped onion
1 (10¾-ounce) can cream of
  chicken soup (undiluted)

2 cups sour cream
1 teaspoon salt
1 teaspoon pepper
1 (8-ounce) package grated
  sharp Cheddar cheese
2 cups crushed cornflakes

Pour frozen hash brown potatoes in a large shallow casserole dish to defrost. In a saucepan, melt butter or margarine. Add chopped onions, cream of chicken soup, and sour cream. Remove from heat. Add salt and pepper. Mix this mixture well with potatoes. Top with grated cheese, and top with crushed cornflakes. Bake at 350° for about 1 hour—until hot and bubbly. Do not overbake. May divide in half and freeze part. Serves 6–8.

The Pick of the Crop (Mississippi)

Editor's Extra: A classic, this recipe is sometimes called Funeral Potatoes because it is so often brought to feed the mourners.

How to say the number one in ten different languages:
1. French – un
2. Spanish – uno
3. German – eins
4. Chinese – yi
5. Japanese – ichi
6. Dutch – een
7. Irish Gaelic – a haon
8. Latin – unus
9. Greek – ena
10. Czech – jeden

★★★★★★★★★★★ ★★★★★★★★★★★

Ham and Potato Scallops

5 cups sliced potatoes
2 slices ham, chopped
1 (10¾-ounce) can cream of
  mushroom soup
¼ cup milk
½ cup chopped onion

¼ cup chopped green bell
  pepper
½ teaspoon salt
Dash of pepper
Butter

Place potatoes in greased casserole dish. Combine chopped ham, soup, milk, onion, and green pepper; add seasonings. Pour mixture over potatoes; dot with butter. Cover. Bake at 350° for 1 hour. Remove from oven; uncover and bake 45 minutes longer or till potatoes are done.

Down Home Country Cookin' (Idaho)

Garlic Roasted Potatoes

4 large baking potatoes, peeled
4 garlic cloves
6 tablespoons butter

¾ cup grated Parmesan cheese,
  divided
Salt and pepper to taste

Cut potatoes in half lengthwise; slice ¼ inch thick. Rinse in cold water; drain thoroughly on paper towels. Mince garlic or put through press. Melt butter in small saucepan; add garlic and cook on medium heat for one minute. Place potatoes in large bowl; add butter/garlic, half the cheese, and seasonings. Stir until potatoes are well coated; pour into shallow pan. Top with remaining cheese; bake at 400° uncovered until golden brown, about 30 minutes. Do not stir or turn during baking. Serves 8.

175th Anniversary Quilt Cookbook (Ohio)

★★★★★★★★★★★   ★★★★★★★★★★★

Ranch Potato Casserole

5 cups cooked, cubed
  potatoes, drained
1 cup sour cream
½ cup ranch dressing
1¼ cups shredded Swiss
  cheese, divided

¼ cup chopped onion
2 tablespoons minced parsley
½ teaspoon dill
1 teaspoon chives
Paprika

In a bowl, combine potatoes, sour cream, dressing, 1 cup cheese, onion, parsley, dill, and chives; transfer to a greased baking dish. Sprinkle with remaining cheese and paprika. Bake, uncovered, at 350° until bubbly. Serves 8.

Cabbage to Caviar (North Carolina)

Sweet Potato and Cashew Bake

½ cup packed brown sugar
⅓ cup broken cashews
½ teaspoon salt
¼ teaspoon ground ginger
2 pounds sweet potatoes,
  cooked, peeled, and cut
  crosswise into thick pieces

1 (8-ounce) can peach slices,
  well drained
3 tablespoons butter or
  margarine

Preheat oven to 350°. Combine brown sugar, cashews, salt, and ginger. In a 10x6x2-inch baking dish, layer half the sweet potatoes, half the peaches, and half the brown sugar mixture. Repeat layers. Dot with butter or margarine. Bake, covered, in preheated oven 30 minutes. Uncover and bake mixture about 10 minutes longer. Serves 6–8.

A Cook's Tour of Iowa (Iowa)

Editor's Extra: Use a 15-ounce can peaches for more peachy flavor. And try chopped pecans or peanuts for a change as well.

Oven-Roasted Sweet Potatoes and Onions

4 medium sweet potatoes, peeled
  and cut into 2-inch pieces
  (about 2½ pounds)
2 medium Vidalia or other sweet
  onions, sliced

2 tablespoons extra virgin olive
  oil
¾ teaspoon garlic-pepper
  blend
½ teaspoon salt

Preheat oven to 425°. Combine all ingredients in a 9x13-inch baking dish, tossing to coat. Bake at 425° for 35 minutes or until tender, stirring occasionally. Serves 6.

Beyond the Grill (Mississippi)

Praline Sweet Potato Casserole

FILLING:

3 cups mashed, cooked sweet
  potatoes
1½ cups sugar
¾ stick margarine
1 cup evaporated milk

3 eggs, beaten
½ teaspoon nutmeg
½ teaspoon cinnamon
½ teaspoon salt
1 teaspoon vanilla

TOPPING:

1 cup crushed cornflakes
½ cup brown sugar

¾ stick margarine, melted
½ cup chopped pecans

Mix all Filling ingredients and put into ungreased 9x13-inch casserole dish. Bake 15 minutes at 375°. Remove from oven and layer Topping over mixture. Return to oven and bake for 15 minutes more.

From Cajun Roots to Texas Boots (Texas II)

White Corn Casserole

10 strips bacon
1 medium onion, chopped
1 (8-ounce) carton sour cream

2 (12-ounce) cans white corn,
  drained

Fry bacon crisp. Sauté onions in bacon grease. Combine 8 strips bacon, onion, sour cream, and corn in greased casserole. Bake at 350° for 20 minutes or until bubbly. Top with remaining 2 strips bacon. Serves 5–6.

Kitchen Sampler (Alabama)

Corn Scallop

1 (15-ounce) can cream corn
2 eggs, beaten
½ cup crushed Ritz Crackers
¼ cup butter or margarine,
  melted
¼ cup undiluted evaporated
  milk
¼ cup finely shredded carrot
1 tablespoon chopped celery

¼ cup chopped green bell
  pepper
1 teaspoon chopped onion
½ teaspoon sugar
½ teaspoon salt
½ cup shredded Cheddar
  cheese
Paprika

Combine corn and remaining ingredients except cheese and paprika. Mix thoroughly and turn into a greased 8x8x2-inch baking dish. Top with cheese and sprinkle with paprika. Bake at 350° for 30 minutes or until mixture is set and top is golden brown. Serves 6–8.

Oregon: The Other Side (Oregon)

★★★★★★★★★★★★   ★★★★★★★★★★★★

Two Corn Casserole

½ cup margarine
¼ cup chopped onion
¾ cup chopped green bell
   pepper
1 (15-ounce) can whole-kernel
   corn (undrained)
1 (15-ounce) can cream-style
   corn

3 eggs, well beaten
1 (8½-ounce) box corn
   muffin mix
1 cup grated Cheddar cheese
   (optional)

Heat oven to 350°. Grease 2-quart casserole. In small skillet, melt margarine. Add onion and pepper. Sauté until crisp.

   In large bowl, combine 2 corns, eggs, and muffin mix. Blend well. Add onion and pepper. Mix. Pour into casserole and sprinkle with cheese, if desired. Bake at 350° for 55–65 minutes or until firm and set. Let stand 5 minutes before serving. Serves 6–8.

The Fruit of Her Hands (Michigan)

Chimayo Corn Pudding

This is a spicy side dish that's sure to become a family favorite . . . delish served with any and all Bar-B-Q.

1½ cups creamed corn
1 cup yellow cornmeal
1 cup (2 sticks) butter, melted
¾ cup buttermilk
2 medium onions, chopped
2 eggs, beaten

½ teaspoon baking soda
2 cups grated sharp Cheddar
   cheese, divided
1 (4-ounce) can green chiles,
   drained

Preheat oven to 350°. Grease a 9-inch square baking pan. Combine first 7 ingredients and mix well. Turn half the batter into the greased pan; cover evenly with half the cheese, all the chiles, then remaining cheese. Top with remaining batter. Bake 1 hour. Let cool 15 minutes before serving. Serves 8–12.

Collectibles III (Texas II)

4th of July Bean Casserole

Made with bacon and ground beef, this is a tasty side dish for a barbe-cue, but could be served as a main dish any time of year.

½ pound bacon, diced
½ pound ground beef
1 cup chopped onion
1 (28-ounce) can pork and beans
1 (15-ounce) can lima beans,
  rinsed and drained
1 (15-ounce) can kidney beans,
  rinsed and drained

½ cup barbecue sauce
½ cup ketchup
½ cup sugar
½ cup packed brown sugar
2 tablespoons mustard
2 tablespoons molasses
1 teaspoon salt
½ teaspoon chili powder

Preheat oven to 350°. In a skillet over medium-high heat, cook bacon, beef, and onion until meat is brown and onion is tender. Remove from heat and drain. Place in a greased casserole dish. Add beans and mix well. In a separate bowl, combine barbecue sauce, ketchup, sugars, mustard, molasses, salt, and chili powder and stir into beef mixture. Cover and bake for 45 minutes. Uncover and bake for 15 minutes longer, or until browned and bubbly. Serves 12 as a side dish.

Note: If serving this savory baked casserole as a main course, offer hot cornbread and a green salad to make a full meal.

In the Kitchen with Kendi (Mid-Atlantic)

The Colorado River has wound its way through the various layers of the Grand Canyon walls for millions of years, carving a gorge of epic proportions. The near-ly forty major sedimentary rock layers exposed in its walls and in the Grand Canyon National Park area range in age from about two hundred million to nearly two billion years old.

Calico Beans

A good dish to take to a picnic or a potluck dinner. Serve with raw or lightly steamed vegetable sticks and a dip for a complete meal.

¼ pound bacon (4–5 slices)
½ cup chopped onion
1 (31-ounce) can pork and
 beans, drained
1 (15-ounce) can black beans,
 drained
1 (15-ounce) can Great Northern
 beans, drained

½ cup crushed pineapple,
 drained
¼ cup chopped green bell
 pepper
½ cup ketchup
¼ cup brown sugar
1 tablespoon cider vinegar
1 teaspoon mustard

Set oven to 325°. Fry bacon, drain grease, and chop or tear into bite-size pieces. Cook onion in a small amount of bacon grease until golden in color. Pour all 3 cans of beans into a 9x13-inch casserole dish. Add bacon, onion, pineapple, and green pepper. In small bowl, mix together ketchup, brown sugar, vinegar, and mustard. Stir ketchup mixture into bean mixture. Bake for 40–50 minutes or until juices bubble. Serves 10–12.

Food for Tots (Washington)

Sweet Sour Baked Beans

8 bacon slices (or hamburger)
4 large onions
½–1 cup brown sugar
1 teaspoon dry mustard
½ teaspoon garlic powder
1 teaspoon salt
½ cup vinegar

2 (15-ounce) cans butter beans
1 (1-pound) can green lima
 beans
1 (1-pound) can dark red
 kidney beans
1 (1-pound, 11-ounce) can New
 England-style baked beans

Pan-fry bacon until crisp; drain and crumble. Cut onions into rings. Put onions in skillet; add sugar, mustard, garlic powder, salt, and vinegar. Cook 20 minutes, covered. Add onion mixture to drained beans. Add bacon. Pour into 3-quart casserole. Bake at 350° for 1 hour. Serves 10–12.

Happy Times with Home Cooking (Virginia)

Curry Green Bean Casserole

3 cups frozen cut green beans
1 cup sliced celery, cut slantwise
½ cup thinly sliced onions
1 cup sliced water chestnuts

½ cup sour cream
¼ cup mayonnaise
⅛ teaspoon curry powder
Salt and pepper to taste

Cook the beans, celery, and onions all together; drain. Add water chestnuts. Mix in sour cream, mayonnaise, and curry powder. Season to your taste. Pour into a shallow casserole and bake at 300° until hot (about an hour). Brown under broiler. Serves 6.

Seasons of Thyme (Kentucky)

Green Bean & Corn Casserole

2 cups crushed Ritz-style
  crackers, divided
2 (14-ounce) cans French-style
  green beans, drained
1 (14-ounce) can shoepeg corn
  (no substitute)
1 (8-ounce) can sliced water
  chestnuts

1 small onion, finely chopped
1 (10¾-ounce) can cream of
  celery soup
8 ounces sour cream
1 cup shredded Cheddar cheese
1 stick butter, melted
1 (2¼-ounce) package slivered
  almonds (optional)

Layer ½ cup crackers, beans, corn, water chestnuts, and onion in a greased 9x13-inch pan. Combine soup, sour cream, cheese, and butter in a small bowl and pour over mixture in pan. Top with remaining 1½ cups crackers and chopped almonds, if desired. Bake in oven at 350° for 30–35 minutes. Serves 6–8.

Smoke in the Mountains Cookbook (Tennessee)

Green Beans with Swiss Cheese

1 tablespoon butter
1 tablespoon flour
½ teaspoon pepper
¼ cup milk
½ teaspoon grated onion
½ cup sour cream

2 (16-ounce) cans green beans, drained
1½ cups grated Swiss cheese
⅓ cup cornflake crumbs
2 tablespoons melted butter

Heat oven to 400°. Melt 1 tablespoon butter in saucepan and blend in flour and pepper; cook, stirring until bubbling. Blend in milk. Remove from heat and stir in onion and sour cream. Combine sauce with green beans and cheese. Turn into buttered 1½-quart casserole. Combine cornflakes with melted butter and spread on top. Bake 20 minutes. Serves 6–8.

Ashton Area Cookbook (Idaho)

Broccoli-Cauliflower Casserole

1 (16-ounce) package frozen broccoli cuts
1 (16-ounce) package frozen cauliflower flowerets
1 large onion, chopped
2 tablespoons margarine
2 tablespoons all-purpose flour
1 teaspoon salt
½ teaspoon garlic powder

½ teaspoon dried basil
¼ teaspoon pepper
1¼ cups milk
2 (3-ounce) cartons cream cheese with chives
¾ cup soft bread crumbs
3 tablespoons grated Parmesan cheese
2 tablespoons melted butter

Cook broccoli and cauliflower according to directions; drain, and set aside. Cook onion in butter until tender. Stir in flour, salt, garlic, basil, and pepper. Add milk; cook until thick and bubbly. Add cream cheese. Stir until cheese melts. Stir into vegetable mixture. Place mixture in 2-quart casserole dish. Toss together bread crumbs, Parmesan cheese, and melted butter. Sprinkle over vegetable mixture. Bake uncovered at 350° for 25–30 minutes. Serves 6–8.

Cooking with People to People (Florida)

Broccoli Hot Dish

1 (16-ounce) package frozen
  chopped broccoli
1–2 cups quick rice (cooked)
1 (15-ounce) jar Cheez-Whiz or
  Cheddar cheese soup
1 (8-ounce) can sliced water
  chestnuts (optional)

Chopped onion and celery
  (optional)
¼ cup milk
1 (10¾-ounce) can cream of
  mushroom or chicken soup
Crushed potato chips or
  French fried onion rings

Mix all except last ingredient together in casserole dish and bake 30–40 minutes at 350°. Cover with crushed potato chips or onions 15 minutes before done. Serves 6.

Variation 1: For Mexican dish, use jalapeño Cheez-Whiz, but be careful!! May add 2 cups grated cheese. Add ⅔ of it to the casserole; top with remaining.

Variation 2: Combine broccoli, 2 cups rice, onion, 8 ounces Cheez-Whiz and ½ cup half-and-half.

Country Cupboard Cookbook (Iowa)

Broccoli Puffs

1 (10-ounce) package broccoli
  cuts
1 (10¾-ounce) can cream of
  mushroom soup
½ cup shredded Cheddar cheese

¼ cup milk
¼ cup mayonnaise
1 egg, beaten
¼ cup bread crumbs
1 tablespoon melted butter

Cook broccoli and drain well. Put in baking dish. Mix together soup, cheese, milk, mayonnaise, and egg; pour over broccoli. Brown bread crumbs in butter; sprinkle on top. Bake at 350° for 45 minutes. Serves 4.

Through Our Kitchen Windows (Florida)

★★★★★★★★★★★★ ★★★★★★★★★★★★

Glazed Broccoli with Almonds

2 pounds fresh broccoli
½ teaspoon salt
1 beef bouillon cube
¾ cup hot water
1 cup half-and-half
¼ cup butter or margarine
¼ cup all-purpose flour
2 tablespoons sherry

2 tablespoons lemon juice
⅛ teaspoon pepper
2 teaspoons monosodium
  glutamate (optional)
½ cup (2-ounces) shredded
  Cheddar cheese
¼ cup slivered almonds

Trim off large leaves of broccoli. Remove tough ends of lower stalks and wash broccoli thoroughly; separate into spears. Cook broccoli, covered, in a small amount of boiling salted water for 10 minutes or until crisp-tender. Drain well and place in a 12x8x2-inch baking dish. Dissolve bouillon cube in ¾ cup hot water; stir in half-and-half and set aside.

Melt butter in a heavy saucepan over low heat; blend in flour, stirring until smooth. Cook 1 minute, stirring constantly. Gradually stir in bouillon mixture; cook over medium heat, stirring constantly until thickened and bubbly. Stir in sherry, lemon juice, pepper, and monosodium glutamate.

Pour sauce over broccoli. Sprinkle with cheese and almonds. Bake at 375° for 25–30 minutes. Serves 6.

Hospitality Heirlooms (Mississippi)

A hole in one is scored once every 3,500 golf rounds. Only 1%–2% of golfers score one during the year. A hole in one on a par four is called an albatross.

Hundred Dollar Broccoli Casserole

2 (10-ounce) packages frozen
  broccoli
1 (8-ounce) package cream
  cheese
1 envelope Lipton Dry Onion
  Soup Mix

1 (8-ounce) carton sour cream
1 (8-ounce) can water
  chestnuts, drained and sliced
Sharp grated cheese
Ritz Cracker crumbs

Cook broccoli until tender in the amount of water called for on one package and drain. Have cream cheese out of refrigerator at least 3 hours to soften. Mash together soup mix, cream cheese, sour cream, and chestnuts. Add to drained broccoli and stir well. Place in lightly buttered casserole dish and top with grated cheese and cracker crumbs; dot with butter. Bake at 275° for 30–35 minutes. Serves 8–10.

Our Favorite Recipes (Illinois)

Quick and Easy Broccoli Potluck

2 (10-ounce) packages frozen
  chopped broccoli, thawed
2 (10¾-ounce) cans cream of
  mushroom soup
1 (8-ounce) can sliced water
  chestnuts, drained

1 (8-ounce) can bamboo shoots,
  drained
1 cup shredded Cheddar
  cheese, divided
1 (3-ounce) can French-fried
  onions, divided

Combine broccoli, soup, water chestnuts, bamboo shoots, half the cheese, and half the onions in bowl; mix well. Add enough water for desired consistency. Spoon into 1½-quart baking dish. Bake, covered, at 350° for 20 minutes. Sprinkle with remaining cheese and onions. Bake, uncovered, for 10 minutes longer. May substitute green beans for broccoli and cream of chicken or celery soup for mushroom soup. Serves 8.

Approximately per serving: Cal 234; Prot 8g; Carbo 18g; Fiber 4g; Total Fat 15g; 57% Calories from Fat; Chol 16mg; Sod 752mg.

Best Bets (Nevada)

★★★★★★★★★★★★   ★★★★★★★★★★★★

Yellow Squash Casserole

2 pounds yellow squash, sliced	2 tablespoons butter
Salt to taste	1 teaspoon salt
½ cup whipping cream	½ teaspoon white pepper
2 tablespoons butter, melted	1½ cups shredded Cheddar
3 eggs, slightly beaten	cheese, divided
1½ cups sliced celery	9 slices bacon, crisp-fried,
1 cup chopped onion	crumbled

Cook squash in boiling water, with salt to taste, in saucepan, until tender; drain. Mash squash in large bowl. Add cream, 2 tablespoons melted butter, and eggs; mix well. Sauté celery and onion in butter in skillet until tender. Add to squash mixture with salt, white pepper, and half the cheese; mix well. Spoon into 9x13-inch baking dish; top with remaining cheese and bacon. Bake at 350° for 45 minutes. Serve immediately. Serves 8–10.

Calling All Cooks, Three (Alabama)

Ranch Squash Casserole

The key to this creamy casserole is the ranch dressing.

2 pounds yellow squash, sliced	1 envelope ranch buttermilk dressing
1 cup sliced onion	1 cup shredded Cheddar
¾ cup mayonnaise	cheese
2 eggs, slightly beaten	2 tablespoons butter, melted
½ cup crushed unsalted soda crackers	½ cup fresh bread crumbs

Cook squash and onion together in water until tender; drain well. In a bowl, mix mayonnaise, eggs, crackers, ranch dressing, and shredded cheese together. Mash squash with a fork and combine with ranch mixture. Pour into a greased casserole dish. Mix melted butter with bread crumbs and put on top of casserole. Bake 20–25 minutes in a 350° oven. Serves 6–8.

Someone's in the Kitchen with Melanie (North Carolina)

★★★★★★★★★★★ ★★★★★★★★★★★

Butternut Squash Soufflé

2 cups cooked, mashed butternut
   squash
3 eggs, beaten
⅓ cup butter, melted
½ cup milk
¾–1 cup sugar
½ teaspoon ground ginger
½ teaspoon coconut extract

Mix all ingredients together. Pour into lightly greased 1½-quart casserole, and bake 1 hour at 350°. Serves 8.

Louisiana Entertains (Louisiana)

Zucchini Moussaka

2 tablespoons vegetable oil
3 zucchini, cut in ¼-inch
   slices
1 onion, sliced
1 pound lean ground beef
1 (8-ounce) can tomato sauce
1 garlic clove, minced
½ teaspoon salt
¼ teaspoon cinnamon
1 egg, slightly beaten
1 cup small-curd cottage
   cheese
¼ cup freshly grated
   Parmesan or feta cheese
Cinnamon
Nutmeg

Put oil in skillet; add zucchini and onion, and brown lightly. Remove from skillet and place in a shallow 1½–2-quart baking dish.

Brown ground beef in same skillet. Drain fat. Stir in tomato sauce, garlic, salt, and cinnamon. Spoon mixture over zucchini and onion in baking dish. Blend egg and cottage cheese. Spoon over meat. Sprinkle Parmesan or feta over cottage cheese mixture. Sprinkle cinnamon and nutmeg over top. Bake at 350° for 30 minutes. Serves 6.

Cooking for Applause (Missouri)

Italian Zucchini Crescent Pie

This recipe is great for picnics or to go with ham, pork chops, etc.

**4 cups thinly sliced unpeeled
   zucchini**
1 cup chopped onions
½ cup margarine or butter
2 tablespoons parsley flakes
¼ teaspoon garlic powder
¼ teaspoon oregano
½ teaspoon salt

½ teaspoon pepper
¼ teaspoon basil leaves
2 eggs, well beaten
**2 cups shredded mozzarella
   cheese**
1 (8-count) can crescent rolls
2 teaspoons mustard

Heat oven to 375°. In 10-inch skillet, cook zucchini and onions in margarine until tender (about 10 minutes). Stir in parsley and seasonings. In large bowl, blend eggs and cheese. Stir in vegetable mixture. Separate dough into 8 triangles. Place in ungreased 11-inch quiche pan. Press over bottom and up sides to form crust. Spread crust with mustard. Pour vegetable mixture evenly into crust. Bake at 375° for 18–20 minutes, or until knife inserted near center comes out clean. Let stand 10 minutes before serving. Serves 6–8.

Note: For extra cheesy flavor, use 3 cups mozzarella instead of 2.

Dutch Pantry Cookin' (West Virginia)

★★★★★★★★★★★ ★★★★★★★★★★★

New England Autumn Casserole

2½ cups thinly sliced pumpkin
  or winter squash, peeled and
  seeded
1½ cups sliced apples
¼ cup butter, melted
3–4 tablespoons brown sugar

1 teaspoon cinnamon
½ cup walnuts or almonds,
  broken up
Salt to taste
Butter to taste

Place a layer of pumpkin, then a layer of apples, in a 2-quart casserole. (The pumpkin or squash will not cook as quickly, so slice it more thinly than the apples.)

Combine ¼ cup melted butter, sugar, cinnamon, nuts, and salt; drizzle some over apples and pumpkin. Continue alternating layers and drizzling with butter-and-sugar mixture until all ingredients have been used. Dot with a bit more butter.

Cover casserole and bake at 350° for 45–60 minutes or until pumpkin and apples are tender. Serves 4.

Apple Orchard Cookbook (New England)

Top Ten Greatest One-Hit Wonders

A one-hit wonder is a person or act known mainly for only a single success. The term is most often used to describe music performers with only one hit single.

1. Los del Río — "Macarena" (1996)
2. Soft Cell — "Tainted Love" (1982)
3. Dexys Midnight Runners – "Come On Eileen" (1983)
4. Right Said Fred — "I'm Too Sexy" (1992)
5. Toni Basil — "Mickey" (1982)
6. Baha Men — "Who Let the Dogs Out?" (2000)
7. Vanilla Ice — "Ice Ice Baby" (1990)
8. A-ha — "Take On Me" (1985)
9. Gerardo — "Rico Suave" (1990)
10. Nena — "99 Luftballons" (1983)

★★★★★★★★★★★ ★★★★★★★★★★★

Oven Roasted Vegetables

1 pound red skin potatoes, cut
  into 1-inch pieces
1 (16-ounce) bag peeled baby
  carrots
1 medium onion, sliced
3 garlic cloves, minced
2 tablespoons dried oregano
2 tablespoons finely chopped
  fresh basil
1 teaspoon salt

1 teaspoon pepper
½ cup olive oil
3 tablespoons fresh lemon juice
1 zucchini, cut into ½-inch
  wide strips
1 large red bell pepper, cut into
  ½-inch strips
1 large green bell pepper, cut
  into ½-inch strips

Preheat oven to 450°. In a 9x13-inch pan, combine potatoes, carrots, and onion. Mix all spices, oil, and lemon juice, and drizzle over vegetables. Toss to coat. Bake, uncovered, 30 minutes, turning occasionally.

Remove from oven and add remaining vegetables. Return to oven and bake an additional 15–20 minutes. If vegetables are too dry, add more olive oil and toss. Serves 6–8.

Three Rivers Renaissance Cookbook IV (Pennsylvania)

Mixed Vegetable Casserole
(Cate's)

1 (20-ounce) package frozen
  mixed vegetables (cook as
  directed)
1 cup chopped onion
1 cup chopped celery

1 stick margarine, melted
1 cup grated Cheddar cheese
1 cup mayonnaise
1 sleeve Ritz Crackers

Put cooked vegetables in greased casserole. Sauté onion and celery in part of the margarine. Mix with cheese and mayonnaise and spread over vegetables. Mix crushed crackers with rest of margarine. Spread over casserole. Bake 30 minutes at 350°.

The Wyman Sisters Cookbook (Kentucky)

★★★★★★★★★★★ ★★★★★★★★★★★

Robin's Nest Vegetable Pie

3 eggs
⅔ cup milk
½ teaspoon salt
½ cup chopped onion

½ cup chopped mushrooms
1 cup cooked cut broccoli
1 (9-inch) pie shell, unbaked
1 tomato, sliced

Beat eggs, milk, and salt together. Sauté onion and mushrooms together in a small amount of oil, butter, or cooking spray. Add onion, mushrooms, and broccoli to egg mixture; pour into pie shell.

Bake in preheated 400° oven for 35 minutes. Before removing from oven, place tomato slices on top, and bake an additional 5 minutes. Serves 4.

Dining in Historic Kentucky (Kentucky)

Vegetable Pie with Rice Crust

1 cup sliced carrots
¼ cup chopped onion
1 green bell pepper, chopped
1 cup cubed turnips
1½ cups chopped celery

2 cups cubed potatoes
4 tablespoons butter
4 tablespoons flour
1 teaspoon salt
1 cup milk

Cook all vegetables except potatoes in salted water for 15 minutes. Add potatoes. Cook until tender. Drain. Melt butter, and add flour, salt, milk, and vegetables. Put in casserole and cover with Rice Crust. Bake at 400° for 20 minutes.

RICE CRUST:
2 cups cooked rice
⅓ cup milk
2 eggs, separated
1½ cups all-purpose flour

1 tablespoon sugar
1 teaspoon baking powder
½ teaspoon salt
1 tablespoon butter, melted

Mix rice and milk. Beat yolks and add to rice mixture. Sift dry ingredients and add to mixture with butter. Beat well and fold in beaten egg whites. Serves 4–8.

Seasoned with Grace (New England)

★★★★★★★★★★★ ★★★★★★★★★★★

Vegetable Casserole with Cream Cheese

This combination of vegetables makes an attractive and delicious dish.

1 (16-ounce) package frozen
  cauliflower, broccoli, and
  carrots (or vegetables of your
  choice)
4 tablespoons butter
4 tablespoons flour

2 cups milk
1 (8-ounce) package cream
  cheese
Salt and pepper to taste
Grated Parmesan cheese

Cook vegetables until almost done. In saucepan add butter, flour, milk, cream cheese, salt and pepper to taste. Heat and stir until creamy and smooth. Pour over vegetables in casserole dish and sprinkle with Parmesan cheese. Bake at 350° for 30 minutes. Serves 4.

Tastes of Country (Washington)

Baked Tomatoes Rockefeller

2 (10-ounce) packages frozen
  chopped spinach
2 cups seasoned bread crumbs
6 green onions, chopped
6 eggs, slightly beaten
¾ cup butter, melted
½ cup grated Parmesan cheese
¼ teaspoon Worcestershire

½ teaspoon minced garlic
1 teaspoon salt
½ teaspoon black pepper
1 teaspoon thyme
1 teaspoon monosodium
  glutamate (optional)
¼ teaspoon Tabasco
12 thick tomato slices

Cook spinach according to directions. Add remaining ingredients except tomato. Arrange tomato slices in a single layer in buttered 9x13-inch baking dish. Mound spinach mixture on tomato slices. Sprinkle lightly with more Parmesan cheese. Bake at 350° for 15 minutes. The spinach mixture may be made well in advance and it freezes well. Serves 12.

Vintage Vicksburg (Mississippi)

★★★★★★★★★★★ ★★★★★★★★★★★

Beaufort Tomato Pie

1 (9-inch) deep-dish frozen pie
  shell, baked, cooled
2–3 large ripe tomatoes,
  thickly sliced
Salt and pepper to taste
Dried sweet basil to taste
Chives to taste
3 green onions, chopped
1 cup (scant) Miracle Whip
1 cup shredded sharp Cheddar
  cheese

Fill pie shell with tomato slices. Sprinkle with salt, pepper, basil, chives, and green onions. Mix Miracle Whip and cheese. Spread over tomatoes, sealing to the edges. Bake 35 minutes at 350°. Serves 6–8.

Dining Under the Carolina Moon (South Carolina)

Tomato Casserole

2 (16-ounce) cans diced
  tomatoes, or 2 pounds fresh
  tomatoes, diced
½ cup chopped onion
¼ cup chopped bell pepper
1 cup cornbread stuffing
¾–1 cup firmly packed light
  brown sugar
1 tablespoon Worcestershire
¾ teaspoon Creole or Cajun
  seasoning
1 cup (4 ounces) shredded
  sharp Cheddar cheese
  (optional)

Combine tomatoes, onion, bell pepper, cornbread stuffing, brown sugar, Worcestershire, and seasoning, stirring well. Pour into a greased 9x13-inch baking dish, and bake at 350° for 30 minutes or until bubbly. Top with cheese, if desired. Serves 12.

Worth Savoring (Mississippi)

★★★★★★★★★★★ ★★★★★★★★★★★

Tomato Okra Casserole

6 tablespoons chopped onion
2 tablespoons bacon grease
1 pound okra, sliced
1 quart tomatoes, peeled
   and cooked (or canned)
¼ teaspoon curry powder
½ teaspoon paprika

1 tablespoon sugar
1½ teaspoons salt
¼ teaspoon red pepper flakes
2½ tablespoons grated
   Parmesan cheese
8 butter crackers, crumbled

Sauté onion in bacon grease. Add okra, and cook until tender. Add tomatoes and seasoning. Pour into greased casserole dish. Top with cheese, then cracker crumbs. Bake at 350° for 35 minutes. Serves about 12.

Welcome Back to Pleasant Hill (Kentucky)

Tony's Cabbage Casserole

1 medium head cabbage
4 tablespoons margarine
1 pound lean ground meat
1 medium onion, chopped
2 garlic cloves, minced
Tony's Creole Seasoning

1 (10¾-ounce) can cream of
   mushroom soup
¼ cup chopped green onions
1 cup steamed rice
¼ cup bread crumbs

Cut cabbage into small chunks. Boil in salted water in a medium pot until tender, but still green. Drain and reserve the liquid. Melt margarine in a deep skillet, and fry ground meat with onion and garlic until brown. Add Tony's Creole Seasoning. In a large bowl, mix cabbage with meat, adding mushroom soup, green onions, and rice.

Pour mixture into greased, flat baking dish. Top with bread crumbs. If you think the casserole is too dry, add some of the water from the boiled cabbage. Bake at 300° for 20–30 minutes. Serves 6.

Tony Chachere's Second Helping (Louisiana II)

Cabbage Casserole

1 stick margarine
2 cups crumbled cornflakes
6–7 cups shredded cabbage
2 cups chopped onions

1 (8-ounce) can sliced water
   chestnuts, drained
   (optional)
2 cups grated Cheddar cheese

Mix margarine and cornflakes. Place ½ of mixture in bottom of 9x13-inch dish. Spread cabbage over cornflakes and sprinkle with onions and water chestnuts, if desired.

SAUCE:

1 (8-ounce) container sour
   cream, or ½ cup mayonnaise
1 cup milk

1 (10¾-ounce) can cream
   of celery soup
Salt and pepper to taste

Mix all ingredients and pour over cabbage. Top with remaining cornflake mixture. Bake in 350° oven 30–40 minutes. Remove from oven. Top with grated cheese. Allow to melt before serving. Serves 8–10.

The Best of Mayberry (North Carolina)

GWEN McKEE

The Eiffel Tower, named after its designer, engineer Gustave Eiffel, is nicknamed *La dame de fer*, the iron lady, for its puddle iron lattice tower. It is the tallest building in Paris—1,063 feet—about the height of an 81-story building. It was built in 1889 as the entrance arch to the World's Fair. It has become both a global icon of France and one of the most recognizable structures in the world. The Eiffel Tower is the most-visited paid monument in the world.

★★★★★★★★★★★ ★★★★★★★★★★★

Smothered Cabbage

1 medium cabbage
½ cup finely chopped green
  bell pepper
¼ cup finely chopped onion
¼ cup butter, melted
¼ cup all purpose flour
2 cups milk

½ teaspoon salt
⅛ teaspoon pepper
½ cup mayonnaise
¾ cup shredded medium
  Cheddar cheese
3 tablespoons chili sauce

Cut cabbage into wedges, removing core. Cover, and cook for 10 minutes in a small amount of slightly salted boiling water; drain well. Place wedges in a 9x13x2-inch dish; set aside. Sauté green pepper and onion in butter until vegetables are tender. Add flour, and cook 1 minute, stirring constantly. Gradually add milk; cook over medium heat, stirring constantly, until thickened and bubbly. Then, stir in salt and pepper, and pour mixture over cabbage. Bake at 375° for 20 minutes.

While cabbage is baking, combine mayonnaise, cheese, and chili sauce; mix well. When casserole comes out of the oven, spoon cheese mixture over cabbage wedges, and bake for 5 minutes or more. Serves 8.

Great Flavors of Mississippi (Mississippi)

In 1941 *Wonder Woman* made her debut in All Star Comics #8. Her super powers include super strength, a razor sharp tiara, unbreakable silver bracelets, invisible vehicles made at will, and flight. Wonder Woman's ability to create invisible vehicles can also be stretched to make a complete fortress, known as the Wonderdome.

Apple-Carrot Casserole

This is a not-too-sweet and colorful casserole. Pretty any time, but especially on a buffet table.

2 tablespoons flour
¼ cup sugar
1 pound carrots, cut diagonally
½ teaspoon salt
½ cup water
4 medium cooking apples,
  peeled, cored, and cut into
  ½-inch slices

¼ cup butter or margarine,
  thinly sliced, divided
¼ cup frozen orange juice,
  mixed with ½ cup water

Mix flour and sugar together in a small bowl. Set aside. Combine carrots, salt, and water in small saucepan. Cover and bring to a boil; reduce heat and simmer just until crisp-tender. Drain and set aside. Layer half of carrots, then half of apples in a lightly greased, shallow 2-quart baking dish. (I use a 10x6x2-inch Pyrex dish.) Sprinkle with half the flour mixture and dot with half the butter. Repeat layers. Drizzle with orange juice mixture. Bake at 350° for about 35 minutes or until apples are tender, gently pressing apples down into syrup midway of cooking. Serves 8.

Raleigh House Cookbook 11 (Texas II)

Scalloped Asparagus

1½–2 pounds asparagus
6 tablespoons butter
6 tablespoons flour
1 teaspoon salt
⅛ teaspoon pepper
2 cups milk

¾ cup grated mild or sharp
 Cheddar cheese, divided
2 tablespoons chopped onion
5 hard-boiled eggs, sliced
½ cup buttered bread crumbs

Steam asparagus until just tender. Drain and set aside.

Make a white sauce by melting butter. Stir in flour and add salt and pepper. Add milk, stirring constantly, and cook over low heat until smooth. Blend in ½ cup grated cheese, stirring until smooth. Combine white sauce with asparagus, onion, and eggs. Pour mixture into a 1½-quart greased casserole. Top with crumbs and remaining ¼ cup cheese. Bake at 350° for 15–20 minutes or until casserole is bubbly and cheese melts. Serves 8.

The Central Market Cookbook (Pennsylvania)

Spinach Pauline

2 (10-ounce) packages frozen
 chopped spinach, cooked
 and well drained
6 tablespoons finely minced
 onion
¼ cup margarine, melted
1 teaspoon salt
¾ teaspoon black pepper

6 tablespoons heavy cream or
 evaporated milk
6 tablespoons grated Parmesan
 cheese
2 tablespoons cream cheese,
 softened
Tabasco (optional)
Italian bread crumbs

Cook spinach according to package directions in unsalted water. Drain. Sauté onion in margarine. Add drained spinach, salt, and pepper. Pour in milk. Add cheeses and Tabasco, if desired. Mix well. Before serving, place in baking dish and top with buttered Italian bread crumbs; bake at 375° for 10–15 minutes. Season to taste. Freezes well. Serves 4–6.

River Road Recipes II (Louisiana)

★★★★★★★★★★★ ★★★★★★★★★★★

Sensational Spinach

**3 (10-ounce) packages frozen
  chopped spinach**
1 pint sour cream

1 envelope onion soup mix
Bacon bits (optional)

Cook and drain the spinach well. Combine all ingredients in a greased baking dish and bake 25 minutes at 350°. May top with bacon bits. (Also good with chopped broccoli.) Serves 6.

Amazing Graces (Texas II)

Spanacopita
(Spinach Pie)

**4 (4-ounce) packages frozen
  chopped spinach, drained**
1 bunch scallions, chopped
1 onion, chopped
1 cup oil
1 pound feta cheese
**4 (8-ounce) packages cream
  cheese, softened**

6 eggs
Dill to taste
Salt to taste
1 pound filo dough
1 cup butter, melted

In a pan, sauté spinach, scallions, and onion in oil until onion is transparent. Remove from heat; let stand. In a bowl, mix feta cheese, cream cheese, and eggs till smooth. Add the spinach mixture, and mix well; add dill and salt to taste. Lay out filo dough in 13x15-inch pan; brush the entire sheet with melted butter. Repeat this until half the dough has been used. Add mixture; smooth it out so that it covers the pan. Add remaining filo dough, remembering to butter every sheet when finished. Score the top into 2-inch pieces; sprinkle with water. Bake at 325° for 45 minutes or until golden brown on top. Cool and serve. Serves 10–12.

The Bronx Cookbook (New York)

Cheese and Onion Bake

Good side dish with roasts. Also good for breakfast buffet.

2 large onions, sliced
2 tablespoons butter
1 (10¾-ounce) can cream
  of chicken soup
1 soup can milk

½–¾ cup grated Swiss
  cheese
Salt and pepper to taste
6 slices French bread, buttered
  (preferably sourdough)

Slowly cook onions in butter until limp and golden, about 20 minutes. Place in a 2-quart casserole. Combine soup, milk, cheese, salt and pepper. Heat. Pour ½ the mixture over the onions. Place bread on top (if bread is too fresh, toast slightly). Pour remaining soup mixture over bread. May be made a day ahead. Bake at 350° for 1½ hours. Serves 8.

Soupçon I (Illinois)

Onion Shortcake

An Epicurean delight!

2 large onions, sliced thin
⅓ cup butter or margarine
1 cup sour cream
½ teaspoon dried dill
¼ teaspoon salt
1 cup grated Cheddar cheese
  (4-ounces), divided
1 (15-ounce) can creamed
  corn, undrained

⅓ cup milk
1 (8½-ounce) package corn
  muffin mix
1 egg, slightly beaten
4 drops red pepper sauce or
  to taste

Preheat oven to 425°. Sauté onions in butter or margarine. Stir in sour cream, dill weed, salt, and half the Cheddar cheese. In a separate bowl, combine corn, milk, dry muffin mix, egg, and hot pepper sauce. Put corn mixture in buttered 10-inch oven-proof dish. Spread onion mixture over the top. Sprinkle with remaining Cheddar cheese. Bake for 30–40 minutes or until cheese is golden brown. Serves 6.

Still Gathering (Illinois)

French Onion Casserole

5 medium onions, sliced
5 tablespoons butter or
  margarine, divided
2 tablespoon all-purpose flour
Pepper to taste
1 cup beef bouillon

¼ cup dry sherry
1½ cups plain croutons
¼ cup shredded Swiss cheese
2 tablespoons grated Parmesan
  cheese

Cook onions in 3 tablespoons butter till tender. Blend in flour and dash of pepper. Add bouillon and sherry; cook and stir till thick and bubbly. Turn into 1-quart casserole; cover. Toss croutons with remaining 2 tablespoons melted butter; chill croutons until needed.

Bake casserole, covered, in 350° oven for 30 minutes. Sprinkle with buttered croutons, then cheese. Bake, uncovered, 5–10 minutes more. Serves 6.

Try Me (Alabama)

Cody Carrots

2½–3 pounds carrots, cut in
  strips
1½ cups chicken broth
1 teaspoon minced onion
2 tablespoons butter
1–2 tablespoons horseradish

½ cup mayonnaise
1 cup crushed saltine crackers
3 tablespoons butter
Pepper to taste
Parsley

Steam carrots in broth until barely tender. Remove carrots and transfer to 9x13-inch greased baking dish. To broth, add onion, butter, horseradish, and mayonnaise. Blend with whisk until smooth; pour over carrots. Sprinkle crackers over carrots, dot with butter, and sprinkle with pepper and chopped parsley. Bake at 350° for 20 minutes. Serves 6–8.

The Great Entertainer Cookbook (Big Sky)

Eggplant Parmigiana

2 eggs, beaten
1 teaspoon salt, divided
⅛ teaspoon pepper
1 cup grated Parmesan cheese, divided
2 tablespoons parsley, divided
2 cups bread crumbs

½ teaspoon garlic powder
1 medium eggplant
Olive oil
4 cups marinara sauce, divided
1½ cups shredded mozzarella, divided

In a small bowl, beat eggs, ½ teaspoon salt, pepper, 1 tablespoon Parmesan cheese, and 1 tablespoon parsley. In another bowl, mix bread crumbs, remaining Parmesan cheese, garlic powder, and remaining salt and parsley.

Peel and cut eggplant into round, medium-thick slices. Dip first in egg mixture, then into bread crumbs. Fry in a large frying pan with olive oil. Drain on paper towels to absorb the oil, and set aside.

In a medium to large rectangular pan, line bottom with about a cup of marinara sauce. Arrange one layer of eggplant, then cover with more sauce; add a layer of mozzarella cheese, then sprinkle with Parmesan cheese. Continue to layer. Cook in 350° oven 25–30 minutes. Serve as a side dish with pasta. Serves 6.

The Bridge from Brooklyn (Tennessee)

WIKIPEDIA.ORG

The Brooklyn Bridge is one of the oldest suspension bridges in the United States and one of the United States Wonders. Completed in 1883, it connects the New York City boroughs of Manhattan and Brooklyn by spanning the East River. It was the longest suspension bridge in the world from its opening until 1903, and the first steel-wire suspension bridge. Since its opening, it has become an iconic part of the New York skyline.

Mexican Eggplant

2 garlic cloves, chopped fine
1 large green bell pepper,
  chopped fine
2–4 green chile peppers, chopped
¼ cup olive oil, divided
1 (6-ounce) can tomato paste
1 can of water
Salt and pepper to taste
1 eggplant, peeled, sliced
  ¼-inch thick
2 eggs, beaten
Grated yellow cheese

Sauté garlic, green pepper, and green chile peppers until soft in 1 tablespoon olive oil. Add tomato paste, water, and salt and pepper to taste, and simmer until sauce thickens. Dip eggplant into the eggs and sauté until golden brown in remaining olive oil. Place eggplant slices in a baking dish and cover with the sauce and grated yellow cheese. Bake at 350° for 30 minutes. Serves 6.

San Antonio Cookbook II (Texas)

Ratatouille

2 small eggplants
3 medium-size tomatoes
2 bell peppers
3 small zucchini squash
2 onions
2 yellow squash
3 tablespoons olive oil
Salt and pepper to taste
1 teaspoon garlic powder
¼ cup water

Slice eggplants, tomatoes, peppers, zucchini, onions, and squash about ¼–½ inch thick. Layer vegetables in casserole dish that has been oiled with 1 tablespoon olive oil, starting with onions, bell pepper, and vegetables as desired. Repeat until all vegetables are used. Sprinkle salt and pepper, remaining olive oil, and garlic powder over vegetables. Pour ¼ cup water over casserole. Cover and bake in 275° oven for 1½ hours. Test vegetables for tenderness. Good cold or hot. Serves 8–10.

Waddad's Kitchen (Mississippi)

Sherried Baked Fruit

Elegant for buffet dinner parties, large or small.

2 (20-ounce) cans chunk
   pineapple
1 (29-ounce) can sliced
   freestone peaches
1 (17-ounce) can apricots,
   sliced
1 (16-ounce) can pitted Bing
   cherries or blueberries

2 (15-ounce) jars spiced apple
   rings
½ cup butter
4 tablespoons all-purpose
   flour
1 cup brown sugar
¼ cup sherry

Preheat oven to 350°. Drain fruit. Arrange in layers in a 3-quart baking dish. Melt butter. Add flour and stir until well blended. Add brown sugar and sherry. Cook until thick. Pour over fruit. Bake 30 minutes. Serves 20.

Necessities and Temptations (Texas II)

The Taj Mahal is widely considered one of the most beautiful buildings in the world. Located in Agra, India, this mausoleum was built by Mughal emperor Shah Jahan in memory of his third wife, Mumtaz Mahal. It stands as a symbol of eternal love.

Pasta, Rice, Etc.

★★★★★★★ ★★★★★★★

The Taj Mahal. Agra, India.
One of the New Seven Wonders of the World.

Angel Hair Florentine

1 egg, beaten
1 cup sour cream
2 cups heavy cream
4 tablespoons grated Parmesan
  cheese
½ medium–large onion, minced
½ teaspoon salt
½ teaspoon coarsely ground
  black pepper

1 (10-ounce) package chopped
  spinach, thawed and drained
1½ cups shredded Monterey
  Jack cheese
1½ cups shredded sharp
  Cheddar cheese
4 ounces angel hair pasta,
  cooked, drained

Combine egg, sour cream, heavy cream, Parmesan, onion, salt, and pepper. Add spinach and blend well. Add cheeses and mix well. Fold in pasta. Put in oven-proof casserole, sprinkle with more Parmesan, cover with tin foil, and bake at 350° for 45 minutes to 1 hour or more, until set. Remove tin foil last 10 minutes of cooking. Serves 4–6.

The Hearty Gourmet (Idaho)

Shrimp Casserole

2 large eggs
1 cup evaporated milk
1 cup plain yogurt
8 ounces feta cheese, crumbled
½ pound Swiss cheese,
  shredded
⅓ cup chopped fresh parsley
1 teaspoon dried basil
1 teaspoon dried oregano

4 garlic cloves, minced
½ pound angel hair pasta,
  cooked, divided
1 (16-ounce) jar mild chunky
  salsa
1 pound peeled raw medium
  shrimp, divided
½ pound mozzarella cheese,
  shredded

Blend eggs, milk, yogurt, feta, Swiss cheese, parsley, basil, oregano, and garlic in a large bowl. Spread half of pasta over bottom of a 9x13-inch baking dish that has been coated with nonstick spray. Top with salsa and half of shrimp. Cover with remaining pasta. Pour egg mixture over pasta and top with remaining shrimp. Sprinkle with mozzarella cheese and bake in a preheated 350° oven for 30 minutes. Remove and let stand 10 minutes before serving. Serves 10.

Simple Pleasures from Our Table to Yours (Alabama)

Plenty More in the Kitchen

4 ounces egg noodles	1 tablespoon oil
1 medium onion, chopped	1 pound ground beef
1 garlic clove, minced	

Cook noodles; drain. Fry onion and garlic in oil. Brown meat. Add following ingredients:

1 (15-ounce) can corn	1 (4-ounce) can mushrooms
1 teaspoon brown sugar	1 teaspoon salt
1 teaspoon chili powder	Dash of pepper
¼ teaspoon thyme	1 teaspoon Worcestershire
¼ cup shredded Cheddar cheese	1 (8-ounce) can tomato sauce

Simmer for about 15 minutes. Mix in noodles and put in casserole dish. Top with additional Cheddar cheese. Bake at 350° for 35–45 minutes. Serves 4–6.

Covered Bridge Neighbors Cookbook (Missouri)

Pizza Spaghetti

7 ounces broken spaghetti (break into thirds)	Onion or garlic powder
	1 (32-ounce) jar spaghetti sauce
2 eggs	Sugar
1 cup milk	Pepperoni slices
2 pounds hamburger	Mozzarella cheese

Cook and drain spaghetti. Beat eggs and milk together. Put spaghetti in the bottom of a 9x13-inch greased pan. Pour egg-milk mixture over the spaghetti. Brown hamburger and onion or garlic powder; drain. Mix jar of spaghetti sauce into hamburger; sprinkle a little sugar in. Put on top of spaghetti. Place pepperoni slices on top. Cover with a good layer of mozzarella cheese on top. Bake in 350° oven for 45 minutes, covered, then uncover 10 minutes to set before serving. Serve with garlic toast. Serves 6–8.

A Gathering of Recipes (Nevada)

Baked Chili Spaghetti

1 (12-ounce) package spaghetti
¾ pound ground round steak
5 tablespoons chili powder,
   divided
2 medium onions, chopped
1 green bell pepper, chopped
Bacon drippings or oil
1 (14½-ounce) can diced
   tomatoes
1 (8-ounce) can chopped
   mushrooms
1 tablespoon Worcestershire
8 shakes hot sauce
Salt and pepper to taste
½ pound sharp Cheddar
   cheese, grated
Ketchup to taste
½ cup buttered bread crumbs

Cook spaghetti in boiling water 20 minutes, or until tender. Combine ground steak and 2 tablespoons chili powder; mix well. Brown onions, pepper, and seasoned meat in bacon drippings. Mix with tomatoes, mushrooms, Worcestershire, hot sauce, remaining 3 tablespoons chili powder, salt, pepper, and most of the cheese. Add drained spaghetti; mix well.

Place in buttered baking dish; top with remaining cheese, ketchup, and crumbs. Bake in oven at 350° for 30–45 minutes. Can be mixed beforehand and kept in refrigerator. Serves 8.

The Grace of Patti's (Kentucky)

Depending on what time of the day it is and whether or not there's a moon at night, the Taj Mahal appears to be of a different color every time. Some even believe that this changing pattern of colors depicts the different moods of a woman.

★★★★★★★★★★★   ★★★★★★★★★★★

Chicketti

2 cups bite-size spaghetti
  pieces, cooked, drained
2 cups chopped cooked chicken
1 cup chicken broth
1 (10¾-ounce) can cream of
  mushroom soup
1 cup shredded Cheddar
  cheese, divided
½ onion, chopped
¼ cup pimentos, drained
¼ cup chopped green bell
  pepper
½ teaspoon salt
¼ teaspoon pepper

Combine pasta, chicken, broth, soup, ½ cup cheese, onion, pimentos, green pepper, salt, and pepper in a large bowl and mix well. Spoon into a greased 3-quart baking dish. Sprinkle with remaining ½ cup cheese. Bake at 325° for 45–60 minutes or until cooked through. Serves 8.

Celebrations (Alabama)

Editor's Extra: Boil chicken in 2 cups water to have enough for 1 cup broth.

Chicken Tetrazzini

1¼ cups chopped onion
1 cup chopped celery
½ cup butter
½ cup flour
4 cups chicken broth, heated
1 cup half-and-half, warmed
½ cup grated Parmesan cheese
⅜ teaspoon seasoned salt
⅜ teaspoon white pepper
1 pound mushrooms sliced and
  sauteéd or 1 (16-ounce) can,
  drained
4 cups pulled or diced cooked
  chicken
¼ cup sherry or white wine
12 ounces vermicelli, cooked
2 cups grated Cheddar cheese

Sauté onion and celery in butter. Add flour and cook, stirring. Do not brown. Add hot broth, stirring. Add warm half-and-half, stirring. Add Parmesan. Mix with all other ingredients (including cooked vermicelli), except Cheddar cheese in large bowl. Pour into 3-quart casserole. Top with Cheddar cheese. Bake at 325° for 1 hour or until bubbly and hot. Serves 10.

Without a Doubt (Alabama)

Shrimp Tetrazzini

4 tablespoons butter
2 medium onions, chopped, or
   about 3 tablespoons instant
   minced onion
1 pound fresh or frozen shrimp,
   shelled, deveined
1 pound fresh mushrooms,
   sliced
½ cup all-purpose flour
½ cup mayonnaise

2 teaspoons salt
1 quart milk
½ cup sherry
1 (16-ounce) package thin
   spaghetti, cooked al dente,
   drained
Grated Parmesan cheese
Shredded mozzarella cheese
   (optional)

Preheat oven to 350°. Melt butter in Dutch oven. Sauté onions until just tender. Add shrimp and mushrooms and cook, stirring frequently, until shrimp are just done. Remove from pan (along with liquid) and drain in colander. Blend flour and mayonnaise in pan; add salt, milk, and sherry. Cook until thickened, stirring as you would any cream sauce. Toss with shrimp and spaghetti and turn into 3-quart casserole. Top generously with cheeses. Bake for 30 minutes. Serves 8.

Note: This can be fancied up further if you wish by adding a can or two of artichoke hearts, halved, or hearts of palm, sliced about ½ inch thick.

The Other Side of the House (Virginia)

Mount Rushmore National Memorial

White Lasagna

A tasty variation of a family favorite.

8 ounces lasagna noodles
1 pound ground beef
1 cup finely chopped celery
¾ cup chopped onion
1 garlic clove, minced
2 teaspoons basil
1 teaspoon oregano
¾ teaspoon salt
½ teaspoon pepper
½ teaspoon Italian seasoning
1 cup light cream

3 ounces cream cheese,
  cubed
½ cup dry white wine
2 cups shredded Cheddar
  cheese
1½ cups shredded Gouda
  cheese
1 egg, beaten
12 ounces cottage cheese
12 ounces mozzarella cheese,
  sliced

Cook noodles to al dente. Brown meat and drain grease. Add celery, onion, and garlic. Cook until done. Add herbs, cream, and cream cheese. Cook over low heat to melt cream cheese. Add wine and gradually add Cheddar and Gouda cheeses, stirring until nearly melted. Remove from heat.

Stir egg and cottage cheese together. In greased 9x13-inch pan, layer one-half of each: noodles, meat, cottage cheese, and mozzarella. Repeat layers. Bake, uncovered, in a preheated 375° oven for 30–35 minutes. Let stand 10 minutes before cutting. May be prepared ahead. Freezes well. Serves 6–8.

Simply Sensational (Ohio)

One of the United States Wonders, Mount Rushmore National Memorial is a sculpture carved into the granite face of Mount Rushmore near Keystone, South Dakota. Sculpted by Gutzon Borglum and later by his son Lincoln Borglum, Mount Rushmore features 60-foot sculptures of the heads of former United States presidents (in order from left to right) George Washington, Thomas Jefferson, Theodore Roosevelt, and Abraham Lincoln. Construction on the memorial began in 1927, and the presidents' faces were completed between 1934 and 1939.

Short Cut Spinach Lasagna

This is a wonderful low-cholesterol, low-fat pasta dish that appeals to people of all ages. It is especially appealing to the cook, because it is so quick and easy to make! You don't even have to cook the lasagna first, which saves both time and mess.

1 (10-ounce) package frozen
  chopped spinach
2 cups (1 pound) low-fat or
  nonfat cottage cheese
2 cups (¼ pound) part-skim
  shredded mozzarella cheese,
  divided
1 egg or egg substitute

1 teaspoon oregano
Salt and pepper to taste
1 (29- to 32-ounce) jar spaghetti
  sauce
9 lasagna noodles (¼ pound),
  uncooked
1 cup water

Thaw and drain spinach. In large bowl combine spinach, cottage cheese, 1 cup shredded mozzarella, egg, oregano, salt and pepper. In greased 9x13-inch baking dish, layer 1 cup sauce, ⅓ of noodles, and half the cheese mixture. Repeat. Top with remaining noodles, then remaining sauce. Sprinkle with remaining 1 cup mozzarella. Pour water around edges. Cover tightly with foil. Bake at 350° for 1 hour and 15 minutes or until bubbly. Let stand 15 minutes before serving. Serves 6–8.

Note: May be made up to two days in advance. It also freezes very well.

From Ellie's Kitchen to Yours (New England)

One Flew Over the Cuckoo's Nest is a 1975 American drama film directed by Miloš Forman and based on the 1962 novel by Ken Kesey. The film was the second to win all five major Academy Awards, (Best Picture, Actor in Lead Role, Actress in Lead Role, Director, and Screenplay) following *It Happened One Night* in 1934.

Lasagna

1 large onion, chopped
1 large garlic clove, minced
3 tablespoons olive oil
1 pound Italian sausage
1 pound ground beef
8 ounces pepperoni
1 (32-ounce) jar spaghetti sauce
1 tablespoon oregano
1 tablespoon basil

1 (8-ounce) package lasagna
  noodles
1 (16-ounce) carton cottage
  cheese
3 ounces grated Parmesan
  cheese
1 large egg, beaten
1 (12-ounce) package shredded
  mozzarella cheese

Sauté onion and garlic in oil until onion is tender; do not burn garlic. Break sausage into chunks and add to pan. When sausage is partially cooked, add ground beef, and continue to cook. Cut pepperoni into small chunks and add when meat is done. Cook about 5 minutes. Add sauce, oregano, and basil; reduce heat, and simmer while preparing remaining ingredients.

Preheat oven to 350°. Cook noodles in large pot of water. Mix cottage cheese, Parmesan cheese, and egg in separate bowl. When noodles are done, lay 3 noodles in bottom of pan; layer ¼ cheese mixture, then ¼ meat mixture, and ¼ sauce mixture. Then add layer of mozzarella cheese. Continue process until pan is full. Make sure top layer covers noodles so they will not harden in oven. Bake at 350° for approximately 30 minutes or until mixture boils around edges. Serves 10–12.

A Taste of Tradition (Virginia II)

Chicken Lasagna

SAUCE:

3 tablespoons butter
½ cup chopped onion
½ cup chopped green bell pepper
¼ pound fresh mushrooms, sliced, or 3 ounces canned mushrooms, drained

1 (10¾-ounce) can cream of chicken soup
⅓ cup milk
¼ cup diced pimento, drained
½ teaspoon crumbled dried basil

Heat butter in large skillet over medium heat. Sauté onion, bell pepper, and mushrooms until soft. Add soup, milk, pimento, and basil. Heat until blended.

8 ounces lasagna noodles, cooked and drained
1½ cups cottage cheese, drained
3 cups cooked, diced chicken

2 cups shredded American or Cheddar cheese
½ cup grated Parmesan cheese

In buttered 9x13-inch casserole, place half of noodles; cover with half of Sauce. Top with half of cottage cheese, half of chicken, and half of cheeses. Repeat layering second time. Preheat oven to 375°. Bake 30 minutes or until lightly browned and bubbly. Serves 8.

Sounds Delicious (Oklahoma)!

Spinach Stuffed Manicotti

1 pound ground meat
1 onion, chopped
1 teaspoon chopped garlic
½ bell pepper, chopped
14 ounces chopped spinach
¼ cup cottage cheese

2 eggs, well beaten
14 cooked manicotti shells
1 (26-ounce) jar spaghetti sauce
½ cup grated Parmesan cheese
1 cup shredded mozzarella
  cheese

Cook ground meat, onion, garlic, and bell pepper with seasoning to taste. Drain well and set aside to cool. Cook and drain spinach, cool; add cottage cheese and eggs; mix well. Add to meat mixture. Stuff shells with mixture and place in oiled 9x13-inch pan. Pour spaghetti sauce over manicotti shells. Sprinkle with Parmesan cheese, then the mozzarella cheese. Preheat oven to 350° and bake for 30 minutes. Serves 6–8.

Sisters' Secrets (Louisiana II)

Meaty Manicotti

½ pound ground chuck
½ cup chopped onion
1 garlic clove, minced
½ teaspoon salt
¼ teaspoon oregano
1 slice bread, diced
1 tablespoon parsley flakes

1 (15½-ounce) jar spaghetti
  sauce, divided
½ cup grated Romano cheese
½ pound grated mozzarella
  cheese
1 egg, slightly beaten
8 manicotti shells, parboiled

Brown meat, onion, and garlic in skillet. Spoon off excess fat. Stir in salt, oregano, bread, parsley, ¼ cup spaghetti sauce, and Romano cheese. Cool slightly. Mix in mozzarella cheese and egg. Fill manicotti shells with meat mixture. Spread 1 cup spaghetti sauce in bottom of 7x12-inch baking dish. Arrange shells and cover with remaining sauce. Cover with foil. Bake at 350° for 30 minutes. Remove foil. Sprinkle with additional grated cheese. Bake, uncovered, 10 minutes. Serves 4.

Cookin' with the Stars (West Virginia)

Mama's Monday Night Hamburger Casserole

1 small onion, chopped
1 (8-ounce) can mushrooms,
   or fresh mushrooms, sautéed
1–2 tablespoons olive oil
½–1 pound ground beef,
   cooked and drained
2 tablespoons flour
2 beef bouillon cubes, dissolved
   in 2 cups hot water
3 tablespoons tomato paste
½ bay leaf
½ teaspoon soy sauce
Salt and pepper to taste
1 cup elbow macaroni, cooked
Grated Parmesan cheese

Sauté onion and mushrooms in olive oil until slightly browned. Add drained hamburger. Cover and simmer 10 minutes. Thicken with flour; add bouillon water and cook until thickened, stirring. Add tomato paste, bay leaf, soy sauce, salt and pepper, and cook a few minutes. Add cooked macaroni. Pour into casserole and cover with grated Parmesan cheese. Bake at 350° for 30 minutes. Serves 4–6.

Cooking with My Friends (Kentucky)

Speedy Overnight Casserole

3 cups chopped cooked chicken
   or turkey
2 cups large elbow macaroni,
   uncooked
1 (10¾-ounce) can cream of
   mushroom soup
1 (10¾-ounce) can cream of
   chicken soup
1 soup can milk
1 soup can chicken broth
1 small onion, chopped
1 (8-ounce) can water chestnuts,
   sliced
½ teaspoon salt
½ pound grated Cheddar
   cheese (save some for
   topping)
1 cup crushed potato chips

Mix all ingredients except chips. Put in 9x13-inch pan. Sprinkle reserved cheese and potato chips on top. Cover with foil. Refrigerate overnight. Bake, covered, for 1½ hours at 350°. This freezes well. Serves 6–8.

Home at the Range III (Great Plains)

Shrimp and Crabmeat Casserole

We can't explain why, exactly, but this is the most popular dish we've ever served. Nobody has ever failed to ask for the recipe. It's also easy to make and can be put together in advance, then baked at the last minute.

½ pound macaroni
1 tablespoon salt
1 tablespoon vegetable oil
6 tablespoons butter or
  margarine, divided
½ pound fresh mushrooms,
  sliced
1 cup light cream
1 (10¾-ounce) can cream of
  mushroom soup

¾ cup grated sharp Cheddar
  cheese
1 pound shrimp, cooked,
  shelled, and deveined
1 cup cooked crabmeat
1 cup soft bread crumbs
1 tablespoon butter or
  margarine

Add macaroni, salt, and vegetable oil to 3 quarts boiling water; boil rapidly for 10 minutes. Drain and toss with 4 tablespoons butter or margarine.

Sauté the mushrooms in remaining 2 tablespoons butter or margarine for about 5 minutes, shaking the pan frequently. Mix the cream, mushroom soup, and Cheddar cheese together and add to the macaroni. Add the mushrooms, shrimp, and crabmeat, which have been cut into bite-size pieces.

Place in a buttered 9x13-inch casserole; top with soft bread crumbs, which have been tossed with the 1 tablespoon melted butter or margarine. Bake in a 350° oven for 25 minutes. Season to taste. Serves 6.

The Country Innkeepers' Cookbook (New England)

Pot O' Gold Macaroni and Cheese

This dish is so rich and creamy, I save it for special occasions (like Thursdays, Tuesdays, dinnertime, etc.)!

1 tablespoon vegetable oil
1 pound elbow macaroni
8 tablespoons (1 stick) plus 1
  tablespoon butter, divided
½ cup shredded Muenster
  cheese
½ cup shredded mild Cheddar
  cheese
½ cup shredded sharp Cheddar
  cheese
½ cup shredded Monterey
  Jack cheese
2 cups half-and-half
1 cup small cubes Velveeta
2 large eggs, lightly beaten
¼ teaspoon seasoned salt
⅛ teaspoon freshly ground
  black pepper

Preheat oven to 350°. Lightly butter a deep 2½-quart casserole. Bring a large pot of salted water to a boil over high heat. Add oil, then elbow macaroni, and cook until just tender, about 7 minutes. Drain.

In a small saucepan, melt 8 tablespoons butter. Stir into macaroni. In large bowl, mix Muenster, mild and sharp Cheddar, and Monterey Jack cheeses. To the macaroni, add half-and-half, 1½ cups shredded cheeses, cubed Velveeta, and eggs. Season with salt and pepper. Transfer to buttered casserole. Sprinkle with remaining ½ cup shredded cheeses and dot with remaining tablespoon butter. Bake until it's bubbling around edges, about 35 minutes. Serves 8.

Kitchen Komforts (Tennessee)

★★★★★★★★★★★★ ★★★★★★★★★★★★

Crockpot Macaroni and Cheese

1 (8-ounce) package dry elbow
 macaroni
1 (12-ounce) can evaporated
 milk
1½ cups whole milk
2 eggs

¼ cup butter, melted
1 teaspoon salt
½ teaspoon pepper
3 cups shredded sharp Cheddar
 cheese, divided

Cook macaroni in boiling, salted water 5 minutes. Drain; pour into crockpot. Mix all other ingredients, except 1 cup cheese. Add to macaroni; stir well. Put remaining cup of cheese on top of macaroni. Do not stir. Cook in covered crockpot on HIGH 2 hours. Serves 6.

Favorite Recipes: Barbara's Best Volume II (Virginia II)

Classic Baked Macaroni and Cheese

2 tablespoons cornstarch
1 teaspoon salt
½ teaspoon dry mustard
 (optional)
¼ teaspoon pepper
2½ cups milk

2 tablespoons butter or
 margarine
2 cups American or Cheddar
 cheese, divided
8 ounces elbow macaroni

In medium saucepan, combine cornstarch, salt, mustard, and pepper; stir in milk. Add butter, stirring constantly; bring to a boil over medium-high heat and boil 1 minute. Remove from heat. Stir in 1¾ cups cheese; stir until melted. Cook macaroni 7 minutes and drain; mix with cheese sauce. Pour into greased, 2-quart, casserole. Sprinkle with reserved cheese. Bake uncovered in 375° oven for 25 minutes or until lightly browned. Serves 4–6.

Note: May add 1 cup diced ham before baking.

Bountiful Blessings–DeKalb (Mississippi)

Ski Day Chicken Casserole

Actually, good for any day.

**8 tablespoons butter or
  margarine, divided**
¼ cup flour
1½ cups chicken broth
1 cup sour cream
⅛ teaspoon nutmeg
⅛ teaspoon pepper
Salt to taste
¼ cup dry sherry

**½ pound flat egg noodles,
  cooked and drained**
**4½ cups cut-up cooked
  chicken**
**½ pound mushrooms, sliced
  and sautéed**
1 cup soft bread crumbs
**½ cup freshly grated
  Parmesan cheese**

Melt 4 tablespoons butter; stir in flour, and add broth and sour cream, stirring until thick. Add nutmeg, pepper, and salt. Remove from heat and stir in sherry. Arrange noodles in 9x13-inch baking dish. Cover with chicken, mushrooms, and sauce. Melt remaining 4 tablespoons butter and mix with crumbs. Top casserole with crumbs and cheese. Bake in preheated 350° oven for 30 minutes or until hot and bubbly. May be made a day in advance, refrigerated, and baked when needed. Serves 8.

Merrymeeting Merry Eating (New England)

"What a Wonderful World" is a song written by Bob Thiele (as George Douglas) and George David Weiss. It was first recorded by Louis Armstrong and released as a single in 1968. The song was not initially a hit in the United States, where it sold fewer than 1,000 copies because the head of ABC Records did not like the song, and so, did not promote it. The song was re-released as a single in 1988 and hit #32 on the US Billboard charts.

Chicken Tequila Fettuccine

1 pound spinach fettuccine
½ cup chopped fresh cilantro, divided
2 tablespoons minced garlic
2 tablespoons minced jalapeños
3 tablespoons butter, divided
½ cup chicken stock
2 tablespoons gold tequila
2 tablespoons lime juice
3 tablespoons soy sauce
1¼ pounds chicken breasts, diced
¼ medium red onion, sliced
½ medium red bell pepper, sliced
½ medium green bell pepper, sliced
1½ cups heavy cream

Cook pasta al dente according to package. Cook ⅓ cup cilantro, garlic, and jalapeños in 2 tablespoons butter over medium heat for 5 minutes. Add stock, tequila, and lime juice. Bring mixture to a boil and cook till paste-like; set aside. Pour soy sauce over diced chicken; set aside for 5 minutes. Meanwhile, cook onion and peppers with remaining butter till limp. Add chicken and soy sauce, then add reserved tequila/lime paste and cream. Boil sauce till chicken is cooked through, and sauce is thick. Serve sauce over fettuccine on serving dishes. Serve with cilantro and jalapeños as garnish. Makes 6 or more servings.

Pleasures from the Good Earth (Arizona)

Pizza Casserole

1 pound ground beef
1 (16-ounce) can pizza sauce
1 (4-ounce) can sliced mushrooms, undrained
1 tablespoon oregano
1 tablespoon garlic salt
1 small onion, chopped
1 package sliced pepperoni
2 cups rotini, cooked and drained, or 2 cups twisted macaroni
⅔ cup milk
1 (8-ounce) package shredded mozzarella cheese

Brown ground beef and drain. Stir in pizza sauce, undrained mushrooms, oregano, garlic salt, onion, and pepperoni. Bring to a boil and remove from heat. Combine rotini with milk. In a greased 2-quart casserole, layer ½ of the rotini mixture, ½ meat mixture, and ½ cheese; repeat layers and cover. Bake at 350° for 25–30 minutes. Serves 6.

United Methodist Ministers' Wives Cook Book (West Virginia)

Beef, Noodle & Cheese Casserole

Something like lasagna, but easier to prepare.

1 (8-ounce) package egg noodles
1 pound lean ground beef
3 tablespoons butter, divided
2 (8-ounce) cans tomato sauce
1 cup cream-style cottage
  cheese
¼ cup dairy sour cream

1 (8-ounce) package cream
  cheese, softened
½ cup chopped green onions
1 tablespoon chopped bell
  pepper
1 teaspoon salt

Cook noodles according to package directions. Brown meat in 1 tablespoon butter. Add tomato sauce. Remove from heat and set aside. Combine cottage cheese, sour cream, cream cheese, onions, bell pepper, and salt in a separate bowl. Using a 2-quart buttered casserole, spread with half of the noodles. Cover with the cheese mixture. Spread with the remainder of the noodles. Melt remaining 2 tablespoons butter and drizzle over noodles. Top with meat mixture. Bake 30 minutes in 350° oven. Serves 6.

Calories: 700; Cholesterol: 165mg; Sodium: 1300mg.

Cook 'em Horns: The Quickbook (Texas II)

Do-Ahead Dried Beef Casserole

3 tablespoons diced onion
3 tablespoons diced green
  bell pepper
¼ cup diced celery
1 (4-ounce) can mushrooms
2 tablespoons butter

1 (10¾-ounce) can cream of
  mushroom soup
1 cup milk
1 cup grated Cheddar cheese
1 cup uncooked macaroni
1 (5-ounce) package dried beef

Sauté onion, green pepper, celery, and mushrooms in butter. Stir soup until creamy. Add milk, cheese, sautéed vegetables, uncooked macaroni, and dried beef. Pour into greased 2-quart baking dish. Refrigerate for 3–4 hours or overnight. Bake, uncovered at 350° for 45 minutes or until done. Serves 4–6.

Cardinal Country Cooking (Wisconsin)

★★★★★★★★★★★ ★★★★★★★★★★★

Fellowship Hot Dish

A good dish to take to a potluck or to a family on moving day.

2 pounds ground beef
2 eggs
¼ cup milk
1 pound spaghetti or
  fettuccini noodles, cooked
  and drained
1 (32-ounce) jar spaghetti sauce
1 large onion, chopped fine
2 stalks celery, chopped fine

½ green bell pepper, chopped
  fine
2 teaspoons finely chopped
  garlic
1 tablespoon Italian seasoning
2 cups shredded mozzarella
  cheese
20 or so pieces sliced
  pepperoni

Brown ground beef while boiling spaghetti. Beat eggs and milk; toss with drained spaghetti. Spread in a greased 9x13-inch casserole. Top with sauce.

Sauté chopped onion, celery, green pepper, and garlic in a small amount of oil or butter. Mix with well-browned ground beef. Add Italian seasoning. Spread mixture over sauce. Sprinkle with cheese. Decorate with pepperoni slices. May also use cherry tomatoes and/or green pepper slices. Bake at 350° for 30 minutes. Let stand 5 minutes. Cut into squares. Serves 10–12.

Recipes from St. Michael's (Minnesota)

Wonder, Nevada, was a town in Churchill County, Nevada, approximately 39 miles east of Fallon at an elevation of 5,853 feet. Today Wonder is a deserted ghost town.

Divine Casserole

1 (16-ounce) package small
  egg noodles
2 (10-ounce) packages frozen
  spinach
2 pounds ground chuck
2 (6-ounce) cans tomato paste
2 teaspoons Worcestershire
Few drops Tabasco
Salt to taste
½ teaspoon oregano leaves

1 (12-ounce) carton creamed
  cottage cheese
1 (8-ounce) package cream
  cheese, softened
1 (8-ounce) carton sour cream
2 onions, chopped
2 sticks butter, melted
1 cup grated sharp Cheddar
  cheese

Boil noodles by package directions; drain and rinse under hot water. Cook spinach according to package directions and drain. Add tomato paste, Worcestershire, Tabasco, salt, and oregano to meat. Mix well. Mix cottage cheese, cream cheese, sour cream, and onions. Grease 2 (2-quart) casseroles. Layer ingredients in casserole in following order: noodles, butter, cheese mixture, spinach, noodles, butter, and meat layer on top. Sprinkle ½ cup grated cheese on each casserole. Bake at 350° for 40 minutes or until bubbly. Freezes well. Serves 10–12.

Christmas Favorites (North Carolina)

Frittata with Pasta, Vegetables, and Crab

½ pound capellini
⅓ cup finely chopped zucchini
⅓ cup finely chopped red or
  yellow bell pepper
⅓ cup finely chopped onion
3 tablespoons butter

6 large eggs, whisked
½ cup grated provolone cheese
¼ cup grated Parmesan
  cheese
⅔ cup flaked crabmeat

Cook capellini al dente in boiling salted water. Drain and rinse with cold water. Sauté vegetables in melted butter. Do not overcook. Mix pasta with beaten eggs. Add vegetables, cheeses, and crab. Pour mixture into greased 9x13-inch pan. Cover with foil and bake in preheated 350° oven for ½ hour, or until golden. Serves 8.

Cooking with the Allenhurst Garden Club (Mid-Atlantic)

Broccoli, Tomato, Pasta Bake

8 ounces pasta (shells,
  rigatoni, or macaroni)
1 onion, chopped
1 small red bell pepper, chopped
1 garlic clove, minced
1 tablespoon oil
1 (14½-ounce) can tomatoes
1 teaspoon dried basil

Salt and pepper to taste
1 pound broccoli with stalks
  trimmed off
8 ounces natural yogurt
4 ounces cream cheese, softened
2 eggs, beaten
½ cup grated Cheddar cheese

Cook the pasta in plenty of boiling water until tender. Sauté onion, pepper, and garlic in oil until softened, but not brown. Add tomatoes and basil and simmer until the sauce thickens. Season to taste. Steam broccoli just until tender. Place a layer of tomato sauce on bottom of a large, well-greased oven-proof dish. Cover with a layer of pasta, then broccoli, and a final layer of pasta.

For the topping, beat together yogurt, cream cheese, eggs, and salt and pepper to taste until smooth. Pour mixture over pasta and sprinkle with grated cheese. Bake for 25–30 minutes at 400° until golden brown. Serves 4.

Carnegie Hall Cookbook (West Virginia)

Lazy Man's Pierogi

½ pound bacon, or bacon bits
2 onions, chopped
½ pound chopped mushrooms,
  or 1 (4-ounce) can, drained
1 (16-ounce) jar sauerkraut,
  drained

1 (10¾-ounce) can cream of
  mushroom soup
1 pound spiral noodles, cooked
  and drained well

Fry bacon and crumble. Fry onions and mushrooms in drippings; set aside. Rinse sauerkraut. Combine all together with mushroom soup and noodles in a large casserole dish. Bake at 350° for 45–60 minutes.

Family Collections (Georgia)

★★★★★★★★★★★ ★★★★★★★★★★★

Ham and Cheese Picnic Pie

1 recipe (2-crust) pie pastry
3 eggs
1 (15-ounce) carton ricotta
   cheese
1 (15-ounce) carton small-curd
   cottage cheese, drained
½ cup seasoned bread crumbs
½ cup grated Parmesan cheese
¼ cup minced fresh parsley
1½ teaspoons Creole or Italian
   seasoning, divided

Salt to taste
½–1 teaspoon freshly ground
   pepper
2 or 3 dashes hot sauce
1 pound deli ham, cut into
   ¼-inch cubes
4 ounces mozzarella cheese, cut
   into ¼-inch cubes
1 bunch green onions, thinly
   sliced
1 egg, beaten

Roll half the pastry into an 11-inch circle. Fit into a 10-inch springform pan. Chill in refrigerator.

Beat 3 eggs in a large bowl. Add ricotta cheese, cottage cheese, bread crumbs, Parmesan cheese, parsley, 1 teaspoon Creole seasoning, salt, pepper, and hot sauce, and mix well. Stir in ham, mozzarella cheese, and green onions. Pour into pastry-lined pan. Pull edge of pastry over filling. Brush with ½ of the beaten egg.

Roll remaining pastry into a 12-inch circle. Place over filling, crimping edges of pastry together; the edge will be inside the springform pan. Brush with remaining beaten egg. Sprinkle with remaining ½ teaspoon Creole seasoning. Bake at 375° for 1 hour and 10 minutes. Remove from oven. Let stand until cool. Chill in refrigerator. Serve at room temperature. Serves 12–15.

America Celebrates Columbus (Ohio)

Chicken and Broccoli Casserole

1 (10-ounce) package frozen, chopped broccoli
1 medium onion, chopped
1 tablespoon butter or margarine
2 cups diced or shredded cooked chicken
2 cups cooked white rice
1 cup mayonnaise
Up to 1 teaspoon curry powder
2 teaspoons salt (or less)
¼ teaspoon pepper
2 cups grated Cheddar cheese
2 tablespoons lemon juice

Cook broccoli according to package directions; drain. Sauté onion in butter; add the chicken, rice, and cooked broccoli. In a small bowl, stir together the mayonnaise, curry powder, salt, and pepper. Gently but thoroughly, stir this sauce into the chicken and rice mixture. Spread evenly in greased baking dish. Cook until heated through at 350° for ½ hour. Sprinkle with cheese and lemon juice; cook, uncovered, until melted. Serves 4–6.

Your Favorite Recipes (Washington)

Chicken Spectacular

1 chicken, or 4 large breasts
1 (6-ounce) package Uncle Ben's Long-Grain and Wild Rice
1 (2-ounce) package slivered almonds
1 (1-pound) can French-style green beans, drained
2 tablespoons chopped onion
1 cup water chestnuts, drained and sliced
2 tablespoons chopped pimento
1 (4-ounce) can sliced mushrooms
1 (10¾-ounce) can cream of celery soup
½ cup mayonnaise
Salt and pepper to taste

Stew chicken or breasts; dice. Use chicken broth to cook 1 package rice. Toast almonds in butter and salt under broiler in oven. Mix remaining ingredients along with diced chicken and rice. Place in greased 2-quart casserole dish. Top with slivered almonds. (Almonds may be mixed in with the casserole, if desired.) If dry looking before baking, pour chicken broth over it. This casserole freezes very well. If frozen, thaw, then bake uncovered for 30 minutes at 350°. Serves 6–8.

Entertaining in Texas (Texas)

Oriental Chicken and Rice Casserole

2 cups cooked chicken
1 tablespoon soy sauce
2 tablespoons lemon juice
1 (15-ounce) can bean sprouts,
    drained
1 cup finely chopped celery
¾–1 cup mayonnaise
¼ cup finely chopped green
    onions
1 (8-ounce) can water chestnuts,
    drained and sliced
½ teaspoon salt
⅛ teaspoon black pepper
3 cups cooked rice
1 (3-ounce) can chow mein
    noodles

Sprinkle chicken with soy sauce and lemon juice. Add bean sprouts, celery, mayonnaise, onions, water chestnuts, salt, and pepper. Add the rice. Mix well.

Pour into a buttered 2-quart dish. Bake, uncovered, at 375° for 15–20 minutes. Sprinkle with noodles. Bake 5 minutes more. Serves 6–10.

A Tasting Tour Through Washington County (Kentucky)

Tea Room Chicken

1 (6-ounce) package wild rice
    mix, cooked
1 (16-ounce) package frozen
    chopped broccoli
3 cups cooked diced chicken
1 cup shredded Velveeta
    cheese
1 cup fresh mushrooms, sliced
½ cup mayonnaise
1 can cream of mushroom
    soup
¼ teaspoon dry mustard
¼ teaspoon curry powder
Parmesan cheese
½ cup cracker crumbs
1 tablespoon butter

In a 9x13-inch pan, layer rice, broccoli, chicken, cheese, and mushrooms. In a separate bowl combine mayonnaise, soup, mustard, and curry powder. Pour over chicken mixture. Sprinkle with Parmesan cheese. Sauté crackers with butter and sprinkle over cheese. Bake at 350° for 30–45 minutes or until bubbly. Serves 6–10.

Madison County Cookbook (Iowa)

★★★★★★★★★★ ★★★★★★★★★★★

Shrimp and Wild Rice

1 (6-ounce) package long-grain
  and wild rice
1 (10¾-ounce) can cream of
  mushroom soup
½ cup shredded sharp
  Cheddar cheese
¼ cup chopped green bell
  pepper

¼ cup chopped red bell
  pepper
¼ cup chopped onion
2 tablespoons chopped parsley
½ teaspoon lemon juice
½ tablespoon mustard powder
2 pounds shrimp, peeled,
  deveined

Cook rice according to package directions. Stir in soup, cheese, peppers, onion, parsley, lemon juice, and mustard powder. Gently fold in shrimp. Spoon into a greased 9x13-inch baking dish. Cover and bake in 350° oven 30–35 minutes. Serves 6–8.

Note: To save chopping time, substitute 1 cup frozen seasoning blend in place of onion and peppers.

Dining Under the Carolina Moon (South Carolina)

Shrimp and Rice Rockefeller

1 cup chopped onion
2 tablespoons butter
12 ounces raw shrimp, peeled
  and cut in half
1 (10¾-ounce) can cream of
  mushroom soup, undiluted
1 cup grated Swiss cheese
¼ cup sherry wine
1 (8-ounce) can water chestnuts,
  drained and chopped

3 cups cooked rice
2 (10-ounce) packages frozen
  chopped spinach, cooked
1 tablespoon lemon juice
¼ cup grated Parmesan
  cheese, divided
1 teaspoon salt
1 teaspoon red pepper
½ teaspoon black pepper

In a 3-quart saucepan, sauté onion in butter. Add shrimp; cook until pink. Stir in mushroom soup, cheese, and sherry. Heat thoroughly until mixture is warm. Add water chestnuts, cooked rice, drained spinach, lemon juice, and 2 tablespoons Parmesan cheese. Add salt, red pepper, and black pepper. Pour into a greased shallow 2-quart dish. Sprinkle remaining Parmesan cheese over top. Bake in preheated 350° oven 30 minutes. Serves 6–8.

Voilà! Lafayette Centennial Cookbook 1884–1984 (Louisiana)

Texas Star Crabmeat Casserole

1 pound lump crabmeat
¼ cup lemon juice
½ teaspoon salt
½ cup butter or margarine
2½ tablespoons all-purpose
  flour
1½ cups milk
½ teaspoon garlic salt
½ teaspoon celery salt

1 teaspoon parsley flakes
1 cup grated Cheddar cheese
2 tablespoons white wine
  (optional)
6 cups cooked wild rice or
  Uncle Ben's Wild Rice
  Mixture
1 (4-ounce) can sliced
  mushrooms, drained

Combine crabmeat, lemon juice, and salt in a medium bowl, then refrigerate while preparing sauce.

Melt butter or margarine in a medium saucepan. Add flour; stir and cook for about 1 minute. Add milk slowly, stirring constantly, and cook until sauce thickens. Add seasonings, cheese, and wine, if desired. Stir until cheese is melted and sauce is smooth. Drain crabmeat, add to sauce, and heat until bubbly. Layer cooked wild rice in bottom of a lightly oiled 2-quart casserole dish. Pour crabmeat and sauce over rice. Top with mushroom slices, and bake at 350° for about 30 minutes or until lightly browned. Serve with a crisp green salad and crunchy rolls. Serves 6.

More Tastes & Tales (Texas II)

Baked Chicken and Rice

1 fryer, cut up	½ cup chopped onion
1 teaspoon salt	2 tablespoons butter
¼ teaspoon pepper	3 cups hot chicken broth or
1 teaspoon paprika	boiling water
1 cup uncooked rice	1 teaspoon celery salt

Sprinkle chicken with salt, pepper, and paprika. Brown rice and onion in butter. Spread rice mixture in a buttered 9x13-inch baking dish. Add broth and celery salt. Place chicken on top of rice-broth mixture. Cover dish tightly with foil. Bake at 350° for 1 hour. Remove cover and bake 15 minutes longer, or until meat is tender. Serves 5–6.

The Mississippi Cookbook (Mississippi)

Ham and Rice Casserole

SAUCE:

3 tablespoons butter	1½ teaspoons lemon juice
3 tablespoons flour	1 cup sour cream
1½ cups milk	

Melt butter in saucepan. Stir in flour. Add milk gradually, stirring constantly. Cook and stir over heat until thickens and begins to boil. Stir in lemon juice and sour cream (can use low–fat yogurt).

2 (10-ounce) packages frozen	2 cups cubed ham
broccoli	1½–2 cups cooked rice
½ cup grated Cheddar cheese,	Pepper to taste
divided	

Cook and drain broccoli. Place in greased casserole. Top with half of cheese and ham. Spoon on rice and pour sauce over all. Top with pepper and remaining cheese. Bake at 400° for 20–25 minutes. Serves 4–6.

Dawdy Family Cookbook (Illinois)

★★★★★★★★★★★ ★★★★★★★★★★★

Barbecued Rice

1 stick margarine
1 cup chopped celery
1 medium onion, chopped
2 cups cream of chicken
  soup
1 cup chicken broth
1 teaspoon liquid smoke
Salt and pepper to taste
3 cups cooked rice
¼ teaspoon garlic salt

Melt margarine in skillet; add celery and onion and cook until clear. Add soup, broth, liquid smoke, salt and pepper, and bring to a boil. Pour into casserole dish. Stir in cooked rice and garlic salt. Bake at 350° for 30 minutes. Serves 4–6.

A Heritage of Good Tastes (Arkansas)

Brown Rice Casserole

1 cup brown rice
Boiling water
3 tablespoons chopped onion
3 tablespoons bacon drippings
1 pound ground beef
1 (10¾-ounce) can condensed
  chicken rice soup
1 (4-ounce) can sliced
  mushrooms
½ cup water
⅛ teaspoon each: celery salt,
  onion salt, garlic salt, paprika
  and pepper
1 bay leaf, crumbled

Preheat oven to 325°. Place brown rice in a pot and cover with boiling water; cover the pot and let stand 15 minutes. While rice is sitting, sauté onion in bacon fat until lightly browned, then add ground beef, stirring until brown and crunchy.

In a large bowl, combine chicken rice soup, mushrooms, water, and spices. Combine ground beef mixture and rice, then add them to the soup and spices mixture; mix thoroughly. Pour mixture into a buttered or greased casserole dish. Bake, covered, at 325° for 1 hour. Serves 4–6.

God, That's Good! (Nevada)

Beans and Rice Casserole

1 cup brown rice
1 medium onion, chopped
3 garlic cloves, minced
1 tablespoon olive oil
1 (28-ounce) can seasoned diced
  tomatoes
1 (15½-ounce) can dark red
  kidney beans, drained
1 (15½-ounce) can white
  beans, drained
Parsley, celery seed, basil, white
  pepper, ground cumin to taste
1 bay leaf

Bring 2½ cups water to boil. Add 1 cup brown rice. Cover; reduce to simmer for 45 minutes. Sauté onion and garlic cloves in olive oil in large skillet. Add seasoned tomatoes in juice and drained beans to onion and garlic. Add parsley, celery seed, basil, white pepper, and ground cumin to taste. Add 1 bay leaf. Let simmer for 20 minutes. Add cooked brown rice. Simmer 10–15 additional minutes. Serve with a fresh green salad and cornbread. Serves 4–6.

Gather Around Our Table (New York)

Lowcountry Red Rice

14 slices bacon
2 large red bell peppers,
  chopped
1 medium onion, chopped
4 teaspoons dried thyme
¾ cup tomato paste
3 cups long-grain rice
6 cups canned vegetable or
  chicken broth
1 tablespoon hot pepper sauce

Cook bacon in heavy Dutch oven over medium-high heat until brown. Transfer bacon to paper towels to drain; crumble. Pour off all but 3 tablespoons bacon drippings. Add peppers, onion, and thyme, and sauté 5 minutes. Mix in tomato paste, rice, broth, hot pepper sauce, and bacon. Reduce heat, cover, and simmer until rice is tender, about 30 minutes. Add more hot pepper sauce to taste, if desired. Serves 6–8.

Music, Menus & Magnolias (South Carolina)

Nakatosh Rice Casserole

1 cup uncooked converted rice
2 bunches green onions,
  chopped
1 large green bell pepper,
  chopped
1–2 tablespoons vegetable oil
½ cup margarine
2 (4-ounce) cans sliced
  mushrooms, drained

2 (3-ounce) jars diced
  pimentos, drained
1 tablespoon soy sauce
1 tablespoon Worcestershire
Salt to taste
¼ teaspoon black pepper
1½ teaspoons Italian seasoning
1 teaspoon dry parsley flakes

Prepare rice according to package directions. Sauté green onions and bell pepper in oil and margarine until softened. Combine sautéed vegetables, rice, mushrooms, pimentos, soy sauce, Worcestershire sauce, salt, black pepper, Italian seasoning, and parsley, mixing well. Spread mixture in lightly greased 2-quart casserole. Bake at 350° until hot and bubbly. Unbaked casserole can be stored in refrigerator for up to 2 days. Serves 8.

Cane River's Louisiana Living (Louisiana II)

Milanese Rice

2 tablespoons butter or
  margarine
2 tablespoons olive oil
1 cup raw rice
1 medium onion, chopped
1 garlic clove, minced
1 cup crumbled crisp bacon

2 tablespoons dry white wine
1 (4-ounce) can mushrooms
2 (14½-ounce) cans chicken
  broth
Salt and pepper to taste
½ cup grated Parmesan cheese

Heat butter and oil in heavy skillet. Add rice, onion, and garlic, and brown until rice is golden. Add remaining ingredients; cover and bake at 350° about 45 minutes or until rice is dry. Freezes well. (Be sure to use the olive oil, as it gives the rice a wonderful flavor.) Double or triple the recipe and freeze in zip-lock bags. Serves 4–6.

If It Tastes Good, Who Cares? I (Great Plains)

Eggplant Rice Dressing

2 medium eggplants (2 pounds), peeled and diced
1 large onion, chopped
1 cup chopped celery
2 medium bell peppers, chopped
8 garlic cloves, minced
1 teaspoon salt
1 cup water
3 cups cooked rice
1½ pounds ground pork
2 teaspoons salt
1 teaspoon black pepper
½ teaspoon red pepper
Bread crumbs for sprinkling

Boil eggplants, onion, celery, bell peppers, garlic, salt, and water in Dutch oven until vegetables are tender. Cook rice in separate pot. Place meat in small skillet; brown in its own fat. Drain and add to cooked vegetables. Cook meat and vegetables to a thick consistency. Add rice, salt, black pepper, and red pepper. Place in buttered 2-quart round glass casserole dish. Sprinkle top with bread crumbs. Bake in preheated 350° oven 15 minutes. Serves 12.

Microwave shortcut: After mixture has been placed in 2-quart glass dish, microwave on HIGH (100%) 4 minutes.

Voilà! Lafayette Centennial Cookbook 1884–1984 (Louisiana)

Stevland Hardaway Morris, born May 13, 1950, better known by his stage name Stevie Wonder, is an American singer-songwriter, multi-instrumentalist, record producer, and activist. Despite his being blind since birth, at age 13, he had his first US number one hit single and album with the first live recording to ever top the charts. He is still the youngest person to have reached those number one spots.

Macadamia-Pineapple Rice Pilaf

1 tablespoon unsalted butter
1½ cups long-grain white rice
2 teaspoons minced garlic
1 medium white onion, diced
¼ red bell pepper, seeded
 and diced
¼ yellow bell pepper, seeded
 and diced
3 cups strong chicken stock

½ cup golden raisins
½ cup chopped macadamia
 nuts
1 fresh sage leaf
Salt to taste
⅓ cup chopped fresh cilantro
1 cup diced pineapple, reserve
 juice

Preheat oven to 375°. In a flame-proof casserole, melt butter on medium-high heat and add rice. Stir for a few seconds until rice is coated, but not long enough to let rice change color. Add garlic, onion, and red and yellow bell peppers, and cook for a few more seconds. Add chicken stock and bring mixture to a gentle boil. Add raisins, nuts, sage, and salt. Cover and place in oven and bake for 30 minutes. Remove dish from oven and let it rest (without uncovering) for another 10 minutes. Add the cilantro and pineapple bits. Season, if necessary, and serve at once. Serves 4–6.

Note: May mix chicken stock and syrup from pineapple to make up the 3 cups of liquid needed. If using salted macadamia nuts, remember to adjust seasonings.

Tropical Taste (Hawaii)

Spinach-Cream Cheese Enchiladas

This is a really nice dish for entertaining. The sauce can be made a day ahead and the enchiladas can be filled ahead of time. When your guests arrive, pour the sauce over the filled tortillas, top with cheese, and bake.

SAUCE:

3 tablespoons oil
3 garlic cloves, minced
2 teaspoons dried Mexican
  oregano
1 tablespoon dried ground
  red chile peppers
3 tablespoons unbleached
  flour

1 (6-ounce) can tomato paste
4 cups water
1 teaspoon salt or to taste
1 tablespoon apple cider
  vinegar

In oil, sauté garlic over low heat for 3 minutes. Add oregano, dried ground chiles, and flour, and stir until oil is absorbed. Stir in tomato paste, water, salt, and vinegar, and continue stirring until smooth. Bring to a boil; reduce heat and cook over medium heat until thickened.

FILLING:

1 (8-ounce) package cream
  cheese (room temperature)
1 (10-ounce) package frozen
  chopped spinach, thawed
  and squeezed dry
½ cup roasted, peeled,
  chopped green chile peppers

4 scallions, diced
2 tablespoons lemon juice
12 (8-inch) flour tortillas
½ cup grated Monterey Jack
  cheese

Mix cream cheese, spinach, green chile peppers, scallions, and lemon juice.

Preheat oven to 350°. Grease a 9x13-inch baking pan. Fill each tortilla with 2 tablespoons Filling and roll up. Place in baking pan. Reserving one cup Sauce for serving at table, pour remaining Sauce over filled tortillas. Top with grated cheese. Bake 20 minutes or until Sauce is bubbling. Serve with reserved enchilada sauce. Makes 12 enchiladas. Serves 6.

The Durango Cookbook (Colorado)

Enchilada Casserole

1½ pounds ground beef
1 cup chopped onion
1½ teaspoons cumin
2 garlic cloves, minced
4 teaspoons chili powder
1½ teaspoons salt

½ teaspoon pepper
3 cups enchilada sauce
12 corn tortillas
1 pound Monterey Jack
  cheese
Sour cream

Cook ground beef and onion. Add next 5 ingredients. Simmer 10 minutes. Pour half of sauce in a 9x13-inch baking dish, then layer 6 tortillas, half of meat mixture, and half of cheese. Repeat for next layer, starting with sauce. Cover with foil and bake 40 minutes in a 375° oven. Remove foil; bake another 5 minutes. Serve with sour cream. Serves 6–8.

The Orient Volunteer Fire Department Cookbook (Iowa)

South of the Border
Crustless Quiche

This recipe may be mixed ahead and baked the following day; easy to halve.

8 eggs, beaten
1 cup all-purpose flour
1 teaspoon baking powder
2 cups cottage cheese
½ pound Cheddar cheese,
  grated
½ pound Monterey Jack
  cheese, grated

¼ cup butter, melted
1 (7-ounce) can diced green
  chiles, drained
1 (8-ounce) can sliced water
  chestnuts, drained
½ small onion, chopped

Stir all ingredients together. Pour into greased 2-quart flat baking dish. Bake in 375° oven 30–40 minutes until set. Serves 6–8.

The Best of Mayberry (North Carolina)

Jo Ann's Crustless Quiche

4 cups (16 ounces) grated
  Monterey Jack cheese
4 cups (16 ounces) grated sharp
  Cheddar cheese
1 (5-ounce) can evaporated
  milk

9 eggs
2 or 3 jalapeño peppers,
  chopped
1 (4-ounce) can green chiles,
  chopped

Combine Monterey Jack and Cheddar cheeses, milk, eggs, jalapeño peppers, and chiles, mixing well with wooden spoon. Pour mixture into 9x13x2-inch baking dish. Bake at 350° for 40 minutes. Let stand until cool. Cut into 1-inch squares. Serves 10–12.

Cane River's Louisiana Living (Louisiana II)

Spinach-Mushroom Quiche

CUSTARD MIXTURE:

3 eggs
1½ cups heavy cream
¼ teaspoon pepper

⅛ teaspoon salt
Pinch of nutmeg
1½ cups grated Swiss cheese

Beat eggs and cream in mixing bowl. Stir in remaining ingredients.

SPINACH-MUSHROOM MIXTURE:

1 (10-ounce) package frozen
  chopped spinach, cooked,
  drained
¼ cup diced onion
½ cup sliced mushrooms

2 tablespoons butter, melted
1 (9-inch) unbaked pie crust
2 tablespoons parsley
2 tablespoons grated Parmesan
  cheese

Sauté spinach, onion, and mushrooms in melted butter 10 minutes. Stir into Custard Mixture. Pour into pie crust and top with parsley and Parmesan cheese. Bake 30–35 minutes at 375°, until golden and fluffy. Serves 6–8.

Tasty Treasures from Johnson's Church (Virginia II)

Gourmet Grits Casserole

Grits aren't just for breakfast. This is fabulous for brunch or a side dish with grilled meats.

1½ cups uncooked grits
6 cups boiling water
1 pound longhorn Cheddar
  cheese, shredded
1 (4-ounce) can diced green
  chiles, drained
3 eggs, beaten
¼ cup butter, softened
1 tablespoon savory salt (your
  favorite salt/herb blend)

2–3 garlic cloves, minced
Dash of Tabasco
Dash of Worcestershire
Dash of paprika
Salt and pepper to taste
1 cup crushed cornflakes
¼ cup butter, melted

Cook grits in boiling water according to package directions. Stir in remaining ingredients except cornflakes and melted butter; mix well. Pour into greased 9x13-inch baking dish. Combine cornflakes and butter; sprinkle over casserole. Top with additional paprika, if desired. Bake at 250° for 1½–2 hours, or until set. Serves 10–12.

Note: Casserole can be prepared a day ahead, covered, and refrigerated. Additional baking time may be needed.

Palates (Colorado)

This elliptical amphitheatre in the center of the city of Rome, Italy, is the largest ever built in the Roman Empire. Capable of seating 50,000 spectators, the Colosseum was used for gladiatorial contests and public spectacles such as mock sea battles, animal hunts, executions, reenactments of famous battles, and dramas based on classical mythology.

Poultry

NATHAN CREEL

The Colosseum. Rome, Italy.
One of the Medieval Wonders of the World.

★★★★★★★★★★★★ ★★★★★★★★★★★★

Chicken Parmesan

4 boneless skinless chicken
  breast halves
2 (14½-ounce) cans Italian-style
  stewed tomatoes
½ teaspoon crushed oregano
  or basil

2 tablespoons cornstarch
¼ teaspoon hot pepper sauce
  (optional)
¼ cup grated Parmesan cheese

Place chicken in baking dish. Bake covered for 15 minutes in pre-heated 425° oven; drain. Combine next 4 ingredients in a saucepan, cook, stirring constantly until sauce is thickened. Pour heated sauce over chicken; top with cheese. Bake 5 minutes uncovered. May garnish with fresh parsley. Serves 4.

Tried and True by Mothers of Z's (Ohio)

Peachy Chicken Casserole

This is great for family and entertaining friends.

6 chicken breasts (skinless)
2 teaspoons salt
Pepper to taste
1½ teaspoons paprika
¾ cup all-purpose flour
½ cup butter
½ cup slivered almonds
1 cup water

2 (10-ounce) cans beef
  consommé
2 tablespoons ketchup
2 cups sour cream
1 (20-ounce) can sliced peaches,
  drained
¼ cup grated Parmesan
  cheese

Preheat oven to 350°. Dredge chicken with mixture of salt, pepper, paprika, and flour. Reserve remaining flour mixture. Brown chicken on all sides in hot butter. Place chicken in 3-quart casserole.

Lightly brown almonds in drippings in skillet. Stir in remaining flour. Gradually stir in water and consommé. Add ketchup; cook and stir until thickened. Remove from heat and stir in sour cream. Pour over chicken and bake, uncovered, for about 1 hour. Arrange sliced peaches on top of chicken. Sprinkle with cheese and return to oven for 10 minutes. Serves 8–12.

Four Generations of Johnson Family Favorites (Oklahoma)

Cheesy Chicken Florentine

Always requested for a repeat performance.

3 (10-ounce) packages frozen
  chopped spinach, thawed and
  squeezed dry
6 chicken breast halves,
  cooked, cut into pieces
2 (8-ounce) packages cream
  cheese
14 ounces extra sharp
  Cheddar cheese, grated
2 cups milk

¼ teaspoon salt
¼ teaspoon pepper
½ teaspoon dill
½ teaspoon garlic
1 tablespoon parsley flakes
1 cup grated Parmesan cheese,
  divided
1 cup bread crumbs
¼ cup (½ stick) butter,
  melted

Preheat oven to 375°. Lightly butter a 9x13-inch casserole. Line with uncooked spinach. Add chicken. Set aside.

Make sauce by melting cream cheese, Cheddar cheese, milk, seasonings, and ⅔ cup Parmesan cheese. (Reserve ⅓ cup of Parmesan cheese for bread crumb mixture.) Blend over low heat until smooth. Pour cheese sauce over spinach and chicken. Combine bread crumbs with melted butter. Add remaining ⅓ cup Parmesan cheese. Sprinkle mixture on top of casserole. Bake uncovered for 30 minutes. Serves 4–6.

Moveable Feasts Cookbook (New England)

The name Colosseum has long been believed to be derived from a colossal statue of Nero (which was named after one of the original ancient wonders, the Colossus of Rhodes). Built in the years 72–80 AD, the outer walls of the Roman Colosseum were held together without mortar by 300 tons of iron clamps. It is considered one of the greatest works of Roman architecture and Roman engineering to ever exist. Modern coliseums are modeled after it.

★★★★★★★★★★★★   ★★★★★★★★★★★★

Poppy Seed Chicken Casserole

**4 chicken breast halves,
cooked and diced**
**1 (10¾-ounce) can cream of
chicken soup**
**1 (8-ounce) container sour
cream**

**1–1½ stacks Ritz Crackers,
crushed**
1 stick margarine, melted
2 tablespoons poppy seeds

Mix chicken with soup and sour cream. Spread in casserole dish.
Mix crackers with margarine, and sprinkle over chicken mixture.
Sprinkle poppy seeds on top. Bake at 325° for 25 minutes, or until
bubbly. Serves 4–6.

Home Made with Love (Kentucky)

Party Chicken

**6–8 chicken breast halves,
boned and skinned**
**1 or 2 packages dried chipped
beef**
6–8 slices thin bacon

**1 (10¾-ounce) can cream of
mushroom soup, undiluted**
½ pint sour cream
⅔ cup white wine

Grease an 8x12x2-inch baking dish. Flatten each half breast with
hand; lay slices of beef on top. (I use 2 or 3 slices of dried beef on
each half breast. If beef is too salty, soak 5 minutes and dry.) Roll
up and wrap bacon slices around; flatten. Pin with toothpicks.
Mix soup, sour cream, and wine; pour over all. Marinate in refrigerator several hours or overnight.

Bake at 275° for 3 hours, uncovered. Delicious served with rice,
almond green beans, and Waldorf salad. Serves 6–8.

Holy Chow (Kentucky)

Lynn's Special Chicken

6 chicken breast halves, skinned
   and boned
½ pound fresh mushrooms,
   sliced
2 tablespoons butter
½ pound Swiss cheese, grated
2 eggs, beaten

1 cup flour
1 teaspoon salt
½ teaspoon pepper
½ teaspoon paprika
1 cup Italian bread crumbs
¼ cup grated Swiss cheese
Butter

Pound chicken breasts to ¼-inch thickness. Sauté mushrooms in butter and mix with cheese. Place mixture on each chicken breast and fold in half. Secure with wooden toothpick. Place in freezer until firm, about 20 minutes. Dip in eggs, then in a mixture of flour, salt, pepper and paprika. Dip in a mixture of bread crumbs and Swiss cheese. Sauté in butter in a skillet until lightly browned on all sides. Place in a buttered shallow casserole dish and bake at 325° for 20–30 minutes. Do not overcook. Serves 4–6.

Putting on the Grits (South Carolina)

The Downs

3 cups cooked and diced
   chicken breasts
2 hard-cooked eggs, chopped
¼ cup chopped black olives
¼ cup chopped celery
½ cup mayonnaise
1 tablespoon lemon juice

Salt to taste
12 slices white bread, crusts
   removed
1 (10¾-ounce) can cream of
   chicken soup, undiluted
1 cup sour cream
1 cup grated Cheddar cheese

Combine chicken, eggs, olives, and celery. Blend in mayonnaise and lemon juice. Salt to taste. Spread chicken on bread to make a sandwich. Place 6 sandwiches in a 9x13-inch casserole. Combine soup and sour cream. Pour over sandwiches. Cover and refrigerate overnight. Bake at 325° uncovered for 20 minutes. Add grated cheese and bake until cheese melts. Serves 6.

Fillies Flavours (Kentucky)

Chicken Pot Pie

½ cup liquid butter substitute*
3 tablespoons plain flour
3 cups defatted chicken broth
1 cup skim milk
¼ cup sliced celery
¼ cup chopped onion

3 cups diced chicken breasts
Salt and pepper
1 (16-ounce) package frozen
   mixed vegetables, cooked
   per package instructions
1 (9-inch) pie crust, uncooked

Combine butter substitute and flour in saucepan over low heat. Gradually add chicken broth and milk, stirring constantly until smooth and thickened. Sauté celery and onion in vegetable spray. Stir in chicken, salt, pepper, mixed vegetables, and sautéed onion and celery. Mix well. Pour into a 9x13x2-inch baking dish. Roll pastry to ⅛-inch thickness on lightly floured board and cut into 11-inch wide strips. Arrange in lattice design over chicken mixture. Bake at 350° for 30 minutes or until pastry is golden brown. Serves 8.

*One package Butter Buds mixed with ½ cup water equals ½ cup liquid butter substitute.

Cal 211; Chol 36mg; Sat Fat 1gm; Fat 3gm; Sod 515mg; Pro 18gm; Cho 28gm; Exchanges: 2 meat, 1 bread, ½ vegetable.

Southern But Lite (Louisiana II)

According to the Codex-Calendar of 354, the Colosseum could accommodate 87,000 people (modern estimates say around 50,000) who were seated in a tiered arrangement that reflected the rigidly stratified nature of Roman society, from the Emperor, senators, and knights, to plebians, poor people, and even slaves who were likely in a standing-room-only section. (Banned altogether were grave diggers, actors, and former gladiators.) There were 80 exits at ground level. The Colosseum remained in use nearly 500 years, the last recorded games being held in the 6th century. Today the Colosseum is one of the most popular tourist attractions of Rome.

Country Chicken Pie

4 chicken breast halves,
   cooked and deboned
1 small onion, chopped
2 ribs celery, chopped
1 carrot, chopped
1 small potato, chopped
6 tablespoons butter or
   margarine

6 tablespoons plain flour
2½ cups milk
2 chicken bouillon cubes
1 teaspoon Worcestershire
1 teaspoon salt
Pepper to taste
Biscuits

Boil chicken in enough water to cover until done—about one hour. When cool, remove meat from the bone and chop in bite-size pieces. Chop vegetables into small pieces and boil in a small amount of water about 10 minutes. They should be tender, but not completely done. Drain.

Make sauce by melting butter and adding flour until it is mixed. Gradually add milk, stirring constantly so the sauce will not lump. Add bouillon cubes, Worcestershire, salt, and pepper. Cook over low heat until mixture thickens. Mix chicken, vegetables, and sauce and pour into a greased 2-quart casserole. Top with biscuits rolled about ½ inch thick. (Any biscuit recipe will do, but a mix made according to directions will do as well.) Bake at 400° for 30–40 minutes until the casserole is bubbly and the biscuits are brown. Serves 4–6.

Note: This may be frozen but do not add the biscuits. If frozen, the cooking time will be longer, so the biscuits should be put on top the last 30 minutes of baking.

By Special Request (Louisiana II)

★★★★★★★★★★★   ★★★★★★★★★★★

Turkey Crunch Casserole
Casserole de Dinde Croquée

1½ pounds diced cooked turkey
2 hard-cooked eggs, chopped
1 (4-ounce) can sliced
   mushrooms
1 cup diced celery
½ cup slivered blanched
   almonds

1 tablespoon chopped onion
1 (10¾-ounce) can condensed
   cream of chicken soup
¾ cup low-fat mayonnaise
15 crushed potato chips

Mix together first 6 ingredients. Stir soup into mayonnaise. Toss with turkey mixture. Turn into a 8x8x2-inch baking dish. Sprinkle top with potato chips. Bake at 350° for 30 minutes or until mixture is bubbling. Serves 8.

Per serving: 335 calories. Exchanges per serving = 3 meats, 3 fats, ½ bread, 7½ grams carbohydrates, 22 grams protein, 24 grams fat.

Cooking for Love and Life (Louisiana)

Turkey Mornay

2 (10-ounce) packages frozen
   broccoli spears, cooked
   until tender-crisp
¼ pound thinly sliced
   prosciutto
1 pound sliced cooked turkey
   breast
¼ cup butter
¼ cup flour
1 cup rich chicken broth

1 cup light cream
2 tablespoons grated Parmesan
   cheese
2 tablespoons grated Swiss
   cheese
2 tablespoons sherry
Salt to taste
Dash of cayenne
¼ cup grated Parmesan cheese

Drain broccoli and arrange it in a baking dish. Cover with prosciutto, then turkey. Melt butter and blend in flour. Stir in the chicken broth and cream; cook, stirring constantly, until smooth and thick. Stir in cheeses, sherry, salt, and cayenne. Heat just until cheese is melted. Pour sauce over turkey; sprinkle with ¼ cup grated Parmesan. Bake at 350° until the sauce is hot and the cheese brown and bubbly, about 30 minutes. Serves 6.

Soupçon I (Illinois)

Gobbler Cobbler

PASTRY:

1½ cups flour
⅛ teaspoon salt
½ cup shortening
¼ cup milk
⅓ cup shredded Cheddar
   cheese

Combine flour and salt; cut in shortening. Add milk; blend in cheese and mix lightly. Roll out on floured board, place Pastry in 9-inch pie pan, and prick with a fork. Bake at 425° for 12–15 minutes or until lightly browned.

FILLING:

2 cups chopped cooked turkey
1 cup pineapple chunks, drained
1 cup chopped walnuts
¼ cup chopped celery
¼ cup chopped onion
1 (8-ounce) carton sour cream
⅔ cup mayonnaise
3 tablespoons shredded
   Cheddar cheese
Sliced black olives

Combine turkey, pineapple, nuts, celery, and onion and mix well. In a separate bowl, mix sour cream and mayonnaise. Add just enough sour cream mixture to the turkey mixture to moisten it. Pour turkey mixture into the pie shell; top with remaining sour cream mixture. Garnish with cheese and olives and bake 20 minutes at 350°. Makes 6 large servings.

Recipes and Remembering (Oregon)

Cheesy Tomato Basil Chicken Breasts

SAUCE:

½ teaspoon salt
2 cups cubed tomatoes
⅓ cup chopped onion
1 (6-ounce) can tomato paste

¼ teaspoon pepper
2 teaspoons minced fresh garlic
1 tablespoon basil leaves

In medium bowl, mix Sauce ingredients; set aside.

3 tablespoons butter

**3 whole chicken breasts,
   skinned and cut in half**

Heat oven to 350°. In 9x13-inch baking pan, melt 3 tablespoons butter in oven. Place chicken in baking pan, turning to coat with butter. Spoon Sauce over chicken. Bake for 30–40 minutes or until chicken is no longer pink.

TOPPING:

1 cup fresh bread crumbs
¼ cup chopped fresh parsley
2 tablespoons melted butter

6 ounces mozzarella cheese,
   cut into strips

Stir together all Topping ingredients except cheese. Place cheese strips over chicken; sprinkle with Topping mixture. Continue baking 5–10 minutes or until chicken is fork-tender and bread crumbs are browned. Serves 6.

Blissfield Preschool Cookbook (Michigan)

Friendship Chicken Casserole

6 chicken breast halves,
   boiled tender, cut into
   bite-size pieces
2 (10¾-ounce) cans cream of
   chicken soup
1 (8-ounce) can sliced water
   chestnuts, drained
1 (15-ounce) can chop suey
   vegetables, drained
1 cup chopped celery

1 (7-ounce) can Chinese
   noodles
½ cup Miracle Whip salad
   dressing
1 teaspoon lemon juice
2 tablespoons chopped green
   onions
½–¾ cup chopped cashew
   nuts

Combine all ingredients, except nuts, in large bowl. Place mixture in greased shallow casserole dish. Cover with nuts. Bake at 350° for 30 minutes. Serves 10–12.

Cooking with Friends (Michigan)

The Seven Wonders of the Medieval World

In the 19th and early 20th centuries, some writers claimed that lists of wonders of the world existed during the Middle Ages, although it is unlikely that these lists originated at that time. The word medieval was not invented until the Enlightenment era, and the concept of a Middle Age did not become popular until the 16th century. Many of the structures on these lists were built much earlier than the Middle Ages, but were well known.

1. Stonehenge – United Kingdom
2. Colosseum – Italy
3. Catacombs of Kom el Shoqafa – Egypt
4. Great Wall of China – China
5. Porcelain Tower of Nanjing – China
6. Hagia Sophia – Turkey
7. Leaning Tower of Pisa – Italy

Angel Wings

6 boneless, skinless chicken
  breast halves
3 tablespoons butter or
  margarine, divided
Salt and pepper to taste
1¼ cups chicken broth,
  divided
1 onion, chopped

2 (4-ounce) cans diced green
  chiles
1 garlic clove, minced
1 tablespoon flour
½ cup cream
½ cup shredded Cheddar
  cheese

Brown chicken lightly in half the butter in skillet, and season with salt and pepper. Lay in single layer in greased shallow 9x13-inch baking dish. Splash with ¼ cup chicken broth. Cover tightly and bake in preheated 350° oven for 20 minutes.

While chicken bakes, sauté onion gently in remaining butter until soft. Add chiles to pan with garlic and flour. Stir and cook a minute or so. Stir in remaining cup broth, and simmer until smooth and slightly thickened. Pour into blender or food processor and whirl until puréed. Put back into skillet and stir in cream. Heat just to simmering and pour over chicken. Sprinkle with cheese. Bake in 350° oven an additional 30 minutes, or until baked and cheese is glazed. Serves 6.

Savoring the Southwest (New Mexico)

WIKIPEDIA.ORG

No matter where in the world the president travels, if he flies in an Air Force jet, the plane is called *Air Force One*. Technically, *Air Force One* is the call sign of any Air Force aircraft carrying the president. In practice, however, Air Force One is used to refer to one of two highly customized Boeing 747-200B-series aircraft.

★★★★★★★★★★★ ★★★★★★★★★★★

Chicken-and-Dressing Casserole

FIRST LAYER:

1 (6-ounce) box cornbread
   stuffing mix with seasoning

1 cup chicken broth
1 stick margarine, melted

Combine stuffing mix with seasoning, chicken broth, and melted margarine in a large bowl; mix well. Spoon stuffing mixture into the bottom of a lightly greased, 3-quart casserole dish.

SECOND LAYER:

3 cups chopped, cooked chicken
   (5–6 chicken breasts)
½ cup chopped onion
½ cup chopped celery

1 (8-ounce) can water chestnuts,
   drained, chopped
½ cup mayonnaise
Salt and pepper to taste

Combine chicken, onion, celery, water chestnuts, mayonnaise, salt and pepper in a large bowl; mix well. Spoon on top of First Layer.

THIRD LAYER:

2 eggs, well beaten
1½ cups milk
1 (6-ounce) box cornbread
   stuffing mix with seasoning

1 (10¾-ounce) can cream of
   mushroom soup, undiluted

Combine eggs, milk, and stuffing mix with seasoning in a large bowl; mix well. Spoon on top of Second Layer. Cover and refrigerate overnight.

When ready to cook, evenly spread cream of mushroom soup on top of casserole. Preheat oven to 350°. Bake, uncovered, for 45–60 minutes or until thoroughly heated. Remove from oven, and let stand 20 minutes before serving. Serves 6–8.

Treasured Family Favorites (Mississippi)

Chicken and Stuffing Casserole

4 whole chicken breasts, split,
  skinned, deboned
8 slices Swiss cheese
1 (10¾-ounce) can cream of
  chicken soup (undiluted)

¼ cup white wine
1 cup herb-seasoned stuffing
  mix
¼ cup butter, melted

Place chicken in lightly greased 9x13-inch baking dish. Top with cheese slices. Combine soup and wine; mix well. Spoon sauce over chicken and sprinkle with stuffing mix. Drizzle butter over crumbs. Bake at 350° for 45 minutes, uncovered. Serves 4.

What's Cooking at Trinity (Pennsylvania)

Cornbread Dressing

1 medium onion, chopped
⅔ cup chopped celery
5–6 cups chicken or turkey
  broth
1 pan of cornbread

7 or 8 biscuits
½ teaspoon sage
¼ teaspoon black pepper
2 or 3 eggs, hard-boiled
½ teaspoon salt

Cook onion and celery in broth for about 5 minutes. Crumble cornbread and biscuits with sage and pepper. Add to mixture, stirring until all bread is moist and soft. Add chopped boiled eggs and salt. Beat by hand for 1–2 minutes. Dressing should be rather soft. Pepper and sage can be increased according to taste. Pour into a 2-quart baking dish, and bake in oven at 400° for 45–50 minutes, or stuff inside the holiday bird. Serves 6.

Mrs. Blackwell's Heart of Texas Cookbook (Texas)

★★★★★★★★★★★★   ★★★★★★★★★★★★

Italian Chicken Delight

6 boned and skinned breast
  halves
1 egg, beaten
¾ cup Italian bread crumbs
½ cup oil
1 (16-ounce) can tomato sauce
Salt and pepper to taste

1 tablespoon butter
1 tablespoon basil
Generous amount garlic
  powder
¾ cup grated Parmesan cheese
Mozzarella cheese

Dip chicken into beaten egg, coating well. Roll breasts in bread crumbs. Brown in oil. Drain chicken and place in casserole in single layer.

    To oil in skillet, add tomato sauce, salt, pepper, butter, basil and garlic powder. Simmer and pour over chicken in casserole. Sprinkle with Parmesan cheese. Seal top with foil. Bake at 350° for 30 minutes. Uncover and top with triangles of mozzarella cheese. Bake 10 more minutes. Serves 6.

Bouquet Garni (Mississippi)

Jalapeño Chicken

1½ pounds chicken breast fillets
1½ cups water
2 tablespoons butter
1 box chicken-flavored stuffing
  mix
1 teaspoon ground cumin
  (optional)

1 cup mild or medium salsa
2 cups shredded Monterey Jack
  cheese with jalapeño peppers
¾ cup sour cream
1 chopped jalapeño pepper, or
  to taste

Cook chicken breasts as desired, and slice into thin strips. Bring water and butter to boil in a saucepan; add stuffing mix and cumin. Mix and spread evenly into a greased 7x12-inch baking dish. Layer with chicken, salsa, and cheese.

    Preheat oven to 325°. Bake for 30 minutes. Serve with sour cream and chopped jalapeño. Serves 4–6.

Centennial Cookbook (Idaho)

Chicken Enchiladas

1–2 tablespoons vegetable oil
2 (4-ounce) cans green chiles
1 large garlic clove, minced
1 (28-ounce) can tomatoes
2 cups chopped onions
2 teaspoons salt, divided
½ teaspoon oregano
3 cups shredded, cooked chicken
2 cups dairy sour cream
2 cups grated Cheddar cheese
⅓ cup vegetable oil
15 corn tortillas

Preheat oil in skillet. Chop chiles after removing seeds; sauté with minced garlic in oil. Drain and break up tomatoes; reserve ½ cup liquid. To chiles and garlics add tomatoes, onions, 1 teaspoon salt, oregano, and reserved tomato liquid. Simmer uncovered until thick, about 30 minutes. Remove from skillet and set aside.

Combine chicken with sour cream, grated cheese, and other teaspoon salt. Heat ⅓ cup oil; dip tortillas in oil until they become limp. Drain well on paper towels. Fill tortillas with chicken mixture; roll up and arrange side by-side, seam down, in 9x13x2-inch baking dish. Pour chili sauce over enchiladas and bake at 350° until heated through, about 20 minutes. Makes 15 enchiladas.

Thirty Years at the Mansion (Arkansas)

Karen's Chicken Chalupas

2 (10¾-ounce) cans cream of chicken soup
1 pint sour cream
1 (4-ounce) can diced green chiles
1 bunch green onions, chopped
1 (4-ounce) can sliced black olives (optional)
¾ pound grated Jack cheese
4 large chicken breasts, cooked and cut into pieces
1 dozen flour tortillas
¾ pound grated Cheddar cheese

In large bowl, mix soup, sour cream, chiles, green onions, olives, and Jack cheese. Remove 2 cups of mixture and set aside.

Add chicken to above mixture. Put ½ cup into each tortilla and roll up. Place in large greased casserole or 9x13x2-inch pan. Pour the reserved 2 cups mixture over top of rolled tortillas; cover with grated Cheddar cheese. Bake at 350° until hot and bubbly, approximately 35–45 minutes. Can be made ahead and frozen. Serves 4–6.

Fair Haven Fare (Mid-Atlantic)

Mexicali Chicken

Can do one day ahead.

10 chicken breast halves
1½–2 (7-ounce) cans green
  chile salsa, mild
1 bunch green onions,
  chopped
1½ teaspoons salt
3 ounces cream cheese,
  cubed small
1 (15-ounce) can chili
  without beans

Approximately ¾ cup
  medium-size black
  olives, whole
8 ounces grated Cheddar
  cheese
8 ounces grated Monterey
  Jack cheese

Boil chicken breasts for 45 minutes. Remove bones. Cool and cut into large chunks. In large bowl, combine with salsa, onions, and salt. Place in ungreased 9x13-inch baking dish. Top with cream cheese cubes. Spread chili carefully over all. Place desired amount of olives over chili. Mix together grated cheeses and sprinkle over top. Bake 30 minutes at 350°. Serves 6–8.

Hint: Be sure to cube the cream cheese in small pieces. May be made using 1 bottle of mild salsa and 1 bottle of hot salsa. This is good served with flour tortillas. Recipe may be made the night before and refrigerated.

For Crying Out Loud . . . Let's Eat! (Indiana)

WIKIPEDIA.ORG

Listed as one of the Seven Wonders of the Medieval World, Hagia Sophia is a former Orthodox patriarchal basilica, later a mosque, and now a museum in Istanbul, Turkey.

Famous in particular for its massive dome, it is considered the epitome of Byzantine architecture, and is said to have "changed the history of architecture." It was the largest cathedral in the world for nearly a thousand years, until Seville Cathedral in Spain was completed in 1520.

Puffy Chicken Chile Rellenos

1½ cups chopped cooked
  chicken
3 (4-ounce) cans chopped
  green chiles, drained
4 flour tortillas, cut into halves
16 ounces Monterey Jack
  cheese, shredded
2–3 Roma tomatoes, seeded,
  chopped
8 eggs, lightly beaten
½ cup milk

2 tablespoons flour
½ teaspoon salt
½ teaspoon pepper
½ teaspoon cumin
½ teaspoon garlic powder
½ teaspoon onion salt
Paprika to taste
½ cup sour cream (optional)
¼ cup chopped green onions
  (optional)

Layer half the chicken, half the green chiles, half the tortillas, and half the cheese in a greased 2½-quart baking dish. Top with tomatoes. Repeat layers with remaining chicken, green chiles, tortillas, and cheese. Beat eggs, milk, flour, salt, pepper, cumin, garlic powder, and onion salt in a bowl. Pour over the layers. Sprinkle with paprika.

Bake at 350° for 35–40 minutes or until golden and puffy. Cool for 10–15 minutes before serving. Top with sour cream and green onions, if desired. Serves 6–8.

Taste of the Town (Tennessee)

Company Chicken Casserole

2 tablespoons butter
2 tablespoons flour
¼ teaspoon mustard
1 teaspoon salt
¼ teaspoon black pepper
2 cups milk
1 cup shredded Velveeta or
  grated American cheese

2 cups medium-size noodles,
  cooked
2 cups chopped, cooked chicken
1 (10-ounce) package frozen
  broccoli spears, cooked
⅓ cup slivered almonds

Melt butter and stir in the flour, mustard, salt, pepper, and milk. Cook and stir until thickened. Remove from heat and stir in the cheese; set aside. Arrange layers of noodles, chicken, and broccoli (cut into 1-inch pieces, reserving florets) in a 2-quart casserole dish. Pour cheese sauce over layered ingredients; arrange broccoli florets on top, and sprinkle with the almonds. Bake 20 minutes at 350°. Can be made ahead. Serves 6–8.

A Cookbook of Treasures (Mid-Atlantic)

WIKIPEDIA.ORG

At 150 feet tall, Deno's Wonder Wheel is the centerpiece of Coney Island's Amusement area. Located on the Boardwalk, this amazing attraction gives riders a panoramic view of the Atlantic Ocean, the Jersey Shore, and the New York City Skyline. The ride includes sixteen inner passenger cars that travel freely around curved rails while the wheel is spinning, and eight outer stationary swinging cars. Each year, over 200,000 people of all ages ride the Wonder Wheel.

Saucy Chicken Cordon Bleu

4 skinless, boneless chicken
  breast halves
4 slices ham
4 slices Swiss cheese
1 cup flour
1 teaspoon salt

½ teaspoon pepper
½ teaspoon paprika
2 eggs, beaten
⅓ cup milk
1 cup dry bread crumbs
¼ cup vegetable oil

Preheat oven to 350°. Flatten chicken breasts without breaking through meat. Roll each ham slice in a cheese slice; then roll up in chicken breasts. In a shallow dish or bowl, season flour with salt, pepper, and paprika. In a separate dish or bowl, beat together eggs and milk. Dip chicken rolls in seasoned flour, then egg mixture, then bread crumbs. Heat oil in a large skillet and fry chicken until golden brown. Set aside.

MUSHROOM SAUCE:

1 (10¾-ounce) can cream of
  mushroom soup
½ pound fresh mushrooms,
  sliced

¼ teaspoon garlic powder
¼ cup milk
½ cup sour cream

In a large bowl combine soup, mushrooms, garlic powder, milk, and sour cream. Mix all together. Place chicken in a 9x13-inch baking dish and pour sauce over chicken. Bake for 20–25 minutes or until chicken is completely done. Serves 4.

Favorite Recipes (Big Sky)

Chicken-Chestnut Soufflé

9 slices white bread, crust removed
4 cups cubed, cooked chicken, seasoned to taste
1 (8-ounce) can sliced mushrooms (optional)
¼ cup butter, melted
1 (8-ounce) can sliced water chestnuts
9 slices sharp Cheddar cheese
1 envelope dry onion soup mix
½ cup mayonnaise
4 eggs, well beaten
2 cups milk
1 teaspoon salt
1 (10¾-ounce) can cream of chicken soup
1 (10¾-ounce) can cream of celery soup
1 (2-ounce) jar chopped pimento
2 cups buttered bread crumbs

Line a 9x13-inch dish with bread slices and top with chicken. Sauté mushrooms in butter and spoon over chicken. Top with water chestnuts, cheese, and soup mix. Combine mayonnaise, eggs, milk, and salt, beating well. Pour over cheese. Combine chicken and celery soups and pimento and spoon over casserole. Cover with foil and place in refrigerator overnight.

Bake uncovered for 30 minutes at 350°. Top with crumbs and bake 15–20 minutes longer. Serves 12.

Dixie Dining (Mississippi)

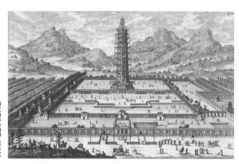

WIKIPEDIA.ORG

The Porcelain Tower of Nanjing in Nanjing, China, was a pagoda constructed in the 15th century during the Ming Dynasty, but was mostly destroyed in the 19th century during the Taiping Rebellion. When it was built, the tower was one of the largest buildings in China, rising up to a height of 260 feet with 9 stories and a staircase in the middle of the pagoda, which spiraled upwards for 184 steps. The tower was built with white porcelain bricks that were said to reflect the sun's rays during the day, and at night as many as 140 lamps were hung from the building to illuminate it. Reconstruction of the tower and temple grounds began in 2010.

Chicken with Marinated Artichoke Hearts

2 (2½- to 3-pound) chickens
2 medium onions, sliced thin
1 pound mushrooms, sliced
1 stick butter
3 (14-ounce) jars marinated
   artichoke hearts, drained
   (reserve oil from 1½ jars)

½–1 cup dry sherry
½ cup flour
1 (10¾-ounce) can cream of
   chicken or mushroom soup

Skin and cut up chicken. Sauté onions and mushrooms in butter. Stir in artichoke hearts. Place chicken pieces in greased casserole and cover with onion mixture. Mix together artichoke oil, sherry, flour, and soup, and pour over top. Bake at 350° for 45–60 minutes. Serves 6–8. May be prepared the night before.

The Woman's Exchange Classic Recipes (Florida)

Editor's Extra: To avoid lumps when mixing flour with liquid, use a whisk, or shake in a jar.

Chicken Jubilee

8 boneless chicken breasts
½ cup butter, melted
1 (16-ounce) can cherries
   packed in syrup, drained
1 cup sweet sherry
½ cup water

1 teaspoon garlic salt
1 (12-ounce) bottle chili sauce
1 tablespoon Worcestershire
2 small onions, sliced
½ cup white raisins

Preheat oven to 325°. Place breasts in 9x13-inch casserole, and pour melted butter over them. Broil until medium brown. Soak cherries in sherry at least 1 hour and set aside. Combine remaining ingredients, and pour over chicken. Cover with foil and bake 1 hour. Remove foil, and add cherries and some of the sherry. Bake 15 minutes longer. Serves 8.

Great Cooks Rise...with the May River Tide (South Carolina)

★★★★★★★★★★★★   ★★★★★★★★★★★★★

Catalina Chicken

6 pieces uncooked chicken
  breasts or parts
5 medium-size potatoes,
  quartered

10 carrots, cut in chunks
1 (8-ounce) bottle Catalina
  dressing

Wash chicken breasts and drain; pat dry. Place in large casserole dish. Put in potatoes and carrots. Cover with Catalina dressing. Cook 90 minutes at 350° in oven. Serves 4–6.

Sharing Our Blessings (North Carolina)

Chicken Curry Hot Dish

2 (8-ounce) packages chopped
  broccoli, cooked and drained
5 cups diced chicken
2 teaspoons lemon juice
3 tablespoons butter
2 (10¾-ounce) cans cream of
  chicken soup
½ cup milk

¾ cup mayonnaise
½ teaspoon curry powder
  (optional)
Mild or sharp Cheddar
  cheese
8 ounces herb stuffing mix
½ cup butter or margarine,
  melted

Put cooked broccoli in a greased baking dish. Top with chicken; sprinkle with lemon juice and dot with butter. Cover with chicken soup (mixed with milk, mayonnaise, and curry powder, if desired). Top with shredded mild or sharp Cheddar cheese. Cover with stuffing mix that has been mixed with the melted butter. Bake at 350° for 30–45 minutes. Serves 6–8.

Sharing Our Best to Help the Rest (Minnesota)

★★★★★★★★★★★   ★★★★★★★★★★★

Hot Chicken Salad

2 cups cooked chicken, in
chunks
1½ cups chopped celery
½ cup slivered almonds
½ teaspoon salt
1 cup mayonnaise

2 tablespoons grated onion
1½ tablespoons lemon juice
½ cup shredded Cheddar
cheese
1 cup crushed potato chips

Combine all but last 2 ingredients, and put in greased shallow casserole dish. Sprinkle with cheese, and top with potato chips. Bake at 425° for 30 minutes. Serves 4–5.

Recipe from Barklin House, Newberry
Palmetto Hospitality Inn Style (South Carolina)

Editor's Extra: Though called "salad," this is generally served on a dinner plate like any chicken casserole. Great on crackers, in a sandwich, or scooped on a pineapple slice as a "salad."

The world's largest reef system is composed of over 2,900 individual reefs and 900 islands stretching over an area of approximately 133,000 square miles. The Great Barrier Reef is located in the Coral Sea, off the coast of Queensland in northeast Australia.

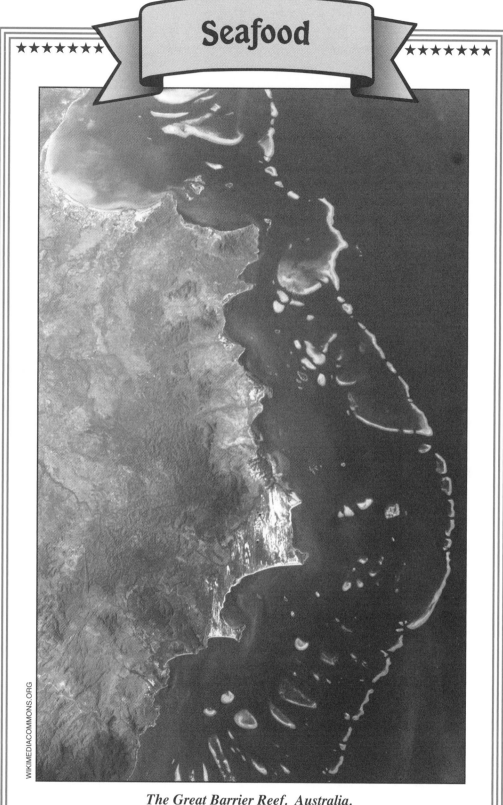

The Great Barrier Reef. Australia.
One of the Wonders of the Natural World.

WIKIMEDIACOMMONS.ORG

★★★★★★★★★★★ ★★★★★★★★★★★

V's Shrimp Casserole

2 pounds shrimp
3–4 slices soft bread, cubed
1¼ cups evaporated milk
1¼ cups mayonnaise
3 large eggs, hard-boiled and
  chopped
3 tablespoons minced fresh
  parsley, or 1 tablespoon
  dry parsley
1 medium onion, diced, or
  1 tablespoon dry minced
  onion

⅛ teaspoon pepper
2 tablespoons sherry
1 tablespoon Ac'cent (optional)
2 dashes red pepper flakes
Salt and pepper to taste
½ cup herb-seasoned
  stuffing mix
Butter

Cook shrimp 2–3 minutes in boiling water until pink. Soak bread in milk while peeling and dicing shrimp. Add all other ingredients except stuffing mix and butter to bread; fold in shrimp. Place in greased 9x13-inch casserole. If not serving immediately, refrigerate at this point and remove 20 minutes before baking. Sprinkle with stuffing mix and dot with butter. Bake at 350° for 30 minutes or until browned. Serves 8.

Variation: For a delicious variation, reduce shrimp to 1 pound and add 1 pound crabmeat.

Let Us Keep the Feast in Historic Beaufort (North Carolina)

Experts opine the Great Barrier Reef was formed around 18 million years ago. Due to various climatic and environmental changes, the reefs that we see today are those that have grown over the earlier reefs since the last Ice Age. Among the species that are seen near the reef, one can notice around 30 species of whales, 215 species of beautiful birds, 6 species of sea turtles, 125 species of sharks and stingrays, 49 species of pipefish, 17 species of sea snakes, and around 1,500 types of fish.

★★★★★★★★★★★ ★★★★★★★★★★★

Roasted Red Pepper and Shrimp Grits

In the White Dog kitchen, we have very few fixed rules about food, however one of them is to never combine fish and cheese. Of course, there are exceptions to every rule, and these rich creamy grits are a glorious one.

2 tablespoons unsalted butter
1 large yellow onion, minced
  (about 2 cups)
1 tablespoon minced garlic
1 cup quick-cooking grits
4 cups whole milk, divided
1 cup water
2 teaspoons salt
½ teaspoon freshly ground
  black pepper

¼ teaspoon Tabasco
2 red bell peppers, roasted,
  peeled, seeded, puréed
8 ounces shrimp, peeled,
  deveined
8 ounces (2 cups) grated
  Cheddar or Monterey Jack
  cheese

Melt butter in a saucepan set over medium heat. Add onion and sauté until soft, about 5 minutes. Add garlic and cook 2 minutes. Stir in grits. Stir in 2 cups of milk and simmer until liquid is absorbed, about 5 minutes. Add remaining 2 cups milk and simmer, stirring occasionally, until it is absorbed, about 5 minutes. Add water and simmer until grits are soft and thick, 35–40 minutes.

Preheat oven to 400°. Add salt, pepper, Tabasco, and puréed bell peppers to grits; mix well. Pour mixture into a 6x10x1¾-inch casserole. (The grits may be prepared to this point 1 day in advance. Let cool to room temperature, cover, and refrigerate overnight. Bring to room temperature before proceeding.)

Spread shrimp evenly over grits and top with grated cheese. Bake on top rack of oven until shrimp are cooked through and cheese is melted, about 15 minutes. Serves 6.

White Dog Cafe Cookbook (Pennsylvania)

Scallop Pie

6 large mushrooms, sliced
¼ cup butter, divided
3 green onions, chopped
3 tablespoons flour
1 teaspoon curry powder
1½ cups milk
¼ cup cooking sherry
12 small whole onions, boiled

2 tablespoons sliced red or
  green bell pepper
½ pound large sea scallops,
  sliced in half lengthwise
Garlic salt
Fresh cracked pepper
Puff or regular pastry

Heat oven to 425°. In saucepan, sauté mushrooms in ⅛ cup butter; add green onions. Blend in flour and curry powder. Add milk; cook until thick, stirring steadily. Remove from heat. Add sherry, whole onions, bell pepper, and drained and dried scallops. Season to taste with garlic salt and cracked pepper; stir to blend. Divide between 4 individual baking dishes or 1 (10-inch) pie plate; dot with remaining butter. Top with pastry. Bake 20–25 minutes. Allow to cool 10 minutes before serving.

A Cook's Tour of Alaska (Alaska)

One of the most interesting facts about the Great Barrier Reef is that this wonderous structure can actually be seen from outer space!

Some of the largest of giant clams can be found at the reef. One of the largest pearls was found in such a clam and was reportedly sold in New York for a whopping $10 million!

Shrimp and Scallop Bake

SAUCE:

6 tablespoons butter
6 tablespoons flour
½ teaspoon salt

2⅓ cups milk
⅔ cup dry white wine
10 ounces Swiss cheese, grated

Melt butter in large saucepan, add flour and salt, and cook until bubbly. Remove from heat and slowly add milk, stirring constantly. Add wine. Return to heat and add Swiss cheese; heat until thickened.

1 pound fresh scallops (bay or
   halved sea scallops)
12 ounces medium shrimp,
   peeled and deveined
8 ounces fresh mushrooms,
   cleaned and sliced

3 tablespoons butter
Melted butter
¼ cup dried bread crumbs
Parmesan cheese

Preheat oven to 350°. In large frying pan, sauté scallops, shrimp, and mushrooms in 3 tablespoons butter until shrimp are just pink and mushrooms look moist. Put scallops, shrimp, and mushrooms into greased 4-quart casserole dish. Top with Sauce and stir. Add enough melted butter to moisten ¼ cup bread crumbs. Sprinkle crumbs over casserole. Top with Parmesan cheese to taste. Bake 20–30 minutes until cheese bubbles. Serves 4–6.

Almost Heaven (West Virginia)

★★★★★★★★★★★★   ★★★★★★★★★★★★

Shrimp and Squash Casserole

1 cup butter
1 cup diced andouille sausage
1½ cups chopped celery
1½ cups chopped onions
1 cup chopped bell pepper
6 garlic cloves, minced
4 cups sliced yellow squash
   (zucchini or eggplant may be
   substituted)

1½ pounds shrimp, boiled and
   peeled
4 tomatoes, each cut into 8
   wedges
Salt and pepper to taste
Italian bread crumbs

Melt butter in a large skillet, and add sausage, celery, onions, bell pepper, and garlic; sauté for 20 minutes. Add squash and sauté for another 15 minutes. Add shrimp and tomatoes and sauté for an additional 5 minutes. Add salt and pepper to taste. Place mixture into a large casserole dish. Sprinkle with bread crumbs, and bake at 400° until crumbs are golden brown. Serves 6.

Lagniappe: Secrets We're Ready to Share II (Mississippi)

Shrimp with Eggplant Casserole

1 large eggplant
16 ounces raw shrimp
1 cup chopped onion
1 cup chopped bell pepper
1 cup chopped celery
1 garlic clove, minced
½ teaspoon black pepper

1 (15-ounce) can Campbell's
   Healthy Request Cream of
   Mushroom Soup
4 ounces shredded light
   Cheddar cheese
½ cup seasoned bread crumbs

Puncture eggplant several times and cook on HIGH in microwave for 3 minutes. Set aside to cool. When cool, pull skin off and chop. Sauté shrimp, onion, bell pepper, celery, and garlic in cooking spray until the shrimp turn pink. Add pepper, soup, and cheese; heat and set aside. Mix with ¼ cup seasoned bread crumbs and chopped eggplant. Top with remaining bread crumbs and spray with cooking spray. Bake at 350° for 25 minutes. Serves 8.

Cal 162; Chol 94mg; Sat Fat 1gm; Fat 4gm; Sod 562mg; Dietary Fiber 1gm; Exchanges: 2 meat, ½ bread, 1 vegetable, ½ fat.

Gone with the Fat (Louisiana II)

Crawfish au Gratin

1 bunch green onion tops,
  chopped
2 tablespoons butter
2 tablespoons flour
½ cup whipping cream
¼ cup white wine
1 teaspoon salt

1 teaspoon cayenne pepper
¼ teaspoon Tabasco
¼ teaspoon garlic powder
6 ounces American cheese,
  grated
3 ounces Swiss cheese, grated
1 pound peeled crawfish tails

Sauté onions in butter in a 2-quart casserole on HIGH 3 minutes. Add flour, cream, wine, salt, pepper, Tabasco, and garlic powder. Microwave on HIGH 1½–2 minutes.

Stir cheeses into hot mixture until melted. Add crawfish. Cover with wax paper and cook on HIGH 6 minutes. Stir halfway through cooking time.

Serve as an entrée in pastry shells or as a dip with Melba rounds. Serves 6.

Tout de Suite à la Microwave I (Louisiana)

Creole Crawfish Casserole

2 large onions, chopped
3 stalks celery, chopped
1 green bell pepper, chopped
½ cup margarine
1 pound cooked crawfish tails,
  peeled
1 egg
1 tablespoon minced parsley
3 cups cooked rice

1 (10¾-ounce) can cream of
  mushroom soup, undiluted
1½ cups (6 ounces) grated
  mozzarella cheese, Cheddar
  cheese, or pasteurized process
  cheese spread
Cajun seasoning salt, or salt
  and black pepper to taste
Bread crumbs

Sauté onions, celery, and bell pepper in margarine in large saucepan until vegetables are softened. Add crawfish and cook for several minutes. Stir in egg, parsley, and rice, mixing well. Add soup and cheese. Season with seasoning salt or salt and black pepper. Spread crawfish mixture in greased 2-quart casserole and sprinkle with bread crumbs. Bake at 375° for 25 minutes. Serves 6.

Cane River's Louisiana Living (Louisiana II)

Oregon Crab Quiche

This simple quiche is so elegant; good at any time, but try it for a special luncheon. It's also a splendid way to stretch and share a small amount of expensive crabmeat.

**1 cup (4 ounces) shredded
  natural Swiss cheese
1 (9-inch) pastry shell, unbaked
½ pound fresh Dungeness
  crabmeat, flaked, or 1
  (7½-ounce) can crabmeat,
  drained and flaked
2 fresh green onions (including
  tops), sliced**

**3 eggs, beaten
1 cup light cream or
  half-and-half
½ teaspoon salt
½ teaspoon grated lemon peel
¼ teaspoon dry mustard
Dash of mace
¼ cup sliced almonds**

Sprinkle cheese evenly over bottom of pastry shell. Spread crabmeat over cheese; sprinkle green onions over crabmeat.

Combine beaten eggs, cream, and seasonings; pour over all. Sprinkle top with sliced almonds. Bake at 325° for about 45 minutes or until set (when knife blade inserted in center comes out clean). Remove from oven and let stand for 10 minutes before cutting and serving. Serves 6–8.

Begged, Borrowed and Stöllen Recipes (Oregon)

WIKIPEDIA.ORG

The Galapagos Islands are a group of volcanic islands near the equator in the Pacific Ocean, 583 miles west of Ecuador. Famed for their vast number of native species, the islands were studied by Charles Darwin. His observations and collections contributed to the inception of Darwin's theory of evolution by natural selection.

Cajun Crab Casserole

1½ cups chopped onion
¼ cup chopped green bell pepper
¼ cup chopped red bell pepper
2 garlic cloves, minced
½ cup chopped celery
1 stick margarine
1 (10-ounce) can tomatoes
  with green chiles
¼ cup chopped pimentos
2 slices bread

1 (10¾-ounce) can cream of
  mushroom soup
1 teaspoon Worcestershire
1 teaspoon hot pepper sauce
3 cups crabmeat
3 cups cooked rice
¼ cup snipped parsley
¼ cup chopped green onion
  tops

Sauté onion, green pepper, red pepper, garlic, and celery in the melted margarine in a saucepan. Add tomatoes and pimentos. Soak the bread in water; squeeze. Add the bread, soup, Worcestershire, hot pepper sauce, and crabmeat. Blend well. Add cooked rice, parsley, and onion tops. Spoon into greased 2½-quart casserole; cover with buttered bread crumbs if you desire. Bake 20 minutes at 400°. Serves 6.

C'est Bon, Encore (Louisiana II)

The Seven Wonders of the Underwater World

This list was drawn up by CEDAM (Conservation, Education, Diving, Awareness, and Marine-research) International, an American-based nonprofit group for divers.

In 1989, CEDAM brought together a panel of marine scientists, including Dr. Eugenie Clark, to pick underwater areas that they considered to be worthy of protection. The results were announced at The National Aquarium in Washington DC by actor Lloyd Bridges, star of the then-popular TV show, *Sea Hunt:*

1. Palau – Pacific Ocean, 2,000 miles south of Tokyo
2. Belize Barrier Reef – Belize
3. Great Barrier Reef – Australia
4. Deep-Sea Vents – Commonly found in ocean basins
5. Galápagos Islands – Pacific Ocean, west of Ecuador
6. Lake Baikal – Russia
7. Northern Red Sea – Lying between Africa and Asia

Crabmeat Casserole

1 (20-ounce) can artichoke hearts
1 pound crabmeat
½ pound fresh mushrooms,
  sautéed
4 tablespoons butter
2½ tablespoons flour
1 cup cream
½ teaspoon salt

1 teaspoon Worcestershire
¼ cup medium dry sherry
Paprika to taste
Cayenne to taste
Pepper to taste
¼ cup grated Parmesan cheese

Preheat oven to 375°. Place artichokes in bottom of 2½-quart baking dish; spread a layer of crabmeat. Add a layer of sautéed mushrooms. Melt butter in a saucepan; add flour, cream, salt, Worcestershire sauce, sherry, paprika, cayenne, and pepper. Stir well after each addition to form a smooth sauce. Pour sauce over artichoke-crab layer and sprinkle with cheese on top. Bake 20 minutes. Serves 8.

Nancy Reagan
(Ronald Reagan participated in 1969 Azalea Festival)
A Cook's Tour of the Azalea Coast (North Carolina)

Sherwood Forest Crabmeat Casserole

1 cup crabmeat (white)
2 cups bread crumbs
  (slightly toasted)
1 cup mayonnaise

½ cup milk
4 hard-boiled eggs, mashed
1 teaspoon chopped onion
Tabasco, lemon juice, and salt

Mix all ingredients. Put in greased casserole. Bake at 350° until bubbly. Serves 4.

The Virginia Presidential Homes Cookbook (Virginia)

Crab Cobbler

½ cup butter	1 cup shredded American
½ cup chopped green bell	cheese
pepper	1 cup crabmeat
½ cup chopped onion	1½ cups drained chopped
½ cup flour	tomatoes
1 teaspoon dry mustard	2 teaspoons Worcestershire
1 teaspoon Ac'cent (optional)	½ teaspoon salt
1 cup milk	

In top of a double boiler, add butter, green pepper, and chopped onion; let cook about 10 minutes. Blend in flour, dry mustard, Ac'cent, milk, and cheese; cook and stir until cheese melts and mixture is very thick. Add crabmeat, tomatoes, Worcestershire, and salt. Pour into a greased 2-quart casserole.

CHEESE BISQUICK TOPPING:

¼ cup shredded cheese	½ cup milk
1 cup Bisquick	

Combine all ingredients and drop by teaspoons on top of crab mixture. Bake in 450° oven 20–25 minutes. Serves 4–6.

NSHSRA High School Rodeo Cookbook (Nevada)

One Day at a Time is an American situation comedy on the CBS network that aired from December 16, 1975, to May 28, 1984. It portrays a divorced mother, played by Bonnie Franklin, raising her two teenage daughters, Mackenzie Phillips and Valerie Bertinelli. The show was created by Whitney Blake and Allan Manings, a husband-and-wife writing duo who were both actors in the 1950s and 1960s. The show was based on Whitney Blake's own life as a single mother, raising her child, future actress Meredith Baxter.

Crab and Shrimp Hot Dish

1½ pounds crabmeat
½ pound small shrimp
½ green bell pepper, chopped
⅓ cup chopped parsley
2 cups cooked rice

1½ cups real mayonnaise
2 (10-ounce) packages frozen
   peas, thawed but not cooked
Salt and pepper to taste

Combine all and toss lightly. Place in greased casserole dish. Refrigerate covered. Bake at 350° covered for 1 hour. Serves 6.

Lost Tree Cook Book (Florida)

Seafood Casserole for a Crowd

3 pounds shrimp, cooked and
   chopped
3 pounds crabmeat (imitation
   or genuine crab)
2 cups finely chopped celery
1 large bell pepper, chopped
1 large onion, chopped

1 tablespoon Worcestershire
2 cups (1 pint) mayonnaise
Dash of hot pepper sauce
2 cups bread crumbs
½ cup (1 stick) margarine or
   butter, melted

Combine shrimp, crab, celery, bell pepper, onion, and Worcestershire sauce; mix well. Spoon mixture into greased extra large (18x14x3-inch) casserole dish.

Mix mayonnaise with dash of hot pepper sauce; mix bread crumbs with melted butter; combine mayonnaise and bread mixtures. Spoon over shrimp mixture. Bake at 350° for 30 minutes. Serves 30.

Coastal Cuisine (Texas II)

Impossible Seafood Pie

2 (10-ounce) packages frozen
   broccoli or asparagus, thawed
   and drained
3 (6-ounce) packages frozen
   crabmeat and (or) shrimp,
   thawed and drained
½ cup sliced green onions
2 (2-ounce) jars chopped
   pimentos, drained

1 cup sour cream
1 (8-ounce) package cream
   cheese
1 cup Bisquick
4 eggs
1 teaspoon Nature's Seasoning
Dash of nutmeg
2 tomatoes
Grated Parmesan cheese

Preheat oven to 350°. Grease 9x13-inch pan. Spread vegetables, seafood, green onions, and pimentos in the pan. Beat sour cream, cream cheese, Bisquick, eggs, and seasonings; pour over ingredients in pan. Top with thin-sliced tomato and sprinkle with Parmesan cheese. Bake 35–40 minutes at 350°. Serves 6–8.

Winniehaha's Favorite Recipes (Minnesota)

Baked Seafood Salad

1 (10- to 12-ounce) package
   frozen shrimp, peeled and
   deveined
1 (6½-ounce) can crabmeat
1½ cups chopped celery
¼ cup finely chopped green
   bell pepper
¼ cup finely chopped onion

1 cup mayonnaise
1 teaspoon Worcestershire
½ teaspoon salt
1½ cups crushed potato chips
½ teaspoon paprika
2 tablespoons butter or
   margarine

Drop shrimp into boiling salted water; cook for 1 minute after water returns to boil, or until pink. If shrimp are large, cut into ½-inch pieces. Combine with crab, celery, green pepper, and onion. Mix mayonnaise with Worcestershire sauce and salt; fold in. Spread in buttered 2-quart baking dish, or into 6 individual casseroles. Bake at 400° for 10 minutes. Blend potato chips with paprika; sprinkle over mixture. Dot with butter; bake for 10 minutes or until potato chips are brown. Serves 6.

A Taste of Heaven (Washington)

Salmon Florentine

**2 cups canned salmon, drained
  (save liquid)**
Milk
¼ cup flour
¼ cup butter, melted
½ teaspoon dry mustard
¼ teaspoon salt
¼ teaspoon Tabasco
**1½ cups grated Cheddar
  cheese, divided**
**1 tablespoon chopped onion
  (optional)**
2 cups cooked, drained spinach

Drain and flake salmon, removing skin and bones. Add enough milk to salmon liquid to make 1½ cups. Add flour to melted butter in saucepan; stir with wire whisk till blended. Meanwhile, bring milk mixture to a boil; add all at once to butter-flour mixture, stirring vigorously with whisk till sauce is thickened and smooth. Season with mustard, salt, and Tabasco. Mix in 1 cup cheese and onion. Place spinach in 4 individual greased casseroles; top with salmon and sauce; sprinkle with remaining cheese. Bake at 425° for 15 minutes uncovered. Serves 4.

Encore (Louisiana)

★★★★★★★★★★★ ★★★★★★★★★★★

Baked Salmon with Carrots and Zucchini

1 tablespoon olive oil
1 onion, chopped fine
2 zucchini, cut in matchstick-size
   pieces or shredded coarsely
2 carrots, shredded coarsely
¼ cup chopped fresh parsley

2 tablespoons chopped fresh
   basil
4 salmon fillets
1 tablespoon lemon juice
½ teaspoon salt
½ teaspoon pepper

Heat oven to 350°. In a nonstick skillet, heat oil. Add onion; sauté until tender. Add zucchini, carrots, parsley, and basil, mixing lightly. Place vegetable mixture into a lightly greased 10x10-inch baking dish. Arrange salmon steaks over vegetables and drizzle with lemon juice, salt, and pepper. Cover; bake 30 minutes. Uncover and bake 10 more minutes. Serves 4.

Thou Preparest a Table Before Me (New York)

No-Flop Flounder

2 (10-ounce) packages frozen
   spinach, thawed and drained
1 cup sour cream
1 tablespoon flour
½ teaspoon salt
¼ teaspoon nutmeg
Dash of pepper

1 pound flounder or orange
   roughy
2 tablespoons butter
¼ teaspoon salt
1½ teaspoons paprika
⅓ cup shredded Swiss cheese

Combine spinach with sour cream, flour, salt, nutmeg, and pepper; mix well. Spoon into shallow greased casserole or baking dish. Rinse fish; dry with paper towel. Place fish on top of spinach mixture in a single layer. Melt butter; brush on fish. Sprinkle fish with salt, paprika, and cheese. Bake at 375° for 30 minutes. Serves 3–4.

From Minnesota: More Than a Cookbook (Minnesota)

Oysters Rockefeller Casserole

6 tablespoons butter, divided
2 (10-ounce) packages frozen
  chopped spinach, thawed,
  drained
1 tablespoon lemon juice
1 tablespoon Worcestershire
Black pepper to taste
Hot pepper sauce to taste
½ medium onion, grated
1 cup saltine or butter cracker
  crumbs

2 garlic cloves, minced
6 crackers
3 quarts oysters, drained
¼ cup grated Parmesan cheese
1 (12-ounce) package grated
  Cheddar cheese
1 (12-ounce) package grated
  mozzarella cheese

Preheat oven to 350°. Heat 2 tablespoons butter over medium heat. Add spinach, and stir until excess butter evaporates. Mix in lemon juice, Worcestershire, black pepper, and pepper sauce.

In a mixing bowl, combine remaining 4 tablespoons butter, onion, cracker crumbs, and garlic. Mix in spinach mixture. Crumble 6 crackers over bottom of a greased shallow baking dish. Layer spinach mixture, oysters, and cheeses, ending with layers of cheeses. Bake 45 minutes. Serve immediately. Serves 8–12.

Faithfully Charleston (South Carolina)

Machu Picchu in Peru is a pre-Columbian, 15th-century Inca site located 7,970 feet above sea level. It is situated on a mountain ridge above the Urubamba Valley in Peru, which is fifty miles northwest of Cusco and through which the Urubamba River flows. Often referred to as "The Lost City of the Incas," it is perhaps the most familiar icon of the Inca World.

Meats

Machu Picchu. Peru.
One of the New Wonders of the World.

★★★★★★★★★★★ ★★★★★★★★★★★

Beef Tips with Wine

It's so easy and very good.

2 pounds beef tips or beef stew
1 (10¾-ounce) can cream of
  mushroom soup
1 soup can red wine

1 package dry onion soup mix
1 (1-pound) carton whole
  mushrooms, washed and left
  whole

Spray deep casserole dish with cooking spray. Add meat and layer with mushroom soup, wine, onion soup mix, and mushrooms. Bake at 300° for 3 hours. Good to serve with rice or egg noodles.

Mama Couldn't Cook (Alabama)

Meat Pot Pie

FILLING:

1 cup diced potatoes
¼ cup chopped onion
2 tablespoons butter
1½ tablespoons flour
2 cups broth

2 tablespoons chopped pimento
4 cups diced cooked beef or
  chicken
½ teaspoon salt

Cook potatoes and onion in a medium-size saucepan with small amount of water 5 minutes. In another medium saucepan, melt butter, add flour, and stir till well blended. Remove saucepan from heat and slowly add broth. Return to flame and cook until mixture begins to thicken. Add vegetables, pimento, meat, and salt. Pour into a buttered baking dish and cover with strips of Biscuit Dough. Bake in 425° oven 12–15 minutes.

BISCUIT DOUGH:

2 cups all-purpose flour
3–4 teaspoons baking powder
1 teaspoon salt

5 tablespoons shortening
¾–1 cup milk

Sift dry ingredients twice. Cut in shortening; add milk. Mix until dough is soft. Turn onto floured board and knead about 20 times. Roll out to ¼-inch thickness. Cut into strips. Serves 6–8.

Lessons from the Lunchroom (Kentucky)

Patchwork Casserole

2 pounds ground beef
2 green bell peppers, chopped
1 large onion, chopped
2 pounds frozen hash brown
  potatoes
2 (8-ounce) cans tomato sauce
1 (6-ounce) can tomato paste
1 cup water
1 teaspoon salt
½ teaspoon basil
¼ teaspoon pepper
1 pound thinly sliced American
  cheese, divided

Brown meat; drain. Add green peppers and onion; cook until tender. Add remaining ingredients except cheese; mix well. Spoon half of meat and potato mixture into 9x13-inch baking dish (or two 1½-quart casserole dishes). Cover with half of cheese. Top with remaining meat and potato mixture. Cover dish with aluminum foil. Bake at 350° for 45 minutes. Uncover. Cut remaining cheese into decorative shapes; arrange in patchwork design on casserole. Let stand 5 minutes or until cheese shapes have melted. Serves 12. Can be frozen.

Sharing Our Bounty Through 40 Years (New York)

Created around 1450 near the height of the Inca Empire, no one knows what the real purpose of Machu Picchu was. Some people speculate it was a prison and some say it was a defensive retreat, but the most common belief is that Machu Picchu was the estate of an Inca emperor. Unlike the Egyptians, the Incas did not use any kind of mortar to bind their stones together. Instead they cut the stones with such precision that they fit together so tightly that you could not even fit a thin knife blade between them.

Chris's Favorite Hamburger Casserole

1 pound ground beef	1 teaspoon salt or to taste
1 medium green bell pepper, chopped	1 (16-ounce) can Franco American spaghetti
1 medium onion, chopped	1 (16-ounce) can whole-kernel corn
1 cup diced celery	
2 teaspoon chili powder	1 cup grated Cheddar cheese

Brown ground beef in large skillet. Add green pepper, onion, and celery to meat and cook until tender. Drain off excess fat and add chili powder; cook for one minute. Add remaining ingredients; mix well. Transfer to a large baking pan and bake at 350° for 30 minutes. Serves 4–6.

Great Plains Cooking (Colorado)

Supper-In-A-Dish

1 pound hamburger or sausage, browned, drained	¼ cup chopped green bell pepper
1 or 2 potatoes, sliced	Salt and pepper to taste
1 carrot, sliced	1 (10¾-ounce) can cream of chicken or mushroom soup
1 cup peas	
¼ cup chopped onion	¼ cup milk
¼ cup chopped celery	⅔ cup grated Cheddar cheese

In greased baking dish, layer meat, potatoes, carrot, peas, onion, celery, and pepper. Season to taste. In mixing bowl, combine soup and milk. Pour mixture over top of layered ingredients. Bake at 350° for 1¼ hours. Sprinkle grated cheese on top and return to oven until melted. Serves 4–6.

Mennonite Country-Style Recipes & Kitchen Secrets (Pennsylvania)

Pizza Pop Up

1 pound ground beef
1 onion, chopped
1 (16-ounce) jar of spaghetti
  sauce
½ pound fresh mushrooms,
  sliced and sautéed in
  1 tablespoon butter

¼ teaspoon oregano
Salt to taste
1 (6-ounce) package mozzarella
  cheese, sliced

Sauté beef and onion; drain. Add sauce, then sautéed mushrooms. Blend in seasonings. Pour into greased 9x13-inch casserole dish. Top with mozzarella cheese. Bake at 400° for 10 minutes. In the meantime, make Pop-Up Batter:

POP-UP BATTER:
1 cup flour
½ teaspoon salt
2 eggs
1 cup milk

1 tablespoon vegetable oil
½ cup freshly grated Parmesan
  cheese for topping

Place flour and salt in a deep bowl. Make well in center of flour. Combine eggs, milk, and oil. Pour into well of flour. Whisk thoroughly. Remove casserole from oven; pour batter over meat mixture. Sprinkle with Parmesan cheese. Bake at 400° for 30 minutes more. Serve immediately. Serves 6–8.

Fillies Flavours (Kentucky)

Chili Chip Casserole

1 pound ground round
1 cup chopped onion
1 package Lawry's chili
  seasoning mix
1 (6-ounce) can tomato paste
¾ cup water

1 (6-ounce) bag corn chips
1 (1-pound) can pinto beans,
  drained
2 (2½-ounce) cans sliced ripe
  olives
2 cups grated Cheddar cheese

Brown beef until crumbly. Mix in onion, chili seasoning mix, tomato paste, and water, and simmer 10 minutes.

Place ½ bag of corn chips in bottom of buttered 2-quart casserole. Spoon ½ chili meat mixture over corn chips. Spread ½ can pinto beans over meat mixture followed by 1 can sliced olives. Sprinkle with 1 cup grated cheese. Repeat meat, pinto beans, and olive layers. Arrange remaining corn chips over top; sprinkle with remaining cheese. Cover casserole and bake at 350° for 30–35 minutes. Uncover and bake an additional 15 minutes. Serves 6–8.

Twentieth Century Club Cook Book (Nevada)

Seven Wonders of the Industrial World

British author Deborah Cadbury wrote *Seven Wonders of the Industrial World*, a book telling the stories of seven great feats of engineering of the 19th and early 20th centuries. In 2003 the BBC made a seven-part documentary series on the book, with each episode dramatizing the construction of one of the wonders. The seven industrial wonders are:

1. *SS Great Eastern* (ship) – United Kingdom
2. Bell Rock Lighthouse – Scotland
3. Brooklyn Bridge – New York, United States
4. London Sewerage System – England
5. First Transcontinental Railroad – United States
6. Panama Canal – Panama
7. Hoover Dam – Arizona/Nevada, United States

Beef-Potato Nacho Casserole

2 pounds ground beef
¾ cup chopped onion, divided
1 (1¼-ounce) package taco
  seasoning mix
¾ cup water
1 (8-ounce) can tomato sauce
1 (4-ounce) can chopped green
  chiles, drained
1 (16-ounce) can red kidney
  beans, rinsed and drained

1 (24-ounce) package frozen
  potatoes, thawed
1 (11-ounce) can nacho cheese
  soup (undiluted)
½ cup milk
¼ cup chopped green bell
  pepper
¼ teaspoon sugar
1 teaspoon Worcestershire
Paprika

Brown beef. Add ½ cup onion in skillet; drain. Stir in taco mix, water, and tomato sauce. Bring to a boil and simmer one minute. Spread meat mixture into greased 9x13-inch pan. Top with green chiles, beans, and potatoes.

In bowl, combine soup, milk, remaining ¼ cup onion, green pepper, sugar, and Worcestershire sauce. Pour over potatoes. Sprinkle with paprika. Cover with foil and bake at 350° for one hour. Remove foil and bake 15 minutes more until light golden brown. Let stand 10 minutes before cutting. Serves 8.

Heavenly Helpings (Michigan)

NATIONAL ARCHIVES AND RECORDS ADMINISTRATION

Hoover Dam
in the Black Canyon of the Colorado River.

Tamale Cornbread Pie

8 ounces extra lean ground
chuck
3 cups whole-kernel corn
2 cups canned tomatoes
1 cup finely chopped green
bell pepper
1 onion, finely chopped
1 tablespoon chili powder
1 teaspoon cumin

¼ teaspoon ground red
pepper
2 cups tomato juice
¼ cup unbleached flour
1½ cups cornmeal
1 tablespoon baking powder
¾ cup skim milk
2 eggs
2 tablespoons olive oil

Brown ground chuck in skillet, stirring until crumbly; drain. Stir in corn, tomatoes, green pepper, onion, chili powder, cumin, and ground red pepper. Add mixture of tomato juice and flour; mix well. Simmer, covered, over low heat for 5 minutes, stirring occasionally. Spoon into 9x13-inch baking dish.

Combine cornmeal and baking powder in bowl; mix well. Whisk milk, eggs, and olive oil in another bowl until blended. Stir into cornmeal mixture until mixed. Spread evenly over prepared layer. Bake at 425° for 20–25 minutes or until cornbread topping is cooked through. Serves 6.

Simple Decent Cooking (Georgia)

WIKIPEDIA.ORG

Bell Rock Lighthouse in the North Sea, eleven miles off the coast of Angus, Scotland, is the world's oldest surviving sea-washed lighthouse. Before being built, it was estimated that the rocks there were responsible for the wrecking of up to six ships every winter, seventy ships in one storm alone. Robert Stevenson proposed and built the lighthouse with his crew between 1807 and 1810 on Bell Rock (also known as Inchcape). At 116 feet high, the light is visible from 35 miles inland. The challenges faced in the building of the lighthouse have led to it being described as one of the Seven Wonders of the Industrial World.

Deep Dish Taco Squares

½ pound ground beef
½ cup sour cream
⅓ cup Miracle Whip Salad
  Dressing
½ cup shredded sharp
  Cheddar cheese (2 ounces)
1 tablespoon chopped onion

1 cup Bisquick
⅓ cup milk
1–2 medium tomatoes, sliced
  thin
½ cup chopped green bell
  pepper
Paprika

Heat oven to 375°. Cook and stir ground beef till brown; drain off fat. Mix sour cream, salad dressing, cheese, and onion; set aside. Mix baking mix and milk till dough forms a ball. Pat into a greased 8x8-inch pan, halfway up sides. Layer beef, tomato, and green pepper; spoon sour cream over top. Sprinkle with paprika. Bake for 25–30 minutes.

Seasoned Cooks II (Michigan)

Burrito Bake

2 pounds ground beef
1 large onion, chopped
1 package taco seasoning
1 teaspoon chili powder
1 teaspoon cumin (optional)
1 (15-ounce) can refried beans
1 (10¾-ounce) can cream of
  chicken soup
1 (10¾-ounce) can tomato
  soup

1 (15-ounce) can enchilada
  sauce
1 (10-count) package flour
  tortillas
Lots of Cheddar cheese
Sour cream and black olives
  (optional)

Brown ground beef and onion; drain. Add seasonings, beans, soups, and enchilada sauce. In a 9x13-inch pan, layer tortillas and meat mixture like lasagna, adding cheese to each layer. Top with cheese. Bake in 9x13-inch pan at 350° for 45 minutes. Top with sour cream and black olives, if desired. Serves 10–12.

Generations of Treasured Recipes! (Michigan)

Tropic Sun Spareribs

3–4 pounds spareribs or
  country-style ribs
3 large garlic cloves, pressed
Salt and pepper to taste
1 large onion, sliced
¼ cup water

1 (20-ounce) can crushed
  pineapple, undrained
1 (12-ounce) bottle chili sauce
½ cup packed brown sugar
1 teaspoon ground ginger
½ teaspoon dry mustard

Rub ribs with garlic. Sprinkle with salt and pepper. Arrange onion in large baking pan. Place ribs on top. Add ¼ cup water to pan. Cover with foil. Bake in a 350° oven for 1½ hours. Combine remaining ingredients. Spoon over ribs. Bake, uncovered, 1 hour longer. Serves 4.

. . . Fire Burn & Cauldron Bubble (California)

Pork Chop Casserole

4–6 pork chops
2–4 potatoes
1 onion, sliced

Salt and pepper to taste
2 (10¾-ounce) cans cream of
  mushroom soup

Brown pork chops in skillet. Put in large casserole dish. Slice potatoes and put on top of pork chops. Add onion, salt and pepper. Put mushroom soup on top. Cover with foil. Cook in 350° oven until potatoes are done, approximately 1–1½ hours. Serves 4–6.

Variation: Add green beans around edges of casserole before pouring on soup. Makes a meal-in-one-dish.

A Taste of Heaven (Mississippi)

Pat's Pork Chop Casserole

1 cup uncooked rice
3 tablespoons butter or
  margarine
2 Granny Smith apples
8 boneless pork chops
1 large white onion, sliced in
  thin rings
½ pound fresh mushrooms,
  sliced
1 (10¾-ounce) can cream of
  mushroom soup
1 (10¾-ounce) can cream of
  celery soup
Parsley for garnish

Cook rice according to package directions; place in 9x13-inch casserole that has been sprayed with nonstick spray. Dot top of rice with butter. Core apples and slice in ½-inch slices. Arrange the apples on top of the rice. Trim chops of all visible fat and place them on top of the apples. Place onion rings on top of the chops, then add the mushrooms. Finally, combine the 2 cans of cream soup and pour over all. Cover. Bake in 375° oven for 45 minutes; remove cover, and continue baking until top has started to brown, usually about 30 minutes. Garnish with parsley. Good served with baked tomatoes. Serves 6–8.

What's Cooking, Flo? (Big Sky)

Pork Chop Corn Bake

4 pork chops
1 tablespoon shortening
¾ teaspoon salt
⅛ teaspoon pepper
1 (16-ounce) can whole-
  kernel corn, drained
Milk
¾ cup coarse cracker crumbs
1 tablespoon prepared
  mustard
1 egg, slightly beaten
2 tablespoons sugar
1 tablespoon instant minced
  onion

Brown pork chops in melted shortening in heavy skillet over low heat. Sprinkle with salt and pepper. Drain liquid from corn, measure, and add enough milk to make one cup. Stir corn and liquid together with remaining ingredients. Spoon into greased 1½- to 2-quart casserole and place browned pork chops on top of corn mixture. Bake at 350° for 50–60 minutes. Serves 4.

Neighboring on the Air (Iowa)

★★★★★★★★★★★★ ★★★★★★★★★★★★

Pork Chops and Potatoes

6 medium potatoes, peeled and
 sliced
1 (10¾-ounce) can cream of
 mushroom soup
1 (13-ounce) can evaporated
 milk, or 1 cup whole milk
2 tablespoons dry onion
Salt and pepper to taste
6 pork chops, thinly sliced

Heat oven to 350°. Grease oblong baking dish. Mix potatoes, soup, milk, dry onion, salt and pepper. Put in baking dish. Arrange pork chops on top of mixture and bake, uncovered, for 1 hour. Serves 6.

The Dog-Gone Delicious Cookbook (Arizona)

Ham and Asparagus Casserole

3–4 tablespoons butter
1 teaspoon grated onion
Dash of garlic salt
1 teaspoon paprika
½ teaspoon salt
⅛ teaspoon pepper
2 tablespoons flour
3 cups milk
2 cups grated sharp Cheddar
 cheese
2 (10-ounce) packages frozen
 asparagus
1 cup poultry stuffing crumbs
2 cups sliced cooked ham

Melt 2 tablespoons butter and blend in grated onion and seasonings along with flour. Slowly add milk and heat, stirring constantly until thickened. Add cheese and stir until melted. Cook asparagus according to directions and cut into 1-inch lengths.

Preheat oven to 375°. In the bottom of 2-quart buttered casserole, sprinkle a layer of stuffing crumbs. Add layer of ham and one of asparagus. Now pour part of cheese sauce over and repeat layer of ham, asparagus, and sauce until ingredients are used. Top with remaining crumbs and butter. Bake 45 minutes or until bubbly and browned. Serves 6 or more.

Recipes & Remembrances II (Michigan)

Ham 'n Hash Browns

1 (12-ounce) package frozen
  hash brown potatoes, thawed
1½ cups shredded Cheddar
  cheese
1 cup finely chopped, fully
  cooked ham
½ cup sliced green onions,
  with tops
1½ cups milk
1 teaspoon salt
1 teaspoon dry mustard
Dash of ground red pepper
6 eggs, beaten
Paprika

Heat oven to 350°. Mix all ingredients except paprika in large bowl. Pour into lightly greased 11x7x2-inch baking dish. Sprinkle with paprika. Bake uncovered until knife inserted in center comes out clean (40–45 minutes). Serves 6.

Our Favorite Recipes / Aurdal Lutheran Church (Minnesota)

Ham and Scalloped Potatoes with Green Chiles

3 cups cooked ham, cut into
  bite-size cubes
3 green onions, chopped
½ cup diced green chiles
6 medium-size potatoes,
  peeled, and thinly sliced
3 tablespoons butter
3 tablespoons all-purpose flour
2 cups milk
1 teaspoon dry mustard
1 teaspoon salt
1 teaspoon ground black
  pepper
¼ cup unseasoned bread
  crumbs
2 teaspoons paprika

Mix together ham, onions, and chiles. Put a layer of sliced potatoes in a well-buttered baking dish and sprinkle some of the ham-and-chile mixture over them. Repeat until sliced potatoes and ham and chile mixture are all used.

  Melt butter in a frying pan, whisk in flour, and then slowly pour in milk, whisking constantly until mixture is smooth and starts to thicken. Whisk in mustard, salt, and pepper, and then pour over potato mixture. Top with bread crumbs; sprinkle paprika on top; cover and bake in a 375° oven for one hour. Uncover and bake for 30 more minutes or until potatoes are done. Serves 6–8.

New Mexico Cook Book (New Mexico)

Hamburger-Potato Bake

2 pounds ground chuck	2 tablespoons ketchup
2 eggs, beaten	4 teaspoons salt
2 cups bread crumbs	4 teaspoons pepper

Combine meat, eggs, bread crumbs, ketchup, salt and pepper. Mix well, adding more crumbs if needed to make mixture firm. Put in an ungreased oblong glass baking dish and bake at 350° for 20–30 minutes or until brown.

TOPPING:

8 medium potatoes	Garlic salt to taste
1 (16-ounce) carton sour cream	Salt and pepper to taste
1 stick butter or margarine, softened	8 ounces grated sharp Cheddar cheese
3 ounces cream cheese, softened	

Cook potatoes until done. Mash, adding sour cream, butter, cream cheese, garlic salt, salt and pepper. Whip. Spread over meat mixture. Sprinkle with Cheddar cheese. Return to oven and bake until cheese melts and is slightly browned. Serves 8 or more.

Jarret House Potpourri (North Carolina)

Hungry Jack Beef and Bean Round-Up

1½ pounds ground beef	1 (10-ounce) can Hungry Jack biscuits
¼ cup chopped onion	½ cup (2 ounces) shredded Cheddar cheese
1 cup barbecue sauce	
1 tablespoon brown sugar	
1 (16-ounce) can baked beans with brown sugar	

Heat oven to 375°. Brown ground beef and onion in skillet. Drain. Stir in barbecue sauce, brown sugar, and beans. Heat until bubbly. Pour into 1½- to 2½-quart casserole. Separate biscuit dough into biscuits. Cut in half, crosswise. Place biscuits, cut-side-down, over hot meat mixture in spoke fashion around edge of casserole. Sprinkle cheese over biscuits. Bake 22–27 minutes, or until biscuits are golden brown. Serves 6.

A Cookbook of Treasures (Mid-Atlantic)

★★★★★★★★★★★ ★★★★★★★★★★★

La Strata

1 (10-ounce) package frozen
chopped spinach, cooked and
well drained
1 pound ground beef
½ cup minced onion
1 (8-ounce) can tomato sauce
1 teaspoon basil
1 teaspoon chopped parsley
¼ teaspoon oregano

Dash of garlic salt
Dash of pepper
1 (4-ounce) can mushrooms,
drained
1 (8-ounce) container cottage
cheese
4 ounces mozzarella cheese,
shredded

Preheat oven to 375°. Cook spinach as directed on package. In medium skillet, sauté ground meat and onion until onion is tender and meat is browned. Drain. Add tomato sauce, basil, parsley, oregano, garlic salt, pepper, and mushrooms. Combine spinach and cottage cheese. In 8-inch square casserole, arrange in layers the spinach mixture, meat mixture, then mozzarella cheese. Repeat layering, ending with cheese. Bake 15–20 minutes or until hot and bubbly. Serves 4–6.

Pass the Plate (North Carolina)

Beef Hash with Corn Muffin Mix

1 (15-ounce) can corned beef
hash
½ cup chopped onion
1 egg, beaten
1 (8½-ounce) package corn
muffin mix

3 tablespoons grated
Parmesan cheese
½ teaspoon salt

Mix hash, onion, and egg. Prepare muffin mix per package directions; add cheese and salt. Spread ½ of muffin mix into a greased 8x8-inch pan. Spread hash mixture next. Top with remaining batter. Bake at 400° for 25 minutes in preheated oven. Good served with gravy or creamed peas on top. Serves 4.

Generations of Good Cooking (Iowa)

Mexican Cornbread Casserole

1 cup yellow cornmeal
½ teaspoon baking soda
½ teaspoon salt
1 cup milk
2 eggs, beaten
1 (17-ounce) can cream corn
2 cups shredded Cheddar
  cheese
1 (4-ounce) can mild green
  chiles, chopped

½ cup chopped onion
1 pound ground beef
1 (16-ounce) can kidney beans
½ (8-ounce) can tomato
  sauce
2 teaspoons chili powder
¼ teaspoon garlic powder
Yellow cornmeal for sprinkling

In a bowl, stir together cornmeal, baking soda, and salt. Stir in milk, eggs, and corn. Stir in cheese, chiles, and onion. Mix until well blended; set aside.

Cook ground beef until browned; drain. Stir in beans, tomato sauce, chili powder, and garlic powder. Cook together until heated through. Grease a 9x13-inch baking dish and sprinkle a thin layer of cornmeal over the bottom. Pour in ½ the batter. Cover this with the meat mixture. Top with remaining batter. Bake in a 350° oven for 45 minutes or until top is browned. Serves 6.

Tried & True Recipes from Covington, Georgia (Georgia)

The present design of the one dollar bill came off the presses for the first time in 1957. An individual dollar bill is also less formally known as a one, a single, a buck, a bone, and a bill. The average dollar bill has a life span of 18–22 months.

★★★★★★★★★★★★ ★★★★★★★★★★★★

Reuben Sandwich Casserole

1 large onion
1 small (1-pound) head cabbage
2 tablespoons vegetable oil
¼ teaspoon salt
½ cup water
⅓ cup mayonnaise
⅓ cup chili sauce
¼ cup milk

1 tablespoon sweet pickle relish
½ pound thin-sliced deli
  corned beef
¼ pound thin-sliced Swiss
  cheese
½ (8-ounce) loaf party
  pumpernickel bread slices

Cut onion into thick slices. Cut cabbage into thin wedges. In a large skillet heat oil and add onion; cook until tender. Remove onion slices. Add cabbage wedges and brown. Add salt and water. Over high heat, heat to boiling. Cover and reduce heat to low. Simmer 10 minutes until cabbage is tender.

In small bowl, combine mayonnaise, chili sauce, milk, and relish. Stir until well blended.

In a 9x13-inch dish, arrange onion, cooked cabbage, corned beef, and cheese, and top with slices of bread. Spread mayonnaise mixture evenly on top of bread slices. Cover and bake at 375° for 20–25 minutes. Serves 8.

Franklin County Homemakers Extension Cookbook (Illinois)

Cabbage and Beef Casserole

2 pounds lean ground beef
1 large onion, chopped
2 tablespoons brown sugar
Salt and pepper to taste

2 (14-ounce) cans tomatoes,
  cut up
1 medium cabbage, chopped
Parmesan cheese

In a large skillet, brown ground beef with onion, brown sugar, and salt and pepper to taste. Add tomatoes. Add chopped cabbage. Bring to a boil, and simmer for 30 minutes. Sprinkle with Parmesan cheese. Serves 6–8.

Cooking with 257 (Florida)

Moussaka

1 pound ground beef
1 garlic clove, minced
1 (16-ounce) can stewed tomatoes
2 (8-ounce) cans tomato sauce
1 envelope onion soup mix
½ teaspoon oregano
1 medium eggplant

2 eggs, beaten with 1 tablespoon
   water
1 cup bread crumbs
Olive oil for frying
½ cup grated Parmesan cheese
½ pound mozzarella cheese,
   cubed

Brown meat. Stir in garlic, stewed tomatoes, tomato sauce, onion soup mix, and oregano. Cover and simmer 15 minutes. Pare eggplant. Cut crosswise in ¼-inch slices. Dip eggplant into egg-water mixture and then into bread crumbs. Brown in hot olive oil. Alternate layers of eggplant, cheeses, and sauce in a greased 9x13-inch pan or casserole dish. Bake at 350° for 30 minutes. Serves 8.

The Gulf Gourmet (Mississippi)

Potato Pizza

1 (24-ounce) package frozen
   hash browns, diced
1 pound ground beef, browned
1 (15-ounce) jar Prego spaghetti
   sauce

1 (10¾-ounce) can Cheddar
   cheese soup (undiluted)
1 (8-ounce) package mozzarella
   cheese

Spray a 9x13-inch pan lightly with Pam. Line with frozen hash browns. Mix ground beef, Prego, and Cheddar cheese soup. Heat through. Pour over hash browns. Cover with foil and bake at 375° for 45 minutes. Take foil off and cover with mozzarella. Bake 15 minutes more. Let stand 10 minutes before serving.

If desired, you can add a pizza topping of your choice to the hamburger mixture.

The Ultimate Potato Cookbook (Minnesota)

★★★★★★★★★★★ ★★★★★★★★★★★

Lamb Shanks

½ cup flour
4 whole lamb shanks, trimmed
¼ cup oil
1 tablespoon cornstarch
2 teaspoons salt
½ teaspoon dry mustard
¼ teaspoon pepper
¼ teaspoon ginger

¼ teaspoon cloves
¼ teaspoon onion salt
⅛ teaspoon garlic salt
½ teaspoon celery salt
1 teaspoon paprika
1 teaspoon minced parsley
3 cups chicken stock

Flour shanks; brown in oil. Place in large, greased, oven-proof casserole. Combine cornstarch and seasonings; add to pan drippings; blend. Gradually add stock. Cook over low heat until smooth and thickened. Pour over shanks. Bake, covered, at 350° for about 2½ hours, turning once. Serve with rice. Serves 4.

The Albany Collection: Treasures & Treasured Recipes (New York)

The Grand Canyon took 3–6 million years to form; erosion continues to alter its contours along the 277 miles of the Colorado River. In 2008, a significant flash flood caused the extinction of a well-known waterfall called Navajo Falls. However, the flood also created two new waterfalls, which are unofficially named Rock Falls and New Navajo Falls. The other three waterfalls in the Grand Canyon are Havasu Falls, Mooney Falls, and Beaver Falls.

The Grand Canyon was made a national monument in 1908, and became a national park in 1919.

Veal Anna O'Neal

4 slices peeled eggplant, cut
  lengthwise, salted, rinsed
Egg wash (one beaten egg)
Flavored bread crumbs
¼ cup garlic-flavored extra
  virgin olive oil
1 pound mushrooms, sliced
4 (6-ounce) scallopine of veal

20 ounces marinara sauce, if
  served without pasta (1 quart
  with pasta)
½ cup shredded mozzarella
  cheese
4 teaspoons grated Parmesan
  cheese, divided

Preheat oven to 400°. Dredge eggplant in egg wash and bread crumbs. In a cast-iron skillet, sauté in oil. Set aside.

Sauté mushrooms over low heat; set aside. Dredge veal scallopine in egg wash and bread crumbs. Sauté and set aside.

In a baking dish brushed with olive oil, layer veal, eggplant, marinara sauce, mozzarella, and 1 teaspoon Parmesan per serving. Bake until cheese melts over top and sauce bubbles. Serve with pasta, if desired. Serves 4 or more.

Cooking Italian in Hawaii (Hawaii)

WIKIPEDIA.ORG

The ancient city of Chichen Itza (built about 600 AD) is located in Northern Yucatan, an arid region in Mexico. There are two large, natural sink holes, called cenotes, that could have provided plentiful water year round at Chichen, making it attractive for settlement. The Temple of the Warriors is one of the most impressive structures in the ancient city, featuring the Group of a Thousand Columns.

Cakes & Pies

★★★★★★★ ★★★★★★★

Chichen Itza. Mexico.
One of the New Wonders of the World.

Cherry "Upside-Down" Cake

½ cup firmly packed brown
  sugar
1 (20-ounce) can sour pie
  cherries, drained; reserve
  juice
1¾ cups sifted all-purpose flour
2 teaspoons baking powder

½ teaspoon salt
1 cup sugar
⅓ cup vegetable oil
¾ cup milk
1 teaspoon vanilla
1 egg

All ingredients must be at room temperature.

Grease a 12x8x2-inch pan with butter. Sprinkle brown sugar over bottom of pan. Add drained cherries. Sift together flour, baking powder, salt, and sugar. Add oil, milk and vanilla. Beat for 1½ minutes until batter is well blended. Add egg, unbeaten, and beat for another 1½ minutes. Pour over cherries in pan.

Bake in 350° oven for 35–45 minutes.

CHERRY SAUCE:

½ cup sugar
Reserved juice from cherries
  plus water to equal 1½ cups

2 tablespoons cornstarch
⅛ teaspoon almond extract

Combine sugar, juice, and cornstarch. Cook until thickened, stirring constantly. Remove from heat and add almond extract. Serve warm over warm cake. A fluff of whipped cream for decoration may be added. Serves 12.

A Taste of History (North Carolina)

The name "Chichen Itza" literally means "At the mouth of the well of the Itza." The word Chi stands for "mouth," chen for "well," and Itza for "the Itza tribe."

In Chichen Itza, each of the structures has a name of its own. Pelota Court is the main ball court in Chichen Itza, and is also the largest and best preserved ball court in the world.

Butterscotch Bark Cake

1½ cups boiling water
1 cup quick Quaker Oats
1 cup butterscotch morsels
¾ cup granulated sugar
½ cup firmly packed brown
  sugar
½ cup shortening
2 eggs

1½ cups sifted all-purpose flour
1 teaspoon baking soda
½ teaspoon salt
½ teaspoon cinnamon
¼ teaspoon nutmeg
¾ cup raisins
½ cup chopped nuts

Combine boiling water and quick oats; let stand. Melt the butterscotch chips over hot water; set aside. Combine in a bowl the granulated sugar, brown sugar, and shortening; beat well. Add eggs, beating well. Blend in oat mixture and melted butterscotch. Sift together the next 5 ingredients and add to mixture, mixing well. Stir in raisins and chopped nuts. Pour into a greased 9x13x2-inch pan. Bake in a 350° oven for 35–40 minutes. Cool in pan. Frost with Chocolate Bark Frosting.

CHOCOLATE BARK FROSTING:

¼ cup milk
2 tablespoons butter
⅛ teaspoon salt
1 cup chocolate chips

1 teaspoon vanilla
1½ cups sifted confectioners'
  sugar
1–2 teaspoons milk

Combine ¼ cup milk, butter, and salt. Bring just to a boil over moderate heat; remove from heat. Add chocolate chips and vanilla; stir until chocolate is melted. Blend in confectioners' sugar. Gradually stir in 1–2 teaspoons of milk until mixture is of a soft spreading consistency. Spread evenly over cake. Mark surface by running tines of fork lengthwise in wavy lines to simulate bark.

Fortsville UMC Cookbook (New York)

Apple Dapple

¼ cup butter, softened
1 cup sugar
1 egg
1 cup all-purpose flour
1 teaspoon baking soda

½ teaspoon salt
¾ teaspoon cinnamon
½ teaspoon nutmeg
2 cups grated apples
½ cup chopped nuts

In a mixing bowl, cream together butter and sugar; add egg and beat well. In a separate bowl, sift together flour, baking soda, salt, cinnamon, and nutmeg. Add flour mixture to creamed mixture; stir in apples and nuts. Pour into a buttered 8-inch baking pan. Bake at 350° for 45 minutes.

SAUCE:
½ cup butter   1 cup sugar
½ cup cream

In a saucepan, combine butter, cream, and sugar. Bring mixture to a boil; reduce heat and simmer for 20 minutes, stirring constantly. Serve warm over cake squares.

Ohio Cook Book (Ohio)

The Wonder Years is an American television comedy-drama created by Carol Black and Neal Marlens. It ran for six seasons on ABC from 1988 through 1993. The pilot aired on January 31, 1988, after ABC's coverage of Super Bowl XXII.

Better Than Anything Cake

1 (18¼-ounce) box yellow
  cake mix
1 (8-ounce) can crushed
  pineapple
1 cup sugar
1 (3-ounce) package vanilla
  instant pudding

1 (8-ounce) carton Cool Whip,
  thawed
1 (7-ounce) can flaked coconut
1 cup chopped pecans

Mix cake according to directions; bake in a greased and floured 9x13-inch pan. Mix undrained pineapple and sugar together in a saucepan. Bring to a boil and cook 2–3 minutes. Pour hot mixture over hot cake. Let cool. Mix pudding according to directions on box. Spread over cooled cake. Chill in fridge. When firm, spread Cool Whip over pudding. Sprinkle with coconut and pecans. Refrigerate.

Favorite Recipes (Alabama)

Hilbert's Turtle Cake

1 (18¼-ounce) box German
  chocolate cake mix
1 (14-ounce) package caramels
½ cup evaporated milk

1 cup chocolate chips
1 cup chopped nuts
Butter

Prepare cake mix according to directions using butter instead of oil. Bake ½ of batter in 9x13-inch pan in 350° oven for 15 minutes. In a pan, melt caramels and evaporated milk. Pour over cake; add chocolate chips and nuts. Cover with remaining cake batter. Bake 350° for 20–25 minutes.

Entertaining the Louisville Way, Volume II (Kentucky)

Kentucky Wildcat Cake

2 cups all-purpose flour
2 cups sugar
1 teaspoon baking soda
1 teaspoon vanilla

1 cup chopped walnuts
1 (8-ounce) can crushed
  pineapple with juice
2 eggs, beaten

Heat oven to 350°. Mix all ingredients. Pour into greased 9x13x2-inch pan. Bake 35 minutes. Top with Icing.

ICING:
1 (8-ounce) package cream
  cheese, softened
2 tablespoons melted butter
1 (1-pound) box powdered
  sugar

1 cup flaked coconut
¼ cup chopped walnuts

Cream cheese and butter together until fluffy. Gradually add powdered sugar. Ice cake; sprinkle coconut and walnuts on top.

MTTA's Kitchen Companion (Kentucky)

Old South Lemon Custard Cake

6 tablespoons flour
6 tablespoons butter, melted
2 cups sugar, divided
4 eggs, yolks beaten, whites
  reserved

1½ cups milk
2 tablespoons lemon juice
1 lemon peel, grated
Powdered sugar
Nutmeg

In a large bowl, combine flour, butter, and 1½ cups sugar. Add egg yolks, milk, lemon juice, and lemon peel, and mix completely. Beat egg whites stiff, and fold into cake batter, adding remaining ½ cup sugar as you go.

Pour into a well-oiled 2-quart baking dish or individual ramekins. Either way, place baking dishes into a shallow pan of hot water, and bake at 325° about 1 hour, until brown and bubbly. Sprinkle powdered sugar across top and serve warm. Accent with nutmeg.

Hospitality—Kentucky Style (Kentucky)

Cherry Chocolate Cake

**1 (18¼-ounce) package
  chocolate cake mix**
3 eggs

**1 (21-ounce) can cherry fruit
  filling**

Combine cake mix, eggs, and cherry fruit filling. Mix until well blended. Pour into a greased and floured 9x13-inch pan. Bake at 350° for 35–40 minutes, or until cake springs back when lightly touched.

FROSTING:
1 cup sugar
**5 tablespoons butter or
  margarine**

⅓ cup milk
**1 cup semi-sweet chocolate
  pieces**

In a small saucepan, combine sugar, butter, and milk. Bring to a boil, stirring constantly, and cook one minute. Remove from heat. Stir in chocolate pieces until melted and smooth. Spread over cooled cake.

Alta United Methodist Church Cookbook (Iowa)

DAVID ILIFF, WIKIPEDIA.ORG

Mont Saint-Michel, a Forgotten Wonder of the Medieval World, is a rocky tidal island off the northwestern coast of France. According to legend, the Archangel Michael appeared to St. Aubert, bishop of the nearby town of Avranches, in 708 AD and instructed him to build a church there. The bishop repeatedly ignored the angel's instruction until Michael burned a hole in the bishop's skull with his finger. In the 8th century AD, it became the seat of the Saint-Michel monastery, from which it draws the name. The commune living on the island has a population of 41 as of 2006.

★★★★★★★★★★★★ ★★★★★★★★★★★★

Fat Man's Misery

CAKE:

4 eggs, lightly beaten
2 cups granulated sugar
½ pound butter, softened
1½ cups self-rising flour
2 cups chopped pecans
1 teaspoon vanilla
2 tablespoons cocoa

Preheat oven to 325°. Mix together eggs, sugar, butter, flour, pecans, vanilla, and cocoa. Pour into ungreased 9x13-inch baking pan and bake 45 minutes.

ICING:

1 (1-pound) bag miniature
    marshmallows
4 teaspoons cocoa
½ pound butter, melted
1 (1-pound) box powdered
    sugar
8 teaspoons whipping cream

Place marshmallows on top of cake layer as soon as it comes out of the oven. Place back into oven until marshmallows are melted. Mix cocoa, butter, powdered sugar, and whipping cream together; blend until of spreading consistency. Pour this mixture evenly over marshmallows. Let sit at least 2 hours before cutting into squares. Makes 24 bars.

The Best of Sophie Kay Cookbook (Florida)

During any police lineup, the suspects wear numbers two through nine, because it is considered too suggestive (of guilt) to make anyone display the number one!

Hot Fudge Pudding Cake

1 cup all-purpose flour
¾ cup sugar
2 tablespoons cocoa
2 teaspoons baking powder
¼ teaspoon salt
½ cup milk
2 tablespoons shortening,
  melted

1 cup finely chopped nuts
  (optional)
1 cup packed brown sugar
¼ cup cocoa
1¾ cups hot water

Heat oven to 350°. Measure flour, sugar, 2 tablespoons cocoa, baking powder, and salt into bowl. Blend in milk and shortening; stir in nuts. Pour into ungreased 9x9x2-inch pan. Stir together brown sugar and ¼ cup cocoa; sprinkle over batter. Pour hot water over batter. Bake 45 minutes. While hot, cut into squares; invert each piece onto plate or bowl. Spoon sauce on top. Great with ice cream.

Spitfire Anniversary Cookbook (Iowa)

Pigout Cake

1 yellow cake mix
1 package instant milk
  chocolate pudding mix

2 cups lukewarm water
2 egg whites, slightly
  whipped

Mix and pour into greased 9x13-inch pan. Bake 25–35 minutes at 350°. Cool and frost.

FROSTING:
¼ cup softened margarine
1 cup powdered sugar
1 (8-ounce) carton Cool Whip

Heath or Skor candy bars,
  crushed

Mix margarine and powdered sugar. Fold in Cool Whip. Frost cake and sprinkle crushed Heath or Skor candy bars on top. Refrigerate.

Home Cooking with the Cummer Family (Iowa)

Chocolate Sundae Cake

1 cup brown sugar
½ cup cocoa
2 cups water
2 cups miniature marshmallows

1 (18¼-ounce) package
   devil's food cake mix
1 cup chopped pecans

Combine brown sugar, cocoa, and water; mix well. Pour into a greased 9x13-inch pan. Place marshmallows evenly on top. Make cake batter following package directions. Pour batter into pan. Top with nuts. Bake 50 minutes at 350°.

Feeding the Flock (Shiloh Baptist Church) (North Carolina)

Blueberry Tea Cake

¼ cup margarine, softened
1¼ cups sugar
1 egg
½ cup milk

1 teaspoon salt
2 cups all-purpose flour
2 teaspoons baking powder
2 cups blueberries

Mix margarine, sugar, egg, milk, salt, flour, and baking powder. Fold in blueberries and mix thoroughly. Pour into greased 9x13-inch pan and sprinkle on Topping.

TOPPING:

½ cup sugar
1 teaspoon cinnamon

¼ cup all-purpose flour
¼ cup margarine

Mix ingredients with a pastry blender till well blended. Sprinkle on top of cake. Bake at 375° for 45 minutes or until done.

The Proulx/Chartrand 1997 Reunion Cookbook (New York)

Easy Strawberry Cake

1 (18¼-ounce) box white
  cake mix
4 cups sliced fresh
  strawberries

1 cup granulated sugar
1 pint whipping cream

Prepare batter for 2-layer size cake; mix according to package directions; turn into greased and floured 9x13-inch pan. Cover batter with strawberries; sprinkle strawberries with sugar. Pour whipping cream over ingredients in pan. Bake at 350° for 50–60 minutes or until cake springs back when touched lightly. Cream and strawberries sink to bottom, forming a lush custard layer.

Sharing Our Best (Big Sky)

Punch Bowl Cake

1 baked chocolate cake,
  cut into small pieces
1 large package chocolate
  pudding, prepared
1 (16-ounce) jar caramel sauce

1 (12-ounce) container Cool
  Whip
3 Skor or Heath bars, broken
  into pieces

Put cake pieces in bowl (glass looks best). Mix in chocolate pudding, then caramel sauce. Spread Cool Whip on top. Sprinkle candy on top. Refrigerate. Dip out with ice cream scoop. Rich and very yummy!

Rainbow's Roundup of Recipes (Great Plains)

★★★★★★★★★★★★ ★★★★★★★★★★★★

Creamy Baked Cheesecake

1¼ cups graham cracker
   crumbs
¼ cup sugar
⅓ cup butter, melted
2 (8-ounce) packages cream
   cheese, softened
1 (14-ounce) can sweetened
   condensed milk

3 eggs
¼ cup lemon juice
1 (8-ounce) container sour
   cream
Cherry or blueberry pie filling

Heat oven to 325°. Combine first 3 ingredients; press into 9-inch springform pan. In a large bowl, beat cream cheese until fluffy; beat in sweetened milk until smooth. Add eggs and lemon juice, beating until blended. Bake 50 minutes or until center is set. Top with sour cream; bake 5 more minutes. Cool. Chill and top with cherry or blueberry topping. Refrigerate leftovers.

Great Chefs of Butte Valley (California)

Pretzel Cheesecake

3 cups crushed pretzels
1 stick butter or margarine,
   softened
3 tablespoons sugar
2 (8-ounce) packages cream
   cheese, softened
1 cup powdered sugar

1 (8-ounce) carton Cool Whip,
   thawed
2 (3-ounce) packages
   strawberry Jell-O
2 cups boiling water
2 (10-ounce) boxes frozen
   sliced strawberries

Mix first 3 ingredients and press into bottom of an ungreased 9x13-inch pan. Bake in 350° oven 7 minutes. Cool. Mix cream cheese, powdered sugar, and Cool Whip, and spread over pretzels. Mix Jell-O, water, and strawberries. Pour over cream cheese mixture and refrigerate. Serves 8–10.

Michigan Magazine Family and Friends Cookbook (Michigan)

Janice Williams' Sweet Potato Pie

4 cups grated raw sweet potatoes
¾ cup butter
1 cup self-rising flour
2 cups sugar
1 teaspoon cinnamon or vanilla
4 eggs, beaten
1 cup milk

Preheat oven to 350°. Grate sweet potatoes. Melt butter. Mix flour, sugar, and cinnamon or vanilla. Then add eggs and melted butter. Add milk and beat well. Mix in sweet potatoes, and again, beat well. Pour into 9x13-inch pan and bake 35–40 minutes. Sweet potatoes will rise to the top and will be crunchy. Filling settles to the bottom.

More Than Moonshine: Appalachian Recipes and Recollections
(Kentucky)

Mud Pie

1 box Famous Chocolate Wafers,
** or 1 (15-ounce) package**
** Oreos, crushed**
⅔ cup butter, melted
½ gallon coffee ice cream,
** softened**
4 squares unsweetened chocolate
1 cup sugar
1 (12-ounce) can evaporated
** milk**
2 tablespoons butter
Whipped cream
Nuts for topping

Make crust with chocolate cookies and ⅔ cup melted butter. Press into 2 pie pans or one 9x13-inch pan. Top with coffee ice cream. Freeze hard.

Make chocolate sauce in double boiler. Mix the unsweetened chocolate, sugar, evaporated milk, and butter. Cook until thick. Cool and pour over ice cream. Freeze. Serve pie with whipped cream and nuts.

Note: To make your own coffee ice cream, soften ½ gallon ice cream. Add 2–3 tablespoons powdered instant coffee dissolved in 1 tablespoon vanilla and 1–2 tablespoons rum flavoring. Mix well. Refreeze in sealed container or use to make pie.

Christmas Favorites (North Carolina)

Espresso Pecan Fudge Pie

3 ounces coarsely chopped
  chocolate (unsweetened or
  semisweet)
3 tablespoons butter
1 teaspoon instant espresso
  powder (or French roast)
1 cup sugar

1 cup light corn syrup
3 tablespoons coffee-flavored
  liqueur
1 teaspoon vanilla
3 eggs, lightly beaten
1½ cups chopped pecans
1 pie shell, partially baked

Preheat oven to 350°. Combine chocolate and butter over low heat until butter melts. Remove from heat; whisk chocolate mixture until smooth. Mix in espresso powder until dissolved. Whisk in sugar, corn syrup, coffee liqueur, vanilla, and eggs until smooth. Stir in pecans. Pour into partially baked pie crust. Bake 45 minutes or until set. Cool. Serve with whipped cream. Serves 6–8.

Delicious Recipes from the Nimitz Community (California)

Great Putt Peanut Butter Pie

1 cup crunchy peanut butter
1 cup sugar
1 (8-ounce) package reduced-fat
  cream cheese, softened
1 teaspoon vanilla
2 teaspoons melted butter

1 (8-ounce) tub low-fat frozen
  whipped topping, thawed
1 (9-inch) ready-to-use
  chocolate crumb pie crust
Shaved chocolate or peanuts
  (optional)

Beat peanut butter, sugar, cream cheese, vanilla, and butter thoroughly until creamy. Fold in whipped topping. Pour into pie crust and refrigerate overnight or freeze for several hours. Garnish with shaved chocolate or peanuts. Serves 6–8.

The Golf Cookbook (California)

Brownies & Bars

★★★★★★ ★★★★★★

WIKIPEDIA.ORG

The Great Wall of China.
One of the Wonders of the Medieval World.

Marshmallow Brownies

CAKE:

2 sticks butter, softened
4 eggs
2 cups sugar
2 teaspoons vanilla
4 tablespoons cocoa

1½ cups plain flour
1 cup chopped pecans
1 (7-ounce) jar marshmallow
  crème

Mix butter, eggs, sugar, and vanilla; cream well. Add cocoa, flour (sifted together), and 1 cup pecans (more, if desired). Mix well. Pour into a well-greased 9x13-inch pan and bake at 350° for 25–30 minutes. Remove from oven and immediately spread marshmallow crème on top. Set aside and prepare Topping.

TOPPING:

½ cup butter, softened
3 tablespoons cocoa
1 teaspoon vanilla

2 cups powdered sugar
4 tablespoons evaporated milk

Combine all ingredients and mix well. Spread over marshmallow cream. Swirl. Set in refrigerator until cool; remove and cut as desired.

Shared Treasures (Louisiana II)

The Great Wall of China is a series of stone and earthen fortifications in northern China, built from the 5th century BC to 16th century AD. The longest man-made structure in the world, the Great Wall stretches over 5,500 miles. Forts, passes, and beacon towers along the wall housed soldiers, stored grain and weapons, and were used to transmit military information.

The Great Wall has often been compared to a dragon. In China, the dragon is a protective divinity and is synonymous with springtime and vital energy. The Chinese believed the earth was filled with dragons that gave shape to the mountains and formed the sinew of the land.

Cousin Serena's
Easy Lemon Squares

2 cups plus 6 tablespoons
    all-purpose flour, divided
Pinch of salt
½ cup confectioners' sugar
1 cup butter

2 cups sugar
4 eggs
Juice of 2 lemons
Grated rind of 1 lemon

Combine 2 cups flour, salt, and confectioners' sugar. Cut in butter with a pastry blender or in a food processor fitted with a metal blade. Pat with your hands into a 9x13-inch pan, evenly. Bake in a 350° oven for 20 minutes. While it bakes, mix together 6 tablespoons flour, sugar, eggs, lemon juice, and grated rind. Mix with a spoon or combine in food processor. Pour over the partly baked crust. Bake 35 minutes more. Cool. Cut into squares and dust with powdered sugar. Trim off the edges for a clean look.

Temple Temptations (New York)

The Great Wall of China

★★★★★★★★★★★ ★★★★★★★★★★★

Raspberry Bars

1⅔ cups graham cracker
crumbs
½ cup butter, melted (not
margarine)
2⅔ cups (7 ounces) flaked
coconut
1¼ cups (14 ounces) sweetened
condensed milk

1 cup red raspberry jam or
preserves
⅓ cup chopped nuts
¼ cup melted white baking
bark
½ cup melted chocolate

Mix crumbs and butter. Press into a 9x13-inch pan. Sprinkle coconut on top, and pour condensed milk evenly over it. Bake at 350° for 20–25 minutes, until lightly browned. Cool. Spread jam over and chill 45 minutes. Sprinkle with nuts. Drizzle white bark over, then drizzle melted chocolate over it; keep chilled. Enjoy!

Treasures from Heaven–First Baptist Church (Kentucky)

Frosty Strawberry Squares

1 cup sifted all-purpose flour
¼ cup brown sugar
½ cup chopped walnuts or
pecans
½ cup butter, melted
2 egg whites
1 cup sugar

2 cups sliced fresh strawberries,
or 1 (10-ounce) package
frozen strawberries, partially
thawed
2 teaspoons lemon juice
1 teaspoon almond extract
1 cup heavy cream, whipped

Stir together first 4 ingredients. Spread evenly in shallow pan. Bake 20 minutes in 350° oven, stirring occasionally. Sprinkle ⅔ of this crumbed mixture in a 9x13x2-inch baking pan. Combine egg whites, sugar, berries, lemon juice, and almond extract in a large bowl. Beat at high speed until stiff peaks form, about 10 minutes. Fold in whipped cream. Top with remaining crumbed mixture. Freeze 6 hours or overnight. Cut in squares. Top with fresh strawberries. Makes 16 squares.

Variation: May also me made with frozen peaches.

The Mississippi Cookbook (Mississippi)

★★★★★★★★★★★   ★★★★★★★★★★★

Gooies
Seven-Layer Cookies

Wonderful for waterfront outings where your appetite soars and your activities burn up the calories.

1 stick butter	1 cup chopped pecans
12–15 graham cracker squares	1 (14-ounce) can sweetened
1 cup chocolate chips	condensed milk
1 cup butterscotch morsels	
1 (3½-ounce) can flaked	
coconut	

Preheat oven 350°. Melt stick of butter in 9x13-inch glass baking dish. On top of melted butter place a layer of graham crackers, a layer of chocolate chips, a layer of butterscotch chips, a layer of coconut, and a layer of chopped pecans. Dribble a can of condensed milk on top, and bake until a little brown around the edge, 20–30 minutes. *Cut as soon as you remove from oven.* Let stand at least 4 hours. Better to let stand overnight.

If at first you don't succeed, you're running about average.

Sweet Surrender with Advice á la Carte (Florida)

Easy Oreo Peanut Butter Squares

1 (1-pound) package Oreo	1 (3½-ounce) box vanilla
cookies	instant pudding
1 cup margarine, melted	1 (12-ounce) package semisweet
1 (16-ounce) carton Cool Whip	chocolate chips
2 cups creamy peanut butter	

Grease a 9x13-inch pan with margarine. Grind Oreo cookies in a food processor or blender until gravel-like in texture. Add melted margarine; blend some more. Pat cookie mixture lightly in pan. Bake for 10–15 minutes at 350°. Let cool. With a mixer, blend Cool Whip, peanut butter, dry vanilla pudding, and chocolate chips until a brownish color. Spread carefully over cookie crust. Refrigerate. Cut into squares. Delicious.

A Collection of Favorite Recipes (Florida)

★★★★★★★★★★★   ★★★★★★★★★★★

Caramel Choco-Bars

1 (14-ounce) bag Kraft caramels
⅔ cup evaporated milk, divided
1 (18¼-ounce) box German
   chocolate cake mix

¾ cup butter, melted
½ cup chopped nuts
1 (12-ounce) package chocolate
   chips

Melt unwrapped caramels and ⅓ cup evaporated milk over low heat, keeping warm. Combine cake mix, butter, remaining ⅓ cup evaporated milk, and nuts. Mix well. Spread half of batter in greased 9x13-inch pan. Bake 6 minutes at 350°. Remove from oven; sprinkle with chocolate chips and drizzle with melted caramel mixture. Sprinkle remaining batter over caramel mixture. Bake 15–18 minutes at 350°. Cool 2 hours before cutting. Makes 4 dozen bars.

Ohio Traditions with P. Buckley Moss (Ohio)

Mike's Babe Ruth Bars

1 cup sugar
1 cup light corn syrup
1 cup chunky peanut butter

6 cups Special K Cereal
1 cup chocolate chips
1 cup butterscotch morsels

Combine sugar and corn syrup in saucepan. Place over medium heat and bring to a boil, stirring occasionally. Remove from heat. Add peanut butter and mix well. Stir in cereal until evenly coated. Press mixture into a buttered 9x13-inch pan. Cool. Melt chips. Spread over cooled mixture. Cool; cut into bars.

Recipes from Our Friends (Washington)

Desserts

WIKIMEDIACOMMONS.ORG

The Great Pyramid of Giza. Egypt.
The only remaining one of the original Seven Wonders
of the Ancient World.

Lazy Cherry Cobbler

Sure to be a family favorite.

2 (20-ounce) cans cherry pie
   filling
½ (20-ounce) can water
½ teaspoon almond extract

1½ cups self-rising flour
1 cup sugar
1 cup skim milk

Preheat oven to 375°. Combine cherries, water, and almond extract. Mix well. Place in ungreased 9x13-inch baking pan. In a mixing bowl, combine dry ingredients and mix well. Add milk and stir until well mixed. Pour evenly over cherries. Then run a knife through the mixture as if marbleizing. Bake 40–50 minutes, until golden brown. Serves 12.

Options: Use reduced-sugar pie filling. Use other fruits such as blueberries. To make an 8x8-inch pan, use one can of fruit and ¼ cup water, ¾ cup self-rising flour, ½ cup sugar, and ½ cup milk. Bake at 375° for about 35 minutes.

NUTRITION: (per serving): Cal 242; Sat Fat 0g; Total Fat 0g; Prot 3g; Carb 57g; Chol 0mg; Fiber 0g; Vit A 118 IU; Sod 188mg; Iron 1mg; Vit C 0mg.

"Life Tastes Better Than Steak" Cookbook (Michigan)

Super Blackberry Cobbler

4 cups blackberries
1 cup plus 2 teaspoons sugar,
   divided
¼ cup quick tapioca
1⅓ cups water
2 tablespoons butter

2 cups all-purpose flour
5 teaspoons baking powder
¼ teaspoon salt
6 tablespoons shortening
⅔ cup milk
¼ teaspoon lemon extract

Combine berries, 1 cup sugar, tapioca, water, and butter and let stand while making crust. Sift flour, remaining 2 teaspoons sugar, baking powder, and salt together. Cut in shortening. Add milk all at once. Stir to dampen. Roll out. Cut into 8 (2½-inch) rounds. Sprinkle with sugar. Add lemon extract to berries and pour into buttered baking dish. Place rounds over berries and bake at 425° for 30 minutes.

A Taste from Back Home (Kentucky)

Dutch Oven Peach Cobbler

Campers from other sites come driving over to see what's cooking when they smell this cinnamon peach cobbler. Sometimes, Mr. English adds fresh blueberries. Be sure to share! It's the southern thing to do!

2 (16-ounce) cans sliced peaches
  in heavy or light syrup, or in
  fruit juice, your choice
1 pint fresh blueberries
  (optional)

½ cup Bisquick baking mix
⅓ cup sugar
Ground cinnamon

Spray a Dutch oven with vegetable oil cooking spray. Drain 1 can of peaches. Combine both cans of peaches, including the juice from the undrained can, the blueberries, if using, the Bisquick, sugar, and a sprinkling of cinnamon. Place this mixture into the Dutch oven.

TOPPING:
2¼ cups Bisquick baking mix
¼ cup sugar
¼ cup (½ stick) butter, melted

½ cup milk
Cinnamon sugar

Combine the Bisquick, sugar, butter, and milk in a resealable plastic bag. Using your fingers, drop bits of Topping on top of the peaches. Sprinkle with cinnamon sugar. Place the Dutch oven over about 12 coals, then cover with lid; place about 12 coals on top. Check in 10 minutes; if the dough is brown, there are too many coals on top. If it is not brown at all, add a few coals. The cobbler usually cooks in 30 minutes. Serves about 10 hungry campers.

Paula Deen & Friends (Georgia)

Editor's Extra: Can bake in 350° oven for 45 minutes, or until top is golden.

The Giza Necropolis is an archaeological site on the Giza Plateau, on the outskirts of Cairo, Egypt. This complex of ancient monuments includes the three pyramid complexes known as the Great Pyramids, the massive sculpture known as the Great Sphinx, several cemeteries, a workers' village, and an industrial complex. It is located about five miles inland into the desert from the old town of Giza on the Nile. The pyramids were described in a poem composed about 140 BC by Greek poet Antipater of Sidon who, along with several of his peers, is attributed with listing the Seven Wonders of the Ancient World.

The Famous Cheese Apple Crisp

6 cups sliced apples
¾ teaspoon cinnamon
¾ cup water
2¼ teaspoons lemon juice
1½ cups sugar
1 cup all-purpose flour
¼ teaspoon plus ⅛ teaspoon salt
1 stick butter, softened
6 ounces shredded American cheese from a block

Preheat oven to 350°. Arrange apples in a shallow greased baking pan. Sprinkle with cinnamon. Add water and lemon juice. Combine sugar, flour, and salt; work in butter to form a crumbly mixture. Lightly stir in cheese. Spread mixture over apples, and bake until apples are tender and crust is brown and crisp, 30–40 minutes. Serves 12.

Lessons from the Lunchroom (Kentucky)

Apple-Cranberry Crumble

A proven delight.

1 cup sugar
1 tablespoon all-purpose flour
1 teaspoon cinnamon
½ teaspoon nutmeg
6–8 apples, peeled and sliced
2 cups fresh or frozen cranberries

Combine and mix together. Pour apple mixture in a lightly greased glass 9x13-inch baking dish.

CRUMBLE TOPPING:
1 cup all-purpose flour
1 cup sugar
½ cup margarine
1 cup oatmeal
½ cup chopped nuts

Mix flour and sugar. Cut margarine in with pastry blender. Add remaining ingredients. Pour crumble topping over apple mixture and bake at 350° for 30–40 minutes. Serves 8–10.

Our Favorite Recipes (Minnesota)

★★★★★★★★★★★★ ★★★★★★★★★★★★

Apple Goodie

3 cups sliced or diced apples
¾ cup white sugar
¼ teaspoon baking soda
¼ teaspoon baking powder
⅓ cup butter, melted
1 rounded tablespoon flour

Salt and cinnamon to taste
¾ cup oatmeal
¾ cup flour
¾ cup brown sugar, firmly
  packed

Combine apples and white sugar and put in buttered 8x8-inch baking dish. Mix soda, baking powder, melted butter, flour, and salt and cinnamon to taste. Spread over top of apples. Combine remaining ingredients and crumble over the top. Bake 30–40 minutes at 350°. Cut in squares and serve with hard sauce or whipped cream, if desired.

Neighboring on the Air (Iowa)

Tropical Delight

1 (18¼-ounce) box white
  cake mix
1 (3-ounce) package orange-
  pineapple Jell-O
4 eggs
3 teaspoons flour

⅔ cup vegetable oil
½ cup juice from fruit
1 (11-ounce) can Mandarin
  oranges
½ cup crushed pineapple
½ cup flaked coconut

GLAZE:
1 cup powdered sugar
2 tablespoons lemon juice

Rind from 1 orange, grated

Mix for 4 minutes the cake mix, Jell-O, eggs, flour, oil, and ½ cup juice. Cut the oranges in halves or thirds. Stir in the oranges, pineapple, and coconut. Bake in a greased 9x13-inch pan for 45–50 minutes at 350°. Mix Glaze ingredients. With a meat fork, punch cake all over and pour the Glaze over the hot cake.

From the Cozy Kitchens of Long Grove (Iowa)

Yum Yum Dessert

1 stick butter or margarine
1½ sleeves Ritz Crackers
¼ cup sugar
1 (14-ounce) can sweetened
　condensed milk

1 (8-ounce) carton Cool Whip
1 (6-ounce) can orange juice,
　undiluted
2 (11-ounce) cans Mandarin
　oranges, drained, divided

Melt butter, and crumble in Ritz Crackers; add sugar. Mix well and press mixture (reserving ½ cup) into bottom of 9x13-inch baking dish.

Blend condensed milk, Cool Whip, and orange juice with mixer. With a spoon, stir in 1½ cans Mandarin oranges. Pour this mixture over cracker mixture. Place remaining Mandarin oranges on top, and sprinkle with reserved crumbs. Keep refrigerated.

Good Cooks Sharing (Kentucky)

SHORELANDER, WIKIPEDIA.ORG

The *Disney Wonder* is one of the most revered and recognizable ocean liners in the world, inspiring awe wherever it pulls into port. Along with its sister cruise ship, the *Disney Magic*, the *Disney Wonder* was specially constructed with families in mind, combining sleek style with a splash of fun.

Lisa's Strawberry Dessert

This tastes like strawberry cream pie.

CRUST:

1 cup all-purpose flour
1 stick margarine, softened

⅓ cup powdered sugar

Mix ingredients together; put in a 9x13-inch pan. Bake at 350° for 15 minutes.

FILLING:

1 (8-ounce) package cream
 cheese, softened

1 (8-ounce) carton Cool Whip
1 cup powdered sugar

Mix Filling together. Spread over cooled Crust. Refrigerate until firm.

TOPPING:

2 cups water
1½ cups sugar
⅓ cup white corn syrup
4 tablespoons cornstarch

1 (3-ounce) box strawberry
 Jell-O
1 quart fresh strawberries,
 sliced

Mix the 2 cups water, sugar, corn syrup, and cornstarch together in a saucepan. Bring to a boil. This will become thick and shiny. Remove from heat. Add Jell-O; stir well. Let this cool. Add sliced strawberries. Spoon carefully over Filling layer. Refrigerate until firm.

Titonka Centennial Cookbook (Iowa)

Favorite Raspberry Dessert

Excellent dessert.

CRUST:

1 cup all-purpose flour
¼ cup powdered sugar

1 stick butter, melted
¼ cup chopped pecans

Mix flour, powdered sugar, and melted butter. Add pecans. Butter a 9x13-inch pan. Pat mixture to cover bottom of pan. Bake at 350° for 15–20 minutes. Completely cool Crust.

3 (10-ounce) packages frozen
raspberries, thawed, juice
reserved
2 tablespoons cornstarch
1 (8-ounce) package cream
cheese, softened
1 cup powdered sugar

1 (16-ounce) tub Cool Whip,
divided
1 (16-ounce) package vanilla
instant pudding, prepared per
package instructions
Chopped pecans to sprinkle
over top

Drain fruit juice into a saucepan. Over medium heat, thicken with cornstarch. Cool. Add fruit to mixture and set aside.

In separate bowl, beat together cream cheese, powdered sugar, and ½ the Cool Whip. Spread this mixture over the prepared Crust. Now layer the fruit mixture. Pour prepared vanilla instant pudding over fruit. Add the last of the Cool Whip to the top and sprinkle with chopped pecans. Refrigerate.

From the High Country of Wyoming (Big Sky)

In the English language, there is a word with just ONE vowel that occurs six times: *indivisibility*.

Mississippi Mud Dessert

1 cup all-purpose flour
1 stick margarine, softened
½ cup chopped nuts
1 (8-ounce) package cream
   cheese, softened
1 cup powdered sugar

1 (8-ounce) carton Cool Whip,
   divided
2 (3-ounce) packages chocolate
   instant pudding
3 cups milk
Chopped nuts (optional)

Mix the flour, margarine, and nuts for pie crust. Spread in 9x13-inch pan and bake at 350° for 20 minutes; cool. Cream together cream cheese, powdered sugar, and 1 cup Cool Whip. Spread on crust (hard to spread). Put chocolate pudding and milk in mixer bowl; beat with mixer until thick. Spread over cream cheese layer. Top with remaining Cool whip and sprinkle with nuts, if desired. Refrigerate. Can make a day ahead. Also can use butterscotch pudding.

Thompson Family Cookbook (Iowa)

Cream Puff Dessert

1 stick margarine
1 cup water

1 cup all-purpose flour
4 eggs

Boil margarine in one cup water. Add flour and beat hard until it forms a ball. Add eggs one at a time. Spread in 9x13-inch pan that has been sprayed with Pam. Bake at 400° for 30 minutes. Cool.

FILLING:
2 (3-ounce) packages vanilla
   instant pudding
3 cups milk
1 (8-ounce) package cream
   cheese, softened

1 (8-ounce) carton Cool
   Whip
Hershey's Syrup

Blend pudding with milk and softened cream cheese. Let stand for 15 minutes. Spread over cooled crust. Top with Cool Whip. Drizzle small amount of Hershey's syrup over Cool Whip. Refrigerate.

Our Savior's Kvindherred Lutheran Church (Iowa)

Pioneer Bread Pudding

2 cups stale, but not dry, bread cubes	¼ cup sugar
	2 eggs
2 cups milk	Dash of salt
3 tablespoons butter	¼ teaspoon vanilla

Place bread cubes in a one-quart buttered baking dish. Scald the milk with the butter and sugar. Beat eggs slightly; add the salt, then the warm milk and vanilla. Pour over the bread cubes. Set the baking dish in a pan containing warm water up to the level of the pudding and bake about one hour at 350°, or until a knife comes out clean when inserted in center of pudding. Serve warm with plain cream, currant jelly, or Lemon Pudding Sauce, if desired. Serves 4–6.

LEMON PUDDING SAUCE:

½ cup sugar	1 tablespoon grated lemon rind
2 tablespoons cornstarch	
1 cup boiling water	3 tablespoons lemon juice
2 tablespoons butter	⅛ teaspoon salt

Combine sugar and cornstarch; add boiling water slowly, and stir until dissolved. Cook slowly, stirring constantly, until thickened and clear. Remove from heat and add remaining ingredients. Serve warm.

Neighboring on the Air (Iowa)

The oldest and largest of the three pyramids in the Giza Necropolis, Egypt, is the oldest of the Seven Wonders of the Ancient World, and the only one to remain largely intact. It was the tallest man-made structure in the world for over 3,800 years, the longest period of time ever held for such a record. There have been varying theories about the Great Pyramid's construction techniques.

Creole Bread Pudding

6 slices bread, cubed
3½ cups milk, divided
4 eggs, separated
½ cup sugar, divided
1 tablespoon vanilla extract

Pinch of salt
¼ cup butter or margarine,
  melted
½ cup raisins

Combine bread cubes and 1 cup milk; set aside. Beat egg yolks, 6 tablespoons sugar and remaining 2½ cups milk. Stir in vanilla, salt, butter and raisins. Pour mixture over bread and mix well. Pour into greased shallow 2-quart baking dish. Place dish in a pan of hot water. Bake at 300° about 50 minutes or until knife inserted in center comes out clean. Beat egg whites until stiff; gradually beat in remaining 2 tablespoons sugar. Spread meringue over pudding; bake at 350° about 10 minutes or until golden. Serve with Rum Sauce. Serves 6–8.

RUM SAUCE:
½ cup sugar
2 tablespoons butter or
  margarine

¼ cup water
1 tablespoon rum

Combine sugar, butter, and water in a small saucepan; bring to a boil and boil 1 minute. Remove from heat; stir in rum. Serve warm. Makes about ½ cup.

Auburn Entertains (Alabama)

Apple Bread Pudding
with Bourbon Sauce

8 cups sourdough or French bread (day old is best)
4 tablespoons butter
3 cups low-fat milk, scalded
1 cup brown sugar

1 cup apple pie filling
3 eggs, beaten
1 tablespoon vanilla extract
½ cup raisins

Butter bread and tear into small pieces. Place in a large bowl. Scald milk and then pour over bread to cover. Let soak for 30 minutes.

Once bread has been soaking for about 15 minutes, preheat oven to 350°. Toss the brown sugar and apple pie filling. Add beaten eggs and vanilla and whisk together. Pour over bread mixture. Sprinkle raisins over top and lightly stir to blend. Scrape the mixture into a lightly oiled 2-quart baking dish. Place the baking dish in a larger pan filled with hot water. Place the entire contents into oven. Bake for 60–70 minutes. You may want to loosely cover pudding with foil after 30 minutes of baking to prevent the top from burning. While Bread Pudding is baking, prepare the Bourbon Sauce.

BOURBON SAUCE:
6 tablespoons butter
1 large egg

¾ cup powdered sugar
3 tablespoons bourbon whiskey

Melt butter in a small saucepan. In a small bowl, beat egg, then beat in powdered sugar. Stir into melted butter and whisk mixture until it becomes hot. Do not boil. Remove from heat and let cool to room temperature, stirring occasionally. The sauce will thicken as it cools. Stir in the bourbon. Serve pudding hot or warm, spooning the sauce over each serving. Serves 8.

Drop the Hook, Let's Eat (Alaska)

Biscuit Bread Pudding

2–2½ cups boiling water
6–8 cold biscuits, broken up
4 tablespoons butter, melted
1½ cups sugar
2½ cups evaporated milk
6 eggs, beaten

1½ teaspoons (or to taste)
 vanilla, orange, or almond
 flavoring
Cinnamon to taste
Raisins, apple slices, coconut,
 Mandarin oranges, etc.

Mix water, biscuits, butter, sugar, milk, eggs, flavoring, cinnamon, raisins, etc., and pour into greased 9x13-inch baking dish. Bake at 350° until set, 30–35 minutes. Will be thick and shaky, but settles when it cools. Very rich. Cut in small slices and serve hot or cold with whipped cream.

Lake Guntersville Bed & Breakfast Cookbook (Alabama)

French Silk Dessert

CRUST:
½ cup brown sugar
1 cup all-purpose flour

½ cup chopped pecans
¼ pound butter, softened

Mix all, and pat into 9x13-inch pan; bake at 400° for 15 minutes or until lightly browned. Mix again after taking from oven. Pat down once again.

FILLING:
½ pound butter, softened
1½ cups sugar
2 teaspoons vanilla
3 squares unsweetened
 chocolate, melted

4 eggs
2 cups whipped topping
Chocolate shavings

Cream butter and sugar together. Add vanilla and melted chocolate. Beat in eggs, beating 5 minutes between each egg (very important). Pour mixture over Crust and place in freezer for 20–30 minutes. Remove and spread with whipped topping. Top with chocolate shavings. Store in freezer until ready to serve. Serves 10–12.

Seasons of Thyme (Kentucky)

Chocolate Lush

1 stick margarine, melted
1 cup all-purpose flour
1 cup powdered sugar
1 (8-ounce) package cream
  cheese, softened

2 cups Cool Whip, divided
2 (3-ounce) packages instant
  chocolate pudding mix
3 cups milk
Chopped nuts (optional)

Mix melted margarine and flour; press into greased 9x13-inch pan. Bake 15 minutes at 375°. Mix powdered sugar and cream cheese; fold in 1 cup Cool Whip. Mix pudding with milk in separate bowl. Combine with cream cheese mixture. Pour into prepared crust. Top with remaining 1 cup Cool Whip and nuts, if desired.

A Gift of Appreciation (Georgia)

Snow Peak Lemon Squares

The most heavenly dessert you've ever tasted.

2½ cups graham cracker
  crumbs
1 stick butter or margarine,
  softened
1¼ cups sugar, divided
1 (3-ounce) package lemon Jell-O
1 cup boiling water

1 (8-ounce) package cream
  cheese, softened
1 (12-ounce) can evaporated
  milk, chilled overnight
2 tablespoons lemon juice
½ pint whipping cream,
  whipped with a little sugar

Mix cracker crumbs, butter, and ½ cup sugar (reserve ½ cup mixture to sprinkle on top), and press into a 9x13-inch dish. Dissolve Jell-O in boiling water and mix gradually with cream cheese. Whip chilled evaporated milk, and add remaining ¾ cup sugar and lemon juice. Fold into Jell-O mixture. Pour into crust and chill until set. Top with remaining crumbs and whipped cream. Garnish with a twist of lemon.

The Woman's Exchange Classic Recipes (Florida)

Fresh Peach Dessert

CRUST:

½ cup butter   2 tablespoons sugar
1 cup all-purpose flour

Mix ingredients for Crust until crumbly. Pat in 9x13-inch pan or round quiche dish, and bake at 350° for 10 minutes.

GLAZE:

1 cup sugar   1 cup water
3 tablespoons cornstarch   2–3 cups sliced fresh peaches
3 tablespoons dry peach or
  orange Jell-O

Mix dry ingredients for Glaze and gradually add water. Cook until thick. When cool, add sliced peaches and spread on top of Crust. Refrigerate. Cut in squares and serve with whipped topping.

Winniehaha's Favorite Recipes (Minnesota)

Peaches Eudora

Good with ice cream or whipped topping.

1 cup peeled and sliced   2 tablespoons butter, melted
  fresh peaches   ¼ cup all-purpose flour
½ tablespoon flour   Dash of salt
½ teaspoon orange liqueur,   1 tablespoon shortening
  vanilla, or almond extract   1 tablespoon milk
6 tablespoons sugar   1 tablespoon butter, melted

Mix first 5 ingredients lightly and pour in a small baking dish. For pastry, stir ¼ cup flour and salt together. Cut in shortening with fork till thoroughly mixed in small pea-size bits. Add milk. Roll thin; cut in strips and place over filling. Pour 1 tablespoon melted butter over all. Bake in 350° oven 25 minutes or until golden brown. Serves 1–2.

Quickies for Singles (Louisiana)

Peach Kuchen

½ cup butter
2 cups all-purpose flour
2 tablespoons sugar
½ teaspoon salt
¼ teaspoon baking
  powder

6–8 freestone peaches
½–¾ cup cinnamon sugar
  (2 tablespoons cinnamon to
  ½ cup sugar)
1 cup whipping cream
2 egg yolks

Melt butter and mix together with next 4 ingredients, until crumbly. Pat firmly into pan. Peel and slice 6–8 freestone peaches; put on top of crust. Mix and sprinkle the cinnamon sugar over the top.

Bake 15–20 minutes at 350°. Mix the whipping cream and egg yolks and pour over all. Bake 30 minutes more. Cool and serve with ice cream. (Double for a larger group.)

Arkansas Favorites Cookbook (Arkansas)

Creamy Layered Fruit Sensation

1 (9-ounce) angel food cake
3 tablespoons orange juice
¼ teaspoon almond extract
2½ cups fat-free milk
2 (4-serving) packages vanilla
  instant fat-free/sugar-free
  pudding

1½ cups lite Cool Whip,
  thawed, divided
2 (12-ounce) packages frozen
  mixed berries, thawed,
  well drained

Cut cake into cubes and place in large bowl. Combine orange juice and almond extract. Drizzle over cake cubes and toss lightly. Pour milk into another large bowl and add dry pudding mixes. Beat with wire whisk 2 minutes or until well blended. Gently stir in 1 cup whipped topping.

Layer half the cake cubes in bottom of 2-quart glass serving bowl or 2-quart round baking dish. Reserve a few berries for garnish. Top with layers of half each of the remaining berries and pudding mixture. Repeat layers. Cover with plastic wrap. Refrigerate 2–6 hours before serving. Top with remaining ½ cup whipped topping and reserved berries just before serving.

Thomson-Shore Anniversary Cookbook (Michigan)

Pizza Fruit Platter

CRUST:

1 package (1 layer) yellow
    cake mix
2 tablespoons water
1 egg

2 tablespoons butter, melted
2 tablespoons brown sugar
½ cup chopped nuts

Combine the cake mix, water, egg, butter, and brown sugar. Fold in the nuts and pour batter on heavily greased and floured 12-inch pizza pan. Bake at 375° for 15 minutes and let cool.

SAUCE:

12 ounces cream cheese,
    softened

½ cup sugar
1 teaspoon vanilla

Mix the cream cheese, sugar, and vanilla together. Spread over Crust.

TOPPINGS:

1 pint fresh strawberries,
    cut in half
1 (20-ounce) can pineapple
    tidbits, drained
Medium bunch of green grapes,
    halved

2 bananas, sliced
½ cup apricot preserves
2 tablespoons water

Arrange fruit in circular pattern over cheese mixture. Heat apricot preserves with 2 tablespoons water until the preserves melt. Remove from heat and let cool. Brush apricot glaze on fruit. Cut into wedges and refrigerate until ready to serve. Use whatever fresh fruit is in season. Kiwi is especially attractive and tasty.

Great Plains Cooking (Colorado)

Orange Cream Dessert

CRUST:

¾ cup (1½ sticks) margarine,
  softened
¼ cup firmly packed brown
  sugar

1½ cups all-purpose flour
½ cup chopped nuts

Cream margarine and sugar. Add flour and nuts; mix well. Spread dough in 9x13-inch pan and bake at 375° for 10 minutes. Cool.

FILLING:

1 (8-ounce) package cream
  cheese, softened
¾ cup sugar, or 1 cup
  powdered sugar

1 (8-ounce) carton Cool Whip

Beat cream cheese and sugar. Fold in Cool Whip. Spread Filling evenly on Crust. Chill for ½ hour.

TOPPING:

1 envelope unflavored gelatin
1 cup cold water, divided
1 (6-ounce) package orange
  Jell-O

2 cups hot water
1 pint orange sherbet
2 (11-ounce) cans Mandarin
  oranges, drained

Soften unflavored gelatin in ¼ cup cold water and set aside. In large bowl, dissolve Jell-O with 2 cups hot water; add softened gelatin and remaining ¾ cup cold water and stir until dissolved. Fold in sherbet and Mandarin oranges. Pour Jell-O mixture over cream cheese mixture, and refrigerate.

Friends and Celebrities Cookbook II (Hawaii)

The dramatic prehistoric site of Stonehenge in Wiltshire County, England, was completed about 1500 BC. The first stage began around 3100 BC and was abandoned for nearly 1,000 years. Its original creators and purpose are unclear. The final stage consists of a circular setting of large standing stones brought from 25 miles north. The largest of the Sarsen stones transported to Stonehenge weighs fifty tons. It is unknown how the stones were transported.

Various Lists of Wonders of the World

These lists have been compiled from antiquity to the present day, to catalogue the world's most spectacular natural wonders and manmade structures. The number seven was chosen because the Greeks believed it to be the representation of perfection and plenty. Since ancient times, numerous "seven wonders" lists have been created, the contents of which tend to vary, and none is definitive.

The Seven Wonders of the Ancient World

- The Great Pyramid of Giza (Egypt)
- The Hanging Gardens of Babylon (Iraq)
- The Temple of Artemis at Ephesus (Turkey)
- The Statue of Zeus at Olympia (Greece)
- The Mausoleum at Halicarnassus (Turkey)
- The Colossus of Rhodes (Greece)
- The Lighthouse of Alexandria (Egypt)

The Seven Wonders of the Medieval World
(Architectural Wonders of the Middle Ages)

- Stonehenge (England)
- The Colosseum (Italy)
- The Catacombs of Kom el Shoqafa (Egypt)
- The Great Wall of China (China)
- The Porcelain Tower of Nanjing (China)
- The Hagia Sophia (Turkey)
- The Leaning Tower of Pisa (Italy)

The New Seven Wonders of the World

- Chichen Itza (Mexico)
- Christ the Redeemer Statue (Brazil)
- The Colosseum (Italy)
- The Great Wall of China (China)
- Machu Picchu (Peru)
- Petra (Jordan)
- Taj Mahal (India)
- Giza Necropolis (Egypt) – honorary

The Seven Natural Wonders of the World

- Mount Everest (Nepal, bordering Tibet)
- The Great Barrier Reef (Australia)
- The Grand Canyon (United States)
- Victoria Falls (Africa)
- The Harbor of Rio de Janeiro (Brazil)
- Parícutin Volcano (Mexico)
- The Northern Lights (Arctic region)

The Seven Underwater Wonders of the World

- Palau (Island in Pacific Ocean)
- The Belize Barrier Reef (Belize)
- The Galapagos Islands (Pacific Ocean)
- The Northern Red Sea (Africa)
- Lake Baikal (Russia)
- The Great Barrier Reef (Australia)
- The Deep Sea Vents

The Seven Wonders of the Modern World

- The Empire State Building (United States)
- The Itaipú Dam (Brazil and Paraguay)
- The CN Tower (Canada)
- The Panama Canal (Panama)
- The Channel Tunnel (England and France)
- The North Sea Protection Works (Netherlands)
- The Golden Gate Bridge (United States)

Various Lists of Wonders of the World (continued)

The Seven Wonders
of the Industrial World
• *SS Great Eastern* (ship) (England)
• Bell Rock Lighthouse (Scotland)
• Brooklyn Bridge (United States)
• London Sewerage System (England)
• First Transcontinental Railroad
  (United States)
• Panama Canal (Panama)
• Hoover Dam (United States)

The Seven Forgotten Natural
Wonders of the World
• Angel Falls (Venezuela)
• The Bay of Fundy (Canada)
• Iguaçú Falls (Brazil and Argentina)
• Krakatoa Island (Indonesia)
• Mount Fuji (Japan)
• Mount Kilimanjaro (Africa)
• Niagara Falls
  (United States and Canada)

The Seven Forgotten Wonders
of the Medieval World
• Abu Simbel Temple (Egypt)
• Angkor Wat (Cambodia)
• Taj Mahal (India)
• Mont Saint-Michel (France)
• The Moai Statues (Easter Island)
• The Parthenon (Greece)
• The Shwedagon Pagoda (Burma)

The Seven Forgotten Wonders
of the Modern World
• The Clock Tower–Big Ben (England)
• Eiffel Tower (France)
• The Gateway Arch (United States)
• The Aswan High Dam (Egypt)
• Hoover Dam (United States)
• Mount Rushmore National Memorial
  (United States)
• The Petronas Towers (Malaysia)

The Forgotten Wonders
(on various lists)
• The Aztec Temple (Mexico)
• The Banaue Rice Terraces
  (Philippines)
• The Borobudur Temple (Indonesia)
• The Mayan Temples (Guatemala)
• The Temple of the Inscriptions
  (Mexico)
• The Throne Hall of Persepolis (Iran)
• The Suez Canal (Egypt)
• The Sydney Opera House (Australia)
• The Red Fort (India)
• The Great Sphinx of Giza (Egypt)
• Forbidden City (China)
• Karnak Temple (Egypt)
• Temples of Bagan ªJurma)
• Temples of Bali (Indonesia)
• Teotihucan (Mexico)
• Louvre Museum (France)
• Sistine Chapel (Italy)

United States Wonders
(on various lists)
• National Mall and Memorial Parks
  (Washington DC)
• The Badlands (South Dakota)
• Niagara Falls (New York)
• The Saturn V Rocket (Alabama)
• Yellowstone National Park (Wyoming
  and Montana)
• Arctic National Wildlife (Alaska)
• The Golden Gate Bridge (California)
• The Statue of Liberty (New York)
• The Brooklyn Bridge (New York)
• Hoover Dam (Nevada)
• Mount Rushmore (South Dakota)

Stonehenge. Wiltshire County, England.
One of the Wonders of the Medieval World.

★★★★★★★★★★★★ ★★★★★★★★★★★★

Listed below are the cookbooks that have contributed recipes to the *Recipe Hall of Fame One-Dish Wonders,* along with copyright, author, publisher, city, and state. The information in parentheses indicates the BEST OF THE BEST cookbook in which the recipe originally appeared.

Absolutely á la Carte ©1999 by Charlotte Walton Skelton, Cleveland, MS (Mississippi)

Alaska Women in Timber Cookbook, Alaska Women in Timber, Ketchikan, AK (Alaska)

The Albany Collection ©1997 The Woman's Council of the Albany Institute of History & Art, Albany, NY (New York)

Aliant Cooks for Education ©2004 Morris Press Cookbooks, Aliant Bank, Alexander City, AL (Alabama)

Almost Heaven ©1984 Junior League of Huntington, WV (West Virginia)

Alta United Methodist Church Cookbook, Alta, IA (Iowa)

Amazing Graces ©1993 The Texas Conferences Ministers' Spouses Association, Houston, TX (Texas)

America Celebrates Columbus ©1999 The Junior League of Columbus, OH (Ohio)

Another Taste of Washington State ©2000 Tracy Winters, Washington State Bed & Breakfast Guild, Winters Publishing, Greensburg, IN (Washington)

Apple Orchard Cookbook ©1992 Janet Christensen and Betty Bergman Levin, Lee, MA (New England)

Apples Etc. Cookbook ©1998 Santa Cruz, CA Chapter of Hadassah, Aptos, CA (California)

Arkansas Favorites Cookbook ©1991 J and J Collections, Hot Springs, AR (Arkansas)

Ashton Area Cookbook, Ashton Area Development Committee, Ashton, ID (Idaho)

Auburn Entertains ©1983, 1986 Auburn Entertains, by Helen Bagett, Jeanne Blackwell, and Lucy Littleton (Alabama)

Begged, Borrowed and Stollen Recipes, by Jean Ritter Smith, Eugene, OR (Oregon)

Bell's Best III: Savory Classics ©1992 Telephone Pioneers of America, MS Chapter 36, BellSouth Pioneers, Jackson, MS (Mississippi)

Best Bets ©1993 Nathan Adelson Hospice, Las Vegas, NV (Nevada)

The Best of Mayberry ©1996 by Betty Conley Lyerly, Mount Airy, NC (North Carolina)

The Best of Mennonite Fellowship Meals ©1991 Good Books, by Phyllis Pellman Good and Louise Stoltzfus, Intercourse, PA (Pennsylvania)

The Best of Sophie Kay Cookbook ©1998 by Sophie Kay & Cooking Smart, Inc., Daytona Beach, FL (Florida)

Best Taste of Fairmont, The Woman's Club of Fairmont, WV (West Virginia)

Beyond the Grill ©1997 D.D. Publishing, by Debbye Dabbs, Madison, MS (Mississippi)

Blissfield Preschool Cookbook, Blissfield Preschool Co-op, Blissfield, MI (Michigan)

Bountiful Blessings, DeKalb Parish United Methodist Churches, Daleville, MS (Mississippi)

Bouquet Garni ©1983 Pascagoula-Moss Point Mississippi Junior Auxiliary, Pascagoula, MS (Mississippi)

A Bouquet of Recipes, Homer Flower and Garden Club, Homer, LA (Louisiana)

The Bridge from Brooklyn ©2003 by Bridgette A. Correale, Memphis, TN (Tennessee)

The Bronx Cookbook ©1997 The Bronx County Historical Society, Bronx, NY (New York)

By Special Request © by Leu Wilder, Shreveport, LA (Louisiana)

Cabbage to Caviar, by Ellen Powell, Raidsville, NC (North Carolina)

Calhoun County Cooks, Retired & Senior Volunteer Program, Jacksonville, AL (Alabama)

California Sizzles ©1992 The Junior League of Pasadena, CA (California)

Calling All Cooks, Three ©1994 Telephone Pioneers of America, Alabama Chapter #34, Birmingham, AL (Alabama)

Cane River's Louisiana Living ©1994 The Service League of Natchitoches, LA (Louisiana)

Capitol Cooking, Alabama Legislative Club, Clanton, AL (Alabama)

Cardinal Country Cooking, School District of Brodhead Playground Committee, Brodhead, WI (Wisconsin)

Carnegie Hall Cookbook ©1997 Carnegie Hall, West Virginia, Lewisburg, WV (West Virginia)

Carolina Cuisine Encore! ©1981 The Junior Assembly of Anderson, SC (South Carolina)

Celebrations ©1999 Telephone Pioneers of America, Alabama Chapter #34, Birmingham, AL (Alabama)

Cent$ible Nutrition Cookbook, University of Wyoming Cooperative Extension Service, Laramie, WY (Big Sky)

Centennial Cookbook, Spring Glen United Methodist Church, Jacksonville, FL (Florida)

Centennial Cookbook, Bonners Ferry United Methodist Church, Bonners Ferry, ID (Idaho)

Centennial Cookbook, Welcome Corners United Methodist Church, Hastings, MI (Michigan)

The Central Market Cookbook ©1989 Good Books, Intercourse, PA (Pennsylvania)

C'est Bon, Encore, Vermilion Association for Family & Community Education, Inc., Abbeville, LA (Louisiana)

Christmas Favorites, by Mary Ann Crouch and Jan Stedman, Charlotte, NC (North Carolina)

Coastal Cuisine, Texas Style ©1993 Junior Service League of Brazosport, Lake Jackson, TX (Texas)

Collectibles III, by Mary Pittman, Van Alstyne, TX (Texas)

A Collection of Favorite Recipes, Deercreek Home and Garden Club, Jacksonville, FL (Florida)

Conducting in the Kitchen, The Monmouth Civic Chorus, Red Bank, NJ (Mid-Atlantic)

A Cookbook for My Southern Daughter ©1996 by Patsy Smith, Birmingham, AL (Alabama)

A Cookbook of Treasures, Trinity Presbyterian Church, Claymont, DE (Mid-Atlantic)

Cook'em Horns ©1981 The Ex-Students Association of the University of Texas, Austin, TX (Texas)

Cook'em Horns: The Quickbook ©1986 The Ex-Student's Association of the University of Texas, Austin, TX (Texas)

Cookin' with the Stars, Buffalo #150 Order of Eastern Star, Fraziers Bottom, WV (West Virginia)

Cooking for Applause ©1981 The Repertory Theatre of St. Louis, MO (Missouri)

Cooking for Love and Life ©1979 Recipes for Life, Inc., Lafayette, LA (Louisiana)

Cooking Italian in Hawaii ©1991 by George Sabato "Cass" Castagnola, Honolulu, HI (Hawaii)

Cooking with 257, Boy Scout Troop 257, North Port, FL (Florida)

Cooking with Friends, by Dorothy Jean Bixel Aschenbrenner, Pinckney, MI (Michigan)

Cooking with My Friends ©2003 by LaVece Ganter Hughes, Wind Publications, Nicholasville, KY (Kentucky)

Cooking with People to People, 2002 Student Ambassadors, McDavid, FL (Florida)

Cooking with the Allenhurst Garden Club, The Allenhurst Garden Club, Allenhurst, NJ (Mid-Atlantic)

Cooks Extraordinaires ©1993 Service League of Green Bay, WI (Wisconsin)

A Cook's Tour of Alaska ©1995 A Cook's Tour of Alaska, by Gwen Stetson, Anchorage, AK (Alaska)

A Cook's Tour of Iowa ©1988 University of Iowa Press, Chicago, IL (Iowa)

A Cook's Tour of the Azalea Coast ©1982 The Auxiliary to the Medical Society of New Hanover, Pender and Brunswick Counties, Wilmington, NC (North Carolina)

Country Cooking, Port Country Cousins, Sentinel, OK (Oklahoma)

Country Cupboard Cookbook, Panora Church of the Brethren Women, Panora, IA (Iowa)

The Country Innkeepers' Cookbook ©1992 Wilf and Lois Copping, Country Roads Press, Castine, ME (New England)

Covered Bridge Neighbors Cookbook, Covered Bridge Neighbors, St. Peters, MO (Missouri)

Crab Island Cookbook, by Chef Rebecca Watkins, Destin, FL (Florida)

Crooked Lake Volunteer Fire Department Cookbook, Ladies Auxiliary, Crivitz, WI (Wisconsin)

Culinary Classics ©1981 Young Matron's Circle for Tallulah Falls School, Roswell, GA (Georgia)

Dawdy Family Cookbook, by Kae Dawdy Coates, Roodhouse, IL (Illinois)

Dawn to Dusk ©1998 by Jonna Sigrist Cranebaugh, Olde World Bed & Breakfast, Dover, OH (Ohio)

Delicious Recipes from the Nimitz Community, Nimitz PTA, Sunnyvale, CA (California)

The Des Moines Register Cookbook, ©1995 University of Iowa Press, Chicago, IL (Iowa)

Diamonds in the Desert, Ozona Woman's League, Ozona, TX (Texas)

Dining Door to Door in Naglee Park, The Campus Community Association, San Jose, CA (California)

Dining in Historic Kentucky ©1985 Marty Godbey, McClanahan Publishing House, Kuttawa, KY (Kentucky)

Dining Under the Carolina Moon ©2005 by Deborah Baker Covington, Beaufort, SC (South Carolina)

Dixie Dining ©1982 Mississippi Federation of Women's Clubs, Inc., Jackson, MS (Mississippi)

The Dog-Gone Delicious Cookbook, Humane Society of the White Mountains, Pinetop, AZ (Arizona)

Dorthy Rickers Cookbook: Mixing & Musing, by Dorthy Rickers, Worthington, MN (Minnesota)

Down Home Country Cookin', Center for Discovery, Cottonwood, ID (Idaho)

Drop the Hook, Let's Eat, by Rachel Barth, Petersburg, AK (Alaska)

The Durango Cookbook, by Jan Fleming, Durango, CO (Colorado)

Dutch Pantry Cookin', Dutch Pantry Family Restaurant, Williamstown, WV (West Virginia)

Eat To Your Heart's Content, Too!, by Woody and Berry Armour, Hot Springs, AR (Arkansas)

Elko Arinak Dancers Cookbook, Elko Basque Club, Elso, NV (Nevada)

Encore, Shreveport Symphony Women's Guild, Shreveport, LA (Louisiana)

Encore! Encore! ©1999 Gulf Coast Symphony Orchestra Guild, Gulfport, MS (Mississippi)

Entertaining in Texas ©1982 The Junior League of Victoria, TX (Texas)

Entertaining the Louisville Way, Volume II ©1983 The Queens Daughters Inc. of Louisville, KY (Kentucky)

Fair Haven Fare, Fair Haven PTA, Fair Haven, NJ (Mid-Atlantic)

Faithfully Charleston ©2001 St. Michael's Episcopal Church, Charleston, SC (South Carolina)

Family Celebrations Cookbook, Saline County Homemakers Extension Assn., Harrisburg, IL (Illinois)

Family Collections ©1993 St. Matthew's Episcopal Church Women, Snellville, GA (Georgia)

Favorite Recipes, Baptist Health System Senior Housing, Centre, AL (Alabama)

Favorite Recipes, Ladies of Grace Bible Baptist, Casper, WY (Big Sky)

Favorite Recipes: Barbara's Best Volume II, by Barbara D. Boothe, Lottsburg, VA (Virginia)

Feeding the Flock, Shiloh Baptist Church, Ramseur, NC (North Carolina)

A Festival of Recipes, Annunciation Greek Orthodox Church, Dayton, OH (Ohio)

Fillies Flavours ©1984 The Fillies Inc., Louisville, KY (Kentucky)

Finely Tuned Foods ©1987 Symphony League of Kansas City, Leawood, KS (Missouri)

...Fire Burn & Cauldron Bubble ©1998 Julie Lugo Cerra, Culver City, CA (California)

First Ladies' Cookbook ©1996 by Betty L. Babcock, Helena, MT (Big Sky)

Flavors of Cape Henlopen, Village Improvement Association, Rehoboth Beach, DE (Mid-Atlantic)

Food for Thought ©2005 Alzheimer's Association NW Ohio Chapter, Toledo, OH (Ohio)

Food for Tots ©2001 Janice Woolley and Jennifer Pugmire, Food for Tots Publishing, Vancouver, WA (Washington)

For Crying Out Loud...Let's Eat! ©1988 The Service League of Hammond, IN (Indiana)

Fortsville UMC Cookbook, Cookbook Committee/Fortsville UMC, Ganesvoort, NY (New York)

Four Generations of Johnson Family Favorites, by Ruth Johnson, Oklahoma City, OK (Oklahoma)

Franklin County Homemakers Extension Cookbook, Franklin County Homemakers Extension, Benton, IL (Illinois)

Friends and Celebrities Cookbook II, Castle Performing Arts Center, Kaneohe, HI (Hawaii)

From Cajun Roots to Texas Boots, by Cookie Brisbin, El Paso, TX (Texas)

From Ellie's Kitchen to Yours ©1991 Ellie Deaner, Framingham, MA (New England)

From Hook to Table ©2000 Florida Sportsman, by Vic Dunaway, Stuart, FL (Florida)

From Minnesota: More Than a Cookbook ©1985 Gluesing and Gluesing, Inc., by Laurie and Debra Gluesing, Minnetonka, MN (Minnesota)

From the Cozy Kitchens of Long Grove, Long Grove Civic League, Long Grove, IA (Iowa)

From the High Country of Wyoming, Flying A Guest Ranch, Pinedale, WY (Big Sky)

The Fruit of Her Hands, Temple Israel Sisterhood, West Bloomfield, MI (Michigan)

The Fruit of the Spirit, First Baptist Church of Reno, NV (Nevada)

Gardeners' Gourmet II ©1985 Garden Clubs of Mississippi, Inc., Yazoo City, MS (Mississippi)

Gather Around Our Table, St. Catherine of Siena School and Church, Albany, NY (New York)

A Gathering of Recipes, Western Folklife Center, Elko, NV (Nevada)

Generations of Good Cooking, St. Mary's Parish, Oxford, IA (Iowa)

Generations of Treasured Recipes!, NAHCA, Powers, MI (Michigan)

A Gift of Appreciation ©2004 Dixie Aerospace Employees, Atlanta, GA (Georgia)

Gingerbread...and all the trimmings ©1987 Waxahachie Junior Service League, Waxahachie, TX (Texas)

God, That's Good!, St. Peter's Episcopal Church, Carson City, NV (Nevada)

The Golf Cookbook ©1998 Sharon Gerardi and Nadine Nemechek, Clovis, CA (California)

Gone with the Fat ©1994 Cookbook Resources, by Jen Bays Avis LDN, RD and Kathy F. Ward LDN, RD, West Monroe, LA (Louisiana)

Good Cooks Sharing, Munfordville United Methodist Women, Munfordville, KY (Kentucky)

Good Morning West Virginia! ©1997 Mountain State Association of Bed & Breakfasts, Greensburg, IN (West Virginia)

Gourmet By The Bay ©1989 Dolphin Circle of The King's Daughters and Sons, Virginia Beach, VA (Virginia)

The Grace of Patti's ©2000 Patti's Publishers, by Chip Tullar, Grand Rivers, KY (Kentucky)

Grannie Annie's Cookin' on the Wood Stove, by Ann Berg, Kenai, AK (Alaska)

Great Chefs of Butte Valley, Butte Valley Chamber of Commerce, Dorris, CA (California)

The Great Entertainer Cookbook ©1992, 2002 Buffalo Bill Historical Center, Cody, WY (Big Sky)

Great Flavors of Mississippi, Southern Flavors, Inc., Pine Bluff, AR (Mississippi)

Great Lakes Cookery ©1991 Avery Color Studios, by Bea Smith, Gwinn, MI (Michigan)

Great Plains Cooking, P.E.O. Chapter AA, Wray, CO (Colorado)

The Gulf Gourmet ©1978 The Gulf Gourmet, Westminster Academy, Gulfport, MS (Mississippi)

Happy Times with Home Cooking ©1968-90 Barbara Easter, Barbara Easter's Shenandoah Valley Recipes, Mt. Airy, NC (Virginia)

The Hearty Gourmet, by Diana Swift, Cascade, ID (Idaho)

Heavenly Helpings, Friends of Hospice, Owosso, MI (Michigan)

A Heritage of Good Tastes, Arkansas Post Museum State Park, Gillett, AR (Arkansas)

Hoboken Cooks ©1998 United Synagogue of Hoboken, NJ (Mid-Atlantic)

Holy Chow, Episcopal Churchwomen, Frankfort, KY (Kentucky)

Home at the Range III, Chapter EX. P.E.O., Oakley, KS (Great Plains)

Home Cooking, Truckee Meadows Habitat for Humanity, Reno, NV (Nevada)

Home Cooking with the Cummer Family, Dubuque, IA (Iowa)

Home Made with Love, St. John United Methodist Church, Owensboro, KY (Kentucky)

Hospitality Heirlooms ©1983 South Jackson Civic League, Inc., Jackson, MS (Mississippi)

Hospitality—Kentucky Style ©2003 by Michael Edward Masters, Equine Writer's Press, Bardstown, KY (Kentucky)

If It Tastes Good, Who Cares? ©1992 Spiritseekers Publishing, by Pam Girard, Bismark, ND (Great Plains)

In the Kitchen with Kendi ©1999 Kendi O'Neill, Diversions Publications, Frederick, MD (Mid-Atlantic)

Inncredible Edibles ©2003 by Tracy Winters, Pennsylvania Tourism & Lodging Association, Winters Publishing, Greensburg, IN (Pennsylvania)

Jarrett House Potpourri, The Jarrett House, Dillsboro, NC (North Carolina)

Jim Graham's Farm Family Cookbook for City Folks, College of Agriculture and Life Sciences, Raleigh, NC (North Carolina)

Juicy Miss Lucy Cookbook ©1982 Two Girls From Filly, by Nancy Brail and Kathy Kahan, Longwood, FL (Florida)

Kitchen Komforts ©2003 Threee Hearts Snacks, Inc., by Lulu Roman, Nashville, TN (Tennessee)

Kitchen Sampler ©1985 The Bessemer Junior Service League, Bessemer, AL (Alabama)

La Bonne Cuisine ©1980, 1981 Episcopal Churchwomen of All Saints', New Orleans, LA (Louisiana)

The Lafayette Collection ©1995, Lafayette Arts and Science Foundation, Lafayette, CA (California)

Lagniappe: Secrets We're Ready to Share II, by Patsy Switzer, Ocean Springs, MS (Mississippi)

Lake Guntersville Bed & Breakfast Cookbook, Guntersville, AL (Alabama)

Lessons from the Lunchroom, by Jennifer Nelson, Morton's Gap, KY (Kentucky)

Let Us Keep the Feast in Historic Beaufort ©2001 St. Paul's Episcopal Church Women, Beaufort, NC (North Carolina)

"Life Tastes Better Than Steak" Cookbook ©Avery Color Studios, by Gerry Krag, R.D., Gwinn, MI (Michigan)

Linen Napkins to Paper Plates ©1988 Junior Auxiliary of Clarksville, Clarksville, TN (Tennessee)

Long Hill Bed & Breakfast, Winchester, VA (Virginia)

Lost Tree Cook Book, Lost Tree Chapel, North Palm Beach, FL (Florida)

Louisiana Entertains ©1978, 1983 Rapides Symphony Guild, Alexandria, LA (Louisiana)

Madison Country Cookbook ©1994 St. Joseph's Catholic Church, Winterset, IA (Iowa)

Mama Couldn't Cook ©2005 Mama Couldn't Cook Cookbook, The Oliver Girls, Trussville, AL (Alabama)

Meet Me at the Garden Gate ©2001 Junior League of Spartanburg, SC (South Carolina)

Memories from Brownie's Kitchen ©1989 Bangor Publishing Co., by Mildred "Brownie" Schrumpf, Bangor, ME (New England)

Mennonite Country-Style Recipes & Kitchen Secrets ©1987 Herald Press, by Esther H. Shank, Scottdale, PA (Pennsylvania)

Merrymeeting Merry Eating ©Regional Memorial Hospital, Mid Coast Hospital, Brunswick Auxiliary, Brunswick, ME (New England)

Michigan Magazine Family and Friends Cookbook, Michigan Magazine, Rose City, MI (Michigan)

The Mississippi Cookbook ©1972 University Press of Mississippi, Home Economics Division of the MS Cooperative Extension Service, Jackson, MS (Mississippi)

More Tastes & Tales ©1987 Peg Hein, Heinco, Inc., Austin, TX (Texas)

More Than Moonshine: Appalachian Recipes and Recollections ©1983 University of Pittsburgh Press, Pittsburgh, PA (Kentucky)

Moveable Feasts Cookbook ©1992 Mystic Seaport Museum Stores, Inc., by Ginger Smyle, Mystic, CT (New England)

Mrs. Blackwell's Heart of Texas Cookbook ©1980 Louise B. Dillow, by Louise B. Dillow and Deenie B. Carver, Corona Publishing Company, San Antonio, TX (Texas)

MTTA's Kitchen Companion ©2004 Madison Towers Tenants Association, Richmond, KY (Kentucky)

Munchin' with the Methodists ©2001 Carolina United Methodist Women, Booneville, MS (Mississippi)

Music, Menus & Magnolias ©1996 Charleston Symphony Orchestra League, Charleston, SC (South Carolina)

Necessities and Temptations ©1987 Junior League of Austin, Inc., Austin, TX (Texas)

Neffsville Mennonite Cookbook, Neffsville Women's Missionary & Service Commission, Lancaster, PA (Pennsylvania)

Neighboring on the Air: Cooking with the KMA Radio Homemakers ©1991 University of Iowa Press, Chicago, IL (Iowa)

New Mexico Cook Book ©1990 Lynn Nusom, Golden West Publishers, Phoenix, AZ (New Mexico)

NSHSRA High School Rodeo Cookbook, Nevada State High School Rodeo Association, Battle Mountain, NV (Nevada)

Ohio Cook Book ©2002 Golden West Publishers, by Donna Goodrich, Phoenix, AZ (Ohio)

Ohio Traditions with P. Buckley Moss, Trees of Life-P. Buckley Moss Society, Defiance, OH (Ohio)

175th Anniversary Quilt Cookbook, Oak Grove Mennonite Church (WMSC), Smithville, OH (Ohio)

Only in California ©Children's Home Society of California, Oakland, CA (California)

Oregon: The Other Side, Beta Omicron Chapter, Hines, OR (Oregon)

The Orient Volunteer Fire Department Cookbook, Orient, IA (Iowa)

The Other Side of the House ©1985 Janie Whitehurst, Virginia Beach, VA (Virginia)

Our Best Home Cooking, Roosevelt County Family and Community Educators, Portales, NM (New Mexico)

Our Cherished Recipes Volume II, First Presbyterian Church Deacons, Skagway, AK (Alaska)

Our Daily Bread, Fellowship Memorial Baptist Ladies Aid Society (North Carolina)

Our Favorite Recipes, Union County Hospital Auxiliary, Anna, IL (Illinois)

Our Favorite Recipes, Saint Mary's Hospital Auxiliary, Rochester, MN (Minnesota)

Our Favorite Recipes, Elliott Prairie Community Church, Woodburn, OR (Oregon)

Our Favorite Recipes, Aurdal Lutheran Church, Underwood, MN (Minnesota)

Our Savior's Kvindherred Cookbook, Our Savior's Kvindherred Lutheran Church, Calamus, IA (Iowa)

Our Sisters' Recipe, P.E.O. Sisterhood, Chapter AH, Bowling Green, KY (Kentucky)

Palates ©1995 MVA Colorado Springs Fine Arts Center, Colorado Springs, CO (Colorado)

Palmetto Hospitality Inn Style ©1994 by Tracy M. Winters and Phyllis Y. Winters, Winters Publishing, Greensburg, IN (South Carolina)

Pass the Plate ©1984 Pass the Plate, Inc., by Alice G. Underhill and Barbara S. Stewart, New Bern, NC (North Carolina)

Paula Deen & Friends ©2005 by Paula Deen, Savannah, GA (Georgia)

The Pennsylvania State Grange Cookbook (1992 Green Edition) ©1992 PA State Grange, Lemoyne, PA (Pennsylvania)

Contributors

★★★★★★★★★★★ ★★★★★★★★★★★

The Pick of the Crop ©1978 North Sunflower P.T.A, Drew, MS (Mississippi)

A Pinch of Salt Lake Cookbook ©1986 Junior League of Salt Lake City, UT (Utah)

Pleasures from the Good Earth, Rock of Ages LWML, Sedona, AZ (Arizona)

The Proulx/Chartrand 1997 Reunion Cookbook, Central Square, NY (New York)

Putting On The Grits ©1984 The Junior League of Columbia, SC (South Carolina)

Quickies for Singles ©1980 Quail Ridge Press, Inc., Fellowship Church, Baton Rouge, LA (Louisiana)

Rainbow's Roundup of Recipes, Rainbow Bible Ranch, Sturgis, SD (Great Plains)

Raleigh House Cookbook II ©1995 Raleigh House, by Martha R. Johnson, Kerrville, TX (Texas)

The Rappahannock Seafood Cookbook ©1984 Rappahannock Community College Educational Foundation, Inc., Warsaw, VA (Virginia)

Recipes & Remembrances, Buffalo Lake Lutheran Church WMF, Eden, SD (Great Plains)

Recipes & Remembrances II, Rockwood Area Historical Society, Rockwood, MI (Michigan)

Recipes and Remembering, by Dorothy J. O'Neal, Eugene, OR (Oregon)

Recipes from Our Friends ©2001 Friends of Whitman County Library, Colfax, WA (Washington)

Recipes from St. Michael's, St. Michael's Cookbook Committee, Bloomington, MN (Minnesota)

Recipes from the Kitchens of Family & Friends, Bahari Court #104, Ladies Oriental Shrine of North America, Winston, OR (Oregon)

River Road Recipes II ©1976 The Junior League of Baton Rouge, LA (Louisiana)

San Antonio Cookbook II ©1976 Symphony Society of San Antonio, TX (Texas)

Savor the Moment: Entertaining without Reservations ©2000 The Junior League of Boca Raton, FL (Florida)

Savoring the Southwest ©1983 Roswell Symphony Guild Publications, Roswell, NM (New Mexico)

Seasoned Cooks II, Isabella County Commission on Aging, Mt. Pleasant, MI (Michigan)

Seasoned with Grace: My Generation of Shaker Cooking ©1987 Shaker Village, Inc., by Eldress Bertha Lindsay, Scranton, PA (New England)

Seasons of Thyme ©1979 Charity League of Paducah, KY (Kentucky)

Shared Treasures, First Baptist Church, Monroe, LA (Louisiana)

Sharing Our Best, Kalif Shrine Buckskin Horse Patrol, Sheridan, WY (Big Sky)

Sharing our Best to Help the Rest, Independent School District 196 and United Way of the St. Paul Area, St. Paul, MN (Minnesota)

Sharing Our Best Volume II, Harrietta Area Civic Club, Harrietta, MI (Michigan)

Sharing Our Best: A Collection of Favorite Recipes ©1996 Eagle Historical Society & Museums, Eagle, AK (Alaska)

Sharing Our Blessings, Angier Baptist Church WMU, Angier, NC (North Carolina)

Sharing Our Bounty Through 40 Years, Messiah Lutheran Church, Rochester, NY (New York)

Sharing Traditions from People You Know ©1996 American Cancer Society/Iowa Division, Des Moines, IA (Iowa)

Simple Decent Cooking ©Habitat for Humanity International, Shelton, CT (Georgia)

Simple Pleasures from Our Table to Yours ©1998 Arab Mothers' Club, Arab, AL (Alabama)

Simply Sensational ©1986 The Children's Medical Center TWIGS, Dayton, OH (Ohio)

Sisters' Secrets, Beta Sigma Phi, Ville Platte, LA (Louisiana)

The Smithfield Cookbook ©1978 The Junior Woman's Club of Smithfield, VA (Virginia)

Smoke in the Mountains Cookbook ©2004 by Kent Whitaker, Quail Ridge Press, Brandon, MS (Tennessee)

Contributors

★★★★★★★★★★★ ★★★★★★★★★★★

Someone's in the Kitchen with Melanie ©2004 by Melanie Reid Soles, Greensboro, NC (North Carolina)

Sounds Delicious! ©1986 Volunteer Council of the Tulsa Philharmonic Society, Inc., Tulsa, OK (Oklahoma)

Soupcon I ©1974 The Junior League of Chicago, IL (Iowa)

Soup's On at Quilting in the Country ©1998 Quilting in the County, by Jane Quinn, Bozeman, MT (Big Sky)

South Dakota Sunrise ©1997 Tracy Winters, Bed & Breakfast Innkeepers of South Dakota, Greensburg, IN (Great Plains)

Southern But Lite ©1994 Cookbook Resources, by Jen Bays Avis LDN, RD and Kathy F. Ward LDN, RD, West Monroe, LA (Louisiana)

Southern Settings ©1996 Decatur General Foundation, Decatur, AL (Alabama)

Special Fare by Sisters II, by Ione Burham and Joyce Chorpening, Laurie, MO (Iowa)

Spindletop International Cooks ©1984 Spindletop Oilman's Golf Charities, Inc., (Texas)

Spitfire Anniversary Cookbook, Quimby Spitfire Ladies Auxiliary, Quimby, IA (Iowa)

St. Charles Parish Cookbook, St. Charles Parish, Cassville, WI (Wisconsin)

Still Gathering: A Centennial Celebration ©1991 Infant Welfare Society of Chicago, Auxiliary to the American Osteopathic Assn, Chicago, IL (Illinois)

Stir Crazy! ©1986 Junior Welfare League of Florence, SC (South Carolina)

Sweet Surrender with Advice á la Carte ©1985 McElyea Publications, by Jane Warnock McElyea and Pam McElyea Barnard, Winter Park, FL (Florida)

A Taste from Back Home ©1983 Barbara Wortham, Marathon International Book Company, Madison, IN (Kentucky)

Taste of Clarkston: Tried & True Recipes, Clarkston Area Chamber of Commerce, Clarkston, MI (Michigan)

A Taste of Heaven, Valley Hill Baptist Church, Carrollton, MS (Mississippi)

A Taste of Heaven, Grand Coulee United Methodist Women, Mansfield, WA (Washington)

A Taste of History ©1982 The North Carolina Museum of History Associates, Inc., Raleigh, NC (North Carolina)

A Taste of Kennedy Cook Book, Kennedy Elementary PTSA, Willmar, MN (Minnesota)

Taste of the Town ©1996 Landmark Television of Tennessee, Inc., NewsChannel 5, Nashville, TN (Tennessee)

A Taste of Tradition, Temple Family, Virginia Beach, VA (Virginia)

Tastes of Country ©1987 by Frances A. Gillette, Yacolt, WA (Washington)

A Tasting Tour Through Washington County ©1987 Springfield Woman's Club, Springfield, KY (Kentucky)

Tasty Temptations, The Ladies of the Knights of Columbus, Fremont, CA (California)

Tasty Treasures from Johnson's Church, Women of Johnson's United Methodist Church, Machipongo, VA (Virginia)

Temple Temptations, Temple Shaaray Tefila, New York, NY (New York)

Tennessee Cook Book ©2003 Golden West Publishers, Phoenix, AZ (Tennessee)

Texas Sampler ©1995 by Junior League of Richardson, TX 75080 (Texas)

Thirty Years at the Mansion ©1985 Eliza Jane Ashley, August House Publishers, Little Rock, AR (Arkansas)

Thompson Family Cookbook, by Janice Winter, Lakota, IA (Iowa)

Thompson-Shore 35th Anniversary Cookbook, Dexter, MI (Michigan)

Thou Preparest a Table Before Me, Women of the WELCA, Lutheran Church of the Good Shepherd, Roosevelt, NY (New York)

Three Rivers Cookbook I ©1973 Child Health Association of Sewickley, PA (Pennsylvania)

Three Rivers Renaissance Cookbook IV ©2000 Child Health Association of Sewickley, PA (Pennsylvania)

Through Our Kitchen Windows ©1980 WMSC Council, Sarasota, FL (Florida)

Titonka Centennial Cookbook, Titonka Centennial Committee, Titonka, IA (Iowa)

★★★★★★★★★★★★ ★★★★★★★★★★★★

Tony Chachere's Second Helping ©1995 Tony Chachere's Creole Foods of Opelousas, LA (Louisiana)

Tout de Suite á la Microwave I ©1980 Jean K. Durkee , Lafayette, LA (Louisiana)

Treasured Alabama Recipes ©1967 Kathryn Tucker Windham, Selma, AL (Alabama)

Treasured Family Favorites, by Alisa L. Pate, Cleveland, MS (Mississippi)

Treasures from Heaven ©2001 First Baptist Church, Russell, Flatwoods, KY (Kentucky)

Treat Yourself to the Best Cookbook ©1984 Junior League of Wheeling, WV (West Virginia)

Tried & True Recipes from Covington, Georgia ©2005 Covington, Georgia East Metro Christian Women's Connection, Conyers, GA (Georgia)

Tried and True by Mothers of 2's, Westshore Mothers of Twins Club, Westlake, OH (Ohio)

Trinity Treats, Trinity United Methodist Women, Bradenton, FL (Florida)

Tropical Taste ©2001 by Sonia Martinez, Honomu, HI (Hawaii)

Try Me ©1984 Arthritis Volunteer Action Committee, Mobile, AL (Alabama)

Twentieth Century Club Cook Book, Twentieth Century Club, Reno, NV (Nevada)

The Ultimate Potato Cookbook, Williams Community Commercial Association, Williams, MN (Minnesota)

United Methodist Minister's Wives Cook Book, West Virginia Conference United Methodist Ministers' Wives Association, Buckhannon, WV (West Virginia)

Vintage Vicksburg ©1985 Vicksburg Junior Auxiliary, Vicksburg, MS (Mississippi)

The Virginia Presidential Homes Cookbook ©1987 Williamsburg Publishing Co., by Payne Bouknight Tyler, Charles City, VA (Virginia)

Voilá! Lafayette Centennial Cookbook 1884-1984 ©1983 Jean Kellner Durkee, Lafayette, LA (Louisiana)

Waddad's Kitchen ©1982 Waddad Habeeb Buttross, by Waddad Habeeb Buttross, Natchez, MS (Mississippi)

Washington Street Eatery Cook Book ©1993 Washington Street Eatery, Greenland, NH (New England)

Welcome Back to Pleasant Hill, by Elizabeth C. Kremer, Harrodsburg, KY (Kentucky)

What's Cookin', by Jeanne E Briggs, Rockford, MI (Michigan)

What's Cooking at St. Stephens?, Street Ann's Alter Society, Port Huron, MI (Michigan)

What's Cooking at Trinity, Trinity Evangelical Lutheran Church, Wexford, PA (Pennsylvania)

What's Cooking in Kentucky ©1982 Irene Hayes, T.I. Hayes Publishing Co., Inc., Ft. Mitchell, KY (Kentucky)

What's Cooking, Flo? ©1990 STAMPEDE Cartoon, Inc., by Jerry Palen, Saratoga, WY (Big Sky)

White Dog Café Cookbook, by Judy Wicks and Kevin Von Klause, Philadelphia, PA (Pennslyvania)

Winniehaha's Favorite Recipes, Winnehaha's of Minnesota, Circle Pines, MN (Minnesota)

Without a Doubt ©2000 St. Thomas Episcopal Church, Greenville, AL (Alabama)

The Woman's Exchange Classic Recipes ©2001 The Woman's Exchange of St. Augustine, FL (Florida)

Woodbine Public Library Community Cookbook, Woodbine Public Library, Woodbine, IA (Iowa)

Worth Savoring ©1997 The Union County Historical Society, New Albany, MS (Mississippi)

The Wyman Sisters Cookbook, Edited by Laura F. Tesseneer, Crescent Springs, KY (Kentucky)

Your Favorite Recipes, Mukilteo Presbyterian Church, Mukilteo, WA (Washington)

Index

NATHAN CREEL

The Leaning Tower of Pisa. Italy.
One of the Wonders of the Medieval World.

Index

Index

Index

Index

Index

Index

Index

Index

BEST OF THE BEST STATE COOKBOOK SERIES

  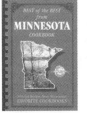  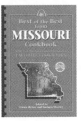